CACHE LEVEL

3

cache
nurturing achievement

pacey
professional association for
childcare and early years

PREPARING TO WORK
IN HOME-BASED
CHILDCARE

Sheila Riddall-Leech

HODDER
EDUCATION
AN HACHETTE UK COMPANY

Orders: please contact Bookpoint Ltd, 130 Milton Park, Abingdon, Oxon OX14 4SB. Telephone: (44) 01235 827720. Fax: (44) 01235 400454. Lines are open from 9.00–5.00, Monday to Saturday, with a 24-hour message answering service. You can also order through our website, www.hoddereducation.co.uk.

British Library Cataloguing in Publication Data

A catalogue record for this title is available from the British Library

ISBN 978 1 4718 4151 4

First Published 2015

Impression number   10 9 8 7 6 5 4 3 2 1

Year   2018 2017 2016 2015

Hachette UK's policy is to use papers that are natural, renewable and recyclable products and made from wood grown in sustainable forests. The logging and manufacturing processes are expected to conform to the environmental regulations of the country of origin.

Cover photo © Igor Emmerich/Getty Images

Typeset in 10.5/15 Palatino LT Std Light by Integra Software Services Pvt. Ltd, Pondicherry, India.

Printed in Great Britain for Hodder Education, an Hachette UK company.

Contents

About the author   iv

Introduction   v

How to use this book   vi

Acknowledgements   viii

Unit 1 Preparing to work as a home-based childcarer   1

Chapter 1 Understand current legislation and regulation in relation to home-based childcare   2

Chapter 2 Understand how to establish a safe and healthy home-based childcare environment   13

Chapter 3 Understand how to support the safeguarding and welfare of children   41

Chapter 4 Understand how to promote equality, diversity and inclusion   58

Chapter 5 Understand how day-to-day care routines promote children's well-being   65

Chapter 6 Understand how to work in partnership to support children's outcomes   80

Chapter 7 Understand children's learning and behaviour in relation to sequence, rate and
stage of development   93

Chapter 8 Understand the value of play in promoting children's learning and development   119

Chapter 9 Understand the role of observation in promoting children's learning and
development   134

Unit 2 Preparing to set up a home-based childcare business   143

Chapter 10 Understand how to lead and manage a home-based childcare setting   144

Chapter 11 Understand how to comply with financial and taxation requirements when
setting up a home-based childcare service   153

Chapter 12 Understand how to create a business plan   158

Chapter 13 Understand how to register with the appropriate regulatory body   170

Common dietary habits   174

Glossary   175

Bibliography   177

Index   179

About the author

Sheila Riddall-Leech began her professional career as a primary school teacher and has worked in many settings in various parts of the UK and abroad. She eventually became a deputy head of a large primary school with a thriving early years unit. Sheila was also a pre-school supervisor and a home-based childcarer for a number of years. She moved into higher and further education in the mid-1990s, teaching on a wide range of early years courses, degree programmes and awards. Until very recently Sheila was a freelance early years inspector. She is an assessor for PACEY Children Come First childminding networks and has worked closely with Telford and Wrekin Council to explore the concept of a childminder agency. She works with CACHE Assessment team to develop assessment materials for various awards.

Currently, Sheila runs her own training company, delivering CACHE awards and professional development events in England and Wales. Sheila writes for professional journals and publishing companies.

Sheila is married to Peter and lives in North Shropshire. She has two grown up daughters and very recently joined the exclusive club for grandparents with the arrival of Thomas Arthur in November 2014. In her spare time, Sheila enjoys gardening, knitting and travel.

Introduction

Working in home-based childcare is a career choice that people may make at many different points in their lives and for many different reasons. Whatever your reason for choosing this path, however, one thing is certain: you are embarking on a journey that will lead to a most fulfilling career. Yes, it is demanding and tiring, sometimes lonely and isolating; but it is also great fun, very enjoyable and provides a hugely valuable service to many children and their families.

It is essential for a home-based childcarer to have a love of children. You also need to have a good understanding of how children develop and learn, and how you can keep them safe, healthy and well cared for. It is important that you understand how to run and manage a business and to provide a professional service.

Studying for this qualification will hopefully enable you to do all of these things with confidence and certainty. This knowledge and qualification will help to raise your professional profile and improve the quality of service you offer to children and their families. So, get reading, learning and enjoy!

How to use this book

This book contains all the information you need to complete the CACHE Level 3 Award in Preparing to Work in Home Based Childcare (QCF). The award has two units, which are divided into learning outcomes. Each chapter will cover a different learning outcome.

Key features in the book

Throughout the book there are key features designed to help you in your course and when studying:

Learning outcome 1

The learning outcomes are written at the start of each chapter, so you will know what is going to be covered in that chapter.

Assessment criteria

Each learning outcome has assessment criteria and these are clearly indicated throughout the book. You must provide evidence for each assessment criteria, as these are the statements detailing what you have learned. There are assessment tasks, which match each of the assessment criteria. You will need to complete successfully and in full each assessment task. The words 'assessment criteria' will be abbreviated to the acronym AC.

Key terms

These will help you understand important words and phrases.

Reflective practice

These boxes will help you to think about your own practice and skills.

In your setting

A checklist of key points and tips to help you develop your professional skills.

Case study

Real-life scenarios to help you understand how ideas work in practice.

Activity

A short task to help you develop a better understanding of an idea or assessment point.

Find out more

Ideas to encourage you to research a topic, subject or idea.

Links to the EYFS

The Early Years Foundation Stage sets the standard for home-based childcarers in England for children form birth to five. Find links to specific parts of the EYFS.

Assessment links

Help and tips to assist you in completing the CACHE assessment tasks.

Discussion point

Topics, subjects or ideas that you can discuss with other people on your course.

pacey says

Ideas and suggestions from PACEY.

Useful resources

Resources, such as websites and other places, where you can research and find out more about a subject or topic.

Building your portfolio

As you work through each learning outcome, you will build a portfolio or file of work items, such as policies and procedures, activity plans, routines, and assignments set by your tutors. These items are usually referred to as 'evidence'. Work that you produce for the assessment tasks can be added to your portfolio and may become a useful resource as your career progresses, for you, or for parents and carers, visitors and regulatory personnel.

Evidence can be scanned, computer-generated or presented in any appropriate format. It is recommended, however, that where possible A4-size documents and paper are used. It is really important that you keep your portfolio organised and up to date. Try to develop the habit of filing, dating and logging work as you go along. It is a very good idea to put the learning outcome and assessment criteria numbers on every piece of work you produce. This way you should be able to find your evidence quickly and, at the same time, have an organised portfolio. Trying to play 'catch-up' at the end of the course is stressful and unnecessary.

Throughout the book the term 'home-based childcarer' is used. This refers to registered childminders and their assistants as well as to nannies working in a child's home. References to parents are intended to include other carers as well.

Acknowledgements

Author acknowledgements

I would like to especially thank Micheal and Joanne Winch for all their assistance with the photoshoot for the book. Also, thanks to the children and families at Mick and Jo's setting, Katie Winch and Emma Bevington for their contributions.

I would also like to thank the editorial team at Hodder Education and to PACEY for their support and helpful suggestions during the writing of this book. Thank you to Jules Selmes who took all the photographs used in this book.

Thanks also go to the many home based childcarers who have trained with me and provided material for the case studies and scenarios. Special thanks to Peter for his continued love and support and remembering my late parents, especially my father Arthur, who encouraged my thirst for learning.

Photo acknowledgements

All photos © Jules Selmes.

UNIT 1

Preparing to work as a home-based childcarer

Chapter 1

Understand current legislation and regulation in relation to home-based childcare

Learning Outcome 1

By the end of this chapter you will be able to:

1 Outline current legislation relevant to the home-based childcarer

2 Summarise current legislation and guidelines in relation to: the health and safety of children; the safeguarding, protection and welfare of children; equality, diversity and inclusion

3 Understand the role of regulatory bodies in relation to home-based childcare

It is important that you start your career in home-based childcare as you mean to carry on. This means that you should be organised, professional and make every effort to keep yourself up to date with legislation and developments in the childcare sector. Legislation does change, as do guidelines and guidance documents. You must be aware of the changes, and you must modify and adapt your practice where necessary.

Key term

Legislation – laws, rules and regulation that have been made by Acts of Parliament

AC 1.1 Outline current legislation relevant to the home-based childcarer

You do not need to know the finer details or small print of current legislation, but you must understand how it impacts on your work and where your professional responsibilities begin and end. There are a large number of relevant regulations, laws and guidelines, some of which are quite old. Many have been updated and replaced, however. For example, the Sex Discrimination Act (1975) was replaced by the Equalities Act (2010). The Equalities Act (2010) is far more wide-ranging than the Sex Discrimination Act (1975); while the older piece of legislation is relevant for you to a certain extent, it is not current.

Tip

The assessment criteria asks you to 'outline' current legislation. An outline is a summary of an idea. AC 1.1 doesn't require you to go into great depth or detail. You need only to cover the key points and main focus of the relevant and current legislation. The most relevant and current pieces of legislation are listed in Table 1.1.

Children Act (1989, 2004)

In 1989 the first Children Act became law. It was a highly significant piece of legislation as it was the first time that the UK had acknowledged children's rights. This Act also covered some values and standards that we now take for granted. These are that:

Table 1.1 Relevant and current pieces of legislation

Legislation	Focus
Children Act (1989, 2004)	The basis of the current child protection system.
	The Children Act (2004) did not replace or change much of the 1989 version. The 2004 revision arose from the Green Paper 'Every child matters', which itself was produced after the murder of Victoria Climbié. 'Every child matters' identifies five outcomes for all children:
	<ul><li>Be healthy</li><li>Stay safe</li><li>Enjoy and achieve</li><li>Make a positive contribution</li><li>Achieve economic well-being.</li></ul>
	The 2004 Act placed a duty on local authorities and partners to work together to safeguard and promote the well-being of children and young people.
Childcare Act (2006)	Introduced the Early Years Foundation Stage (EYFS) framework in England, for children aged 0 to 5 years. It also sets out the statutory assessment of all settings currently carried out by Ofsted.
Equality Act (2010)	Replaced all previous legislation relating to any aspect of equality. It makes sure that all people are protected from discrimination, regardless of age, gender, race, religion or beliefs, sexual orientation or disability.
Children and Families Act (2014)	Includes greater protection to vulnerable children, support for children whose parents are separating, a new system to help children with special educational needs and disabilities (SEND), and help for parents to balance work and family life.
	It also ensures vital changes to the adoption system and reforms for children in care can be put into practice.
Data Protection Act (1998)	Provides a framework to make sure that information is shared appropriately, that records about children are stored securely, and that personal and confidential information about children is not passed on without the written consent of the parents.

- The welfare of the child is paramount
- Children's views and opinions should be considered in regard to matters that affect them
- Parents should care for their children if possible
- Practitioners should work in partnership with parents.

These four standards are essential and should underpin all your responsibilities and work.

By 2003 it was clear that children's services were not working together to protect and identify vulnerable children. This was highlighted by the sad death of Victoria Climbié and the resulting independent inquiry led by Lord Laming. The Laming Report in 2003 was very critical of the approach to protecting children. As a result the Green Paper 'Every child matters' was published, and this led to the Children Act (2004).

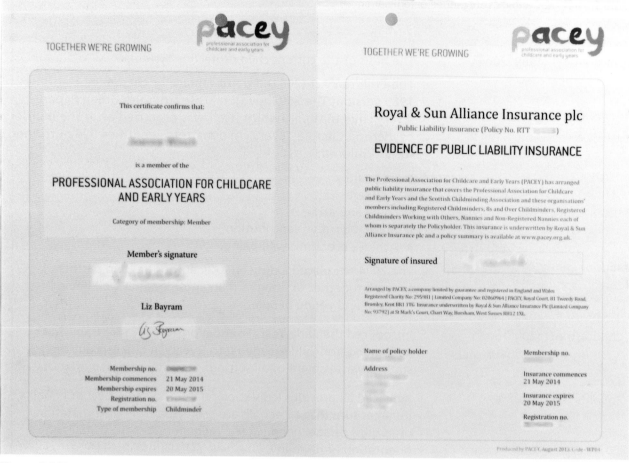

Figure 1.1 You should display your public liability certificate in a prominent position

Childcare Act (2006)

The Childcare Act (2006) defines the new duties imposed on local authorities in respect to improving the 'Every child matters' outcomes for pre-school children. The Act also outlines new rules in relation to childcare for working parents, as well as parental information services. It is aimed at improving the well-being of young children.

This Act introduced the Early Years Foundation Stage (EYFS) into England. The EYFS sets statutory regulatory requirements for all early years professionals. This means all early years practitioners have a legal responsibility to implement all of the EYFS.

Equality Act (2010)

The Equality Act (2010) became law in October 2010. It replaced previous legislation such as the Race Relations Act (1976) and the Disability Discrimination Act (1995). All childcare settings, whether private, voluntary, independent or statutory, including home-based childcarers, must comply with the Act. It aims to ensure consistency in what childcare settings need to do to be fair and to comply with the law.

It sets out the various ways in which it is unlawful to treat someone, such as discrimination. So if you refuse, without very good reasons, to care for a child with a disability or one who doesn't speak the same language as you, you could be breaking the law and not meeting your responsibilities.

Key term

Discrimination – treating someone unequally or differently due to their age, gender, sexual orientation, race, religion or beliefs, or disability

Children and Families Act (2014)

The Children and Families Act (2014) includes greater protection for vulnerable children, such as those in foster care, looked-after children and those with special educational needs and disabilities (SEND). The Act introduced a new system to help children with special educational needs and disabilities. As a result, your local council has to draw up an education, health and care (EHC) plan instead of a statement for children who have been identified as having SEND. Local councils are required to publish a 'local offer' of services and to offer a personal budget to meet the EHC plan. There is also a requirement to offer help for parents to balance work and family life, and to provide support for children whose parents are separating.

The Act also ensures that vital changes to the adoption system can be put into practice, meaning that more children who need loving homes can be placed faster. It also ensures that reforms for looked-after children can be implemented, including giving them the choice to stay with their foster families until their twenty-first birthday.

Your professional responsibilities are around supporting children with SEND, being aware of the support that is available to you and the child's family, and knowing how to access that support.

Data Protection Act (1998)

You will need to keep records for the children for whom you care. You will need their full name, address and date of birth as an absolute minimum. As your business progresses, you may need to store personal information about how children are developing and learning. You must keep all this information confidential, however, and it should not be shared with anyone else without the written permission of the child's parents, except where you suspect a child is at risk of abuse (see Chapter 3). You have a legal responsibility to make sure that you observe confidentiality at all times in all aspects of your work.

Key term

Confidentiality – keeping things private, not disclosing any personal information about children and their families

Discussion point

Can you think of any circumstances when it would be acceptable to share information about a child without the parents' written consent?

The Data Protection Act (1998) requires all businesses, including home-based childcarers, to notify the Information Commissioner's Office (ICO)

unless exempt. Notification is necessary if you are keeping personal information electronically for the provision of childcare, such as on a computer, laptop or tablet. This includes if you take photographs of the children in your care using a digital camera or mobile phone and store them electronically, such as on your hard drive or a memory stick.

Figure 1.2 Do you secure your records in compliance with the Data Protection Act?

In your setting

- Have a lockable filing cabinet, cupboard or drawer where you store confidential materials.
- Make sure that your storage place cannot be accessed by the rest of your family or the children or visitors.
- Password protect your home-based childcare files on a computer, laptop or other mobile device.
- Make back-up copies of your files and store them on a memory stick, portable hard drive, CD or DVD. Make sure these are also password protected.

Find out more

Confidential information that you keep on children in your care must not be destroyed when the child has left your care. Find out how long you need to keep certain records.

Links to the EYFS

Sections 3.68 through to 3.73 (pages 29–30) of the Statutory Framework for the Early Years Foundation Stage (2014) state your statutory responsibilities regarding information and records that you will need to maintain and/or share with parents, other professionals, the police, social services, Ofsted or a childminder agency.

Useful resources

Website

Information Commissioner's Office
The Information Commissioner's Office (ICO) can be contacted at: **www.ico.org.uk/for_organisations/data_protection/registration**

On this website you can find out if you need to register and do so if need be.

AC 1.2 Summarise current legislation and guidelines

Summarise current legislation and guidelines relating to:

- the health and safety of children
- the safeguarding, protection and welfare of children
- equality, diversity and inclusion.

The Children Act (2004) clearly states that the welfare of the child is paramount. For home-based childcarers this means providing a diverse environment where children can develop and learn that is hygienic, safe, secure and not discriminatory. There are many pieces of legislation and guidelines to help you do this. You should know how the legislation and guidelines apply to you in your work and the impact that they may have.

Legislation and guidelines relating to the health and safety of children

The table below gives you a brief summary of the most relevant pieces of legislation and guidelines relating health and safety in the early years.

Table 1.2 Legislation and guidelines relating to the health and safety of children

Legislation or guidelines	Summary
Health and Safety at Work Act (1974)	You must make sure that your workplace is safe and that you understand how to manage health and safety in your home. (This will be covered in greater detail in later chapters.)
Health and Safety (First Aid) Regulations (1981)	You must have a current Paediatric First Aid qualification. This is part of the welfare requirements of the EYFS. Your First Aid qualification has to be renewed every three years.
Children Act (1989, 2004)	The Children Act (1989, 2004) sets out the amount of space that should be available for children. It also covers the numbers and ages of children that one home-based carer can look after at any one time.
Personal Protective Equipment at Work Regulations (1992)	You need to make sure that you have appropriate protective clothing available, such as disposable gloves for dealing with body fluids. This clothing should also be available to any assistant you may have working with you or to students.
Manual Handling Operations Regulations (1992)	You will be lifting and handling children as part of your caring role. There is a risk of injury or accident when doing this if you do not do it properly. These regulations outline safe ways to lift and handle children, play equipment and furniture. They also cover how to reduce these potential risks by carrying out risk assessments. (Risk assessment will be discussed in more detail in Chapter 2.)
Reporting of Injuries, Diseases and Dangerous Occurrences (1995)	These regulations are usually referred to as RIDDOR. Any serious accident that results in injuries needing treatment from a doctor must be reported to the Health and Safety Executive. In addition, outbreaks of a serious disease or the death of a child in your care must be reported. You need to keep an accident book that records any incident that happens to a child while in your care. Parents need to sign the record.
Fire Precautions (Workplace) Regulations (1997, amended 1999)	You need to have an evacuation procedure in place in the event of a fire or other emergency. You should practise this procedure with children and make a record of your practices. This is also part of the Safeguarding and Welfare Requirements of the EYFS. ➜

Table 1.2 Legislation and guidelines relating to the health and safety of children (*Continued*)

Legislation or guidelines	Summary
Care Standards Act (2000)	This Act relates to the standards that must be met in children's residential care homes.
Control of Substances Hazardous to Health Regulations (2002)	These regulations are usually referred to as COSHH. You must make sure that any substances or liquids that are hazardous to health, such as bleach or dishwasher powders, are not accessible to children. You should also know what to do if a child accidently comes into contact with a hazardous substance.
The Regulatory Reform (Fire Safety) Order (2005)	You must carry out a risk assessment of potential fire dangers in your setting. This can be part of your normal risk assessment procedures.
Childcare Act (2006)	This sets out all of the statutory requirements of the EYFS. You will be inspected against this by Ofsted or a childminder agency.

Useful resources

Website
Health and Safety Executive
The Health and Safety Executive's website has a wealth of guidance. The web address is **www.hse.gov.uk**

Legislation and guidelines relating to the safeguarding, protection and welfare of children

Key term

Safeguarding – includes everything that we can do to keep children and young people safe

It is the responsibility of everyone to keep children safe. As you are probably well aware, sometimes people fail in their responsibility and children are put at risk of potential harm. There are several pieces of legislation and guidelines, however, which focus specifically on the safeguarding, protection and welfare of children. Safeguarding will be discussed in more detail in Chapter 3.

The most recent and relevant piece of documentation is 'Working together to safeguard children' (2013). It is quite a straightforward document and you should read it. It clearly states your responsibilities towards safeguarding children and focuses very much on the needs of the child.

Useful resources

Publications
'Working together to safeguard children'
'Working together to safeguard children' can be downloaded from: **www.gov.uk/government/publications/working-together-to-safeguard-children**

'What to do if you are worried a child is being abused' (2006)
'What to do if you are worried a child is being abused' (2006) is a guide for practitioners working with children. It explains the processes and systems of 'Working together to safeguard children' (2013). It can be downloaded from: **www.gov.uk/government/publications/what-to-do-if-youre-worried-a-child-is-being-abused**, reference DFES-04320-2006.

Protection of Children Act (1999)

The purpose of this Act is to give a further level of protection for children. It requires that any organisation involved in the care or supervision of children not employ anyone, in either a paid or unpaid capacity, who is listed on the Department of Health's list as being unsuitable to work with children.

Find out more

A new law was introduced in 2011 following the conviction of Sarah Payne's murderer. It is known as Sarah's Law. Find out how this piece of legislation could help you in your work.

The Disclosure and Barring Service

Any person over the age of 16 years who wants to work with children must have a Disclosure and Barring Service (DBS) check. The DBS replaced the Criminal Records Bureau (CRB) and Independent Safeguarding Authority (ISA). The DBS is a central access point for criminal records checks in the UK.

It is important to remember that before you become a home-based childcarer, **every** member of your household over the age of 16 years must have a DBS check, even if they will not work with the children and will have only minimal contact.

It does not matter if you plan to care for school-aged children only, you will still need a DBS check for yourself and anyone else living in your home who is over 16 years of age.

It is a requirement of the EYFS (England only) that anyone looking after children, and people living in the same home where the care will take place, must meet the suitable people requirements (EYFS Safeguarding and Welfare Requirements 3.9). You will be asked to provide information (as set out in Schedule 1, Part 2 of the Childcare (Early Years Register) (Amendment) Regulations 2012).

Find out more

Check exactly what information you will need to provide to meet the suitable people requirement (EYFS Safeguarding and Welfare Requirements 3.9).

You should also be aware that if you or any member of your household is convicted of a criminal offence, it could impact on whether you would still be considered a suitable person to care for children. You could be disqualified.

Discussion point

Read the scenario below and then consider the implications for the home-based childcarer.

Jess is a single parent and has been a registered home-based childcarer for seven years. Her 17-year-old son, who lives with her, has been arrested and charged with possession of a Class A drug. How might this incident affect Jess's business?

The Children Act (2004)

This Act requires all local authorities to set up Local Safeguarding Children Boards (LSCB). Each local authority has a responsibility to have LSCBs in place. They provide a mechanism for different organisations that have contact with children to work with one another to safeguard and promote the welfare of children. They also have powers to investigate all child deaths in their area as required by 'Working together to safeguard children' (2013). LSCBs will be discussed in more detail in Chapter 3.

The Children Act (2004) also made physical punishment of children an offence. Punishment should not cause mental harm or leave a lasting mark on a child's skin.

Links to the EYFS

Section 3 of the EYFS is called the Safeguarding and Welfare Requirements. This section sets out the instructions that you must follow relating to the safeguarding, protection and welfare of children.

Legislation and guidelines relating to equality, diversity and inclusion

Equality, diversity and inclusion are key components of any childcare practice. They should underpin your professional approach and everything that you do. It is not about treating everyone the same, but treating everyone as an individual. Individuals should be treated with respect, while valuing and recognising the rich heritage of all people. Promoting equality, diversity and inclusion will be discussed in much more detail in Chapter 4.

In order to meet this part of the assessment criteria you are asked to summarise or sum up key legislation and guidelines.

Equality Act (2010)

The main piece of legislation is the Equality Act (2010). This Act replaced all previous legislation, and every childcare setting, including home-based childcarers, must abide by it. Unlawful discrimination is banned and individuals with particular characteristics are protected from discrimination. These characteristics are age, gender, pregnancy, disability, race, religion or beliefs, sexual orientation, marriage and civil partnerships and gender reassignment.

Special Needs and Disability Act (2001) and Code of Practice (2014)

The Special Needs and Disability Act (2001) (SENDA) gives children with disabilities the right to attend mainstream schools wherever possible. Furthermore, all settings should have in place a special educational needs policy and procedures, and have a designated person who is a Special Educational Needs Co-ordinator (SENCO).

United Nations Convention on the Rights of the Child (1989)

The United Nations Convention on the Rights of the Child (1989) (UNCRC) is mentioned earlier in the chapter. Just to remind you, it is not statutory, but underpins much current legislation. It is important, however, that you know and understand the basic requirements in meeting the rights of children and young people up to the age of 18 years.

AC 1.3 Understand the role of regulatory bodies in relation to home-based childcare

In England, all home-based childcarers must be registered with the regulatory body, Ofsted. You can be fined up to £5000 or sent to prison, or both, if you provide childminding services without being registered.

Home-based childcarers in England can also register with an early years childminder agency. The agency will be regulated and inspected by Ofsted. In other parts of the UK, there are different regulatory bodies, as listed on the following page.

UK regulatory bodies

- **England:** Office for Standards in Education (Ofsted), www.gov.uk/register-as-childminder-england
- **Scotland:** Care Inspectorate, www.gov.uk/registering-as-childminder-scotland
- **Wales:** Care and Social Services Inspectorate Wales (CSSIW), www.gov.uk/register-as-childminder-wales
- **Northern Ireland:** Health and Social Services Trust, www.nicma.org/cms/component/content/article/150

The regulatory bodies of the UK have systems and processes to monitor home-based childcare. This is done through:

- **Registration** – this involves checks on you, on other people over 16 years who live with you, and on the premises where you plan to work.
- **Inspection** – inspectors carry out checks on the service offered, using legal requirements and/or standards.
- **Investigation** – an inquiry that is carried out to check the facts if a complaint or concern is raised about you.
- **Enforcement** – the regulatory body can take action against you if you are not meeting the requirements or standards of your country.

Each regulatory body has slightly different requirements but all have the same aims. These are:

- to protect children
- to provide reassurance to parents using childcare
- to ensure that home-based childcare services meet acceptable standards
- to make sure that home-based childcarers can provide an environment that promotes children's development and learning, that is safe and where children are well cared for.

All of the regulatory bodies make sure that home-based childcarers comply with standards for safety, equipment and numbers of children on the premises at any one time. They check references, the health of prospective home-based childcarers and criminal records. How to register with the appropriate regulatory body is covered in detail in Chapter 13.

- In **England and Wales**, registration is a legal requirement for anyone who wants to be paid for looking after children under the age of eight years, for more than two hours per day and in a home that isn't the child's normal home.

Figure 1.3 An inspector will visit your home to check that you meet the requirements for registration

- In **Scotland** registration is a legal requirement for anyone who wants to be paid for looking after children who are 16 years old or younger, for more than two hours per day and in a private home.
- In **Northern Ireland**, registration is a legal requirement for anyone who wants to be paid for looking after children under the age of 12 years, for more than two hours per day and on domestic premises.

In your setting

To find out more about registering as an individual or joining a childminding agency, you may find it helpful to talk to your local authority or other home-based childcarers in your area.

pacey says

You can keep up to date with changes and developments in the sector by regularly accessing the PACEY website, www.pacey.org.uk and others such as The Foundations Years and Ofsted.

Assessment links

This assessment task relates to Learning Outcome 1. This assessment task has two parts. Part 1 links to assessment criteria 1.1 and 1.2, and part 2 links to assessment criteria 1.3.

1 You need to produce a chart that outlines the current legislation that is relevant to you as a home-based childcarer. Your chart should also include a summary of current legislation and guidelines that relate to:
   a the health and safety of children
   b the safeguarding, protection and welfare of children
   c equality, diversity and inclusion.

You can produce your chart in any way that is clear to you. It can be produced on a computer or handwritten, provided it is legible and clear. Remember to keep the language that you use straightforward and uncomplicated.

2 The second part of this assessment task is to produce a chart that outlines the role of regulatory bodies in relation to home-based childcare. You should look at the regulatory body relevant to where you live.

Chapter 2

Understand how to establish a safe and healthy home-based childcare environment

Learning Outcome 2

By the end of this chapter you will be able to:

1 Explain why it is important to take a balanced approach to risk management
2 Explain the principles of safe supervision both in the home-based setting and off-site
3 Describe procedures for the storage and administration of medication, and record keeping in relation to medication

4 Understand how to carry out risk assessments, both inside your home and outdoors
5 Summarise ways to maintain a safe and healthy environment for children in relation to preparation of formula feeds, sterilisation of feeding equipment, preparation and storage of food, safe disposal of waste, and care of pets
6 Explain procedures to follow in the event of accidents, incidents and emergencies

Following Chapter 1 and completing the assessment criteria you will have increased your awareness of how to keep children safe. This chapter will help you develop practices that make sure your home and any outside areas used by the children are safe and hygienic, and promote health and well-being.

Key terms

Explain – give details, make clear, put into plain words

Risk – the possibility or chance of danger or threat to safety. In the context of play, risk can imply new and challenging experiences

AC 2.1 Explain why it is important to take a balanced approach to risk management

No one is in any way suggesting that concerns over children's safety are not real, but sometimes children can become 'over protected' if they are unable to enjoy challenging and risk-taking experiences. In these situations children may not be allowed to try out anything that is challenging or where we believe there may be danger.

When you think about it, every activity that we engage in as humans has a potential risk. For example, every time you eat something, there is a risk that you could choke. Every time you get into your car and drive, there is a risk that you could crash. Every time a child runs about outside, there is the risk that they could fall. Some people enjoy taking part in risky activities, such as mountain climbing or scuba-diving. In risky activities such as these, however, the people doing them have looked at the risks involved and taken appropriate action, such as wearing protective clothing. We also feel that we know which risks are less likely to happen and so carry on with those.

Risks and the possibility of danger are all around us and in every aspect of our lives. As we get older, however, we learn to differentiate between different types of risks. As adults we understand where the most serious dangers may be and we learn what to do about them.

For example, most adults understand that there would be serious risk to our safety in walking down the lanes of a motorway, so we don't do it. In the same way, most adults understand that driving a car around town has possible risks, but we have learned to minimise those risks by driving with care and full attention. If we didn't learn to minimise risks, we would be in a constant state of fear; we could starve for fear of choking and never step outside our doors for fear of being knocked over by a car. Our life experiences have taught us how to take a balanced approach to risks. Taking a balanced approach to risks is important to enable us to learn new things.

Children, however, do not have a wealth of life experiences to help them understand the difference between a slight risk and a major one. It is up to us therefore to help them develop that understanding.

environment that offers them challenge so that their skills can be extended and developed. A risk-free environment lacks stimulation; children need an environment that offers stimulation. Often in an unchallenging and unstimulating environment, children become bored. Their behaviour can deteriorate and their learning will be adversely affected. But they do, of course, still need an environment that is safe.

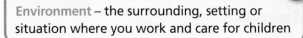

Key term

Environment – the surrounding, setting or situation where you work and care for children

You might feel that telling children about risks and dangers should be enough to make them aware. You tell them not to throw toys, for example, in case someone gets hurt. But this is a rather abstract idea to a young child, who may not understand the idea from words alone. They need to actually see or experience for themselves. This is referred to as 'first-hand experience'.

Key term

First-hand experience – doing something or finding out something yourself

Activity

Think about one 'normal' day. Make a list of all the things that you do during the day that carry a possible risk. Then, next to each possible risk, explain what you do to reduce the risk.

For example:

- Activity: making a cup of tea
- Risk: scalding
- To reduce the risk: stand still when pouring boiling water from a kettle to a mug.

Discussion point

Home-based childcarers are faced with an on-going issue, namely how to balance a child's need to explore and be challenged, with the need to keep children safe. So how can you do this?

Consider:

- Risks that you took as a child and what you learned from them.
- Why children need an element of risk in their play.
- How to balance the need for children to explore with the need to keep them safe.
- How to explain to parents and carers about risky and challenging play.

A totally risk-free environment would be completely safe, but it would be a very boring and uninteresting place to be. Children need an

Figure 2.1 How can you balance a child's need to explore and be challenged with the need to keep children safe?

Useful resources

Website
Rethinking Childhood
www.rethinkingchildhood.com has a blog by Tom Gill about children's need for risk and challenge.

Links to the EYFS

When you are planning and guiding children's activities, it is very important that you think about the different ways in which children learn. The three characteristics of effective teaching and learning are:

● playing and exploring
● active learning
● creating and thinking critically.

When you reflect on these you will realise that having an understanding of risks and challenges are key components in understanding how children learn and develop. These characteristics will be discussed further in Chapter 8.

Publication

Development Matters

This is an essential document for home-based childcarers in England. It gives you details of the three characteristics of effective teaching and learning, and the areas of learning and development in the EYFS. It is strongly recommended that you download a copy from **www.foundationyears.org.uk/ files/2012/03/Development-Matters-FINAL-PRINT-AMENDED.pdf**

In your setting

Think about whether you take a balanced approach to risk management in your own home. Sometimes it can be difficult to answer such a question yourself, so ask the people with whom you live, both adults and children.

AC 2.2 Explain the principles of safe supervision both in the home-based setting and off-site

Supervision of children in your home means that you are aware of what they are doing all the time and that you do everything possible to protect them from harm and dangers. Supervision also has implications for how you manage your time and work; for example, how do you supervise children when one wants to play inside, another wants to go into the garden and a baby is sleeping in a different room? This is a good topic for discussion with others on your course or with other home-based childcarers (read on for answers or possible solutions!).

Key term

Supervision – management, care, protection

As a registered home-based childcarer you are required by law to provide an environment that is safe and secure, both inside and outdoors.

You must also make sure that you do everything possible to prevent accidents and to reduce risks at all times and in any place that you are with children. While children are in your care you have full and complete responsibility for their safety and well-being. When you stop and think about it, this is a huge task; it is also an essential one. The way in which you supervise children in your care directly affects their safety and well-being.

Key term

Well-being – safety, comfort, security, happiness

Supervision of children does not necessarily mean that you are constantly watching every move of every child. This would be impossible. It does mean, however, that you are aware of what they are doing all of the time. You are attentive, alert and mindful. You must be able to see and/or hear all the children. So if you have a sleeping baby in another room, you need a baby monitor where you are, so you can hear them. You should also make frequent and regular visual checks on the baby. This means actually going into the room where the baby is sleeping and checking on them.

There are three different types of supervision:

1 **Constant supervision** – when you are watching and listening to a child all the time. This could be when you are in close contact with them, such as when feeding a baby or when a young child is learning to cut out with scissors or to cut fruit with a knife.
2 **Close supervision** – when you are watching a child; not actually involved but ready to step in immediately if the need arises and their well-being and safety is threatened. You would have close supervision of children on a climbing frame or playing on tricycles.
3 **General supervision** – when you are fully aware of what children are doing and checking on them frequently, keeping an attentive eye on them from a distance. When children are playing on the carpet together you could have general supervision.

Figure 2.2 You have a responsibility to supervise children appropriately at all times

Supervision of children depends on a number of factors:

- **Stage of development** – a lively, curious toddler will need more constant supervision than a seven year old. The older child will still require supervision but because of their age it is more likely to be general.
- **Activities children are involved in and what they are doing** – a sleeping baby will need different supervision to a three year old who is baking cupcakes. This child in turn will need different supervision from a group of after-school children playing football outside.
- **Where children are** – all children will need closer supervision when they are away from your home, especially in less familiar surroundings.
- **Individual and additional needs** – all children have individual needs, but sometimes they also have additional needs, for example,

learning difficulties or impairments. A visually impaired child may need more supervision when away from your home, such as in a supermarket or park.

> **Key term**
>
> **Impairment** – loss or deterioration of a bodily function

Legal requirements for supervision

The regulatory bodies set the maximum numbers of children that home-based childcarers can care for at any one time and in any one place, inside or out. This is to make sure that children can be supervised properly and have their needs met. All four countries of the UK have very similar requirements to ensure safe supervision. A home-based childcarer's own children are always taken into account in the adult-to-child ratios. The ratios can be changed if, for example, you are asked to care for twin babies or siblings. You must get permission from the regulatory body to change your supervision ratios, however. Supervision ratios for older children in school are not regulated, so long as any care provided for them does not adversely affect the younger children. If you work with an assistant or another registered home-based childcarer then the numbers are doubled, so two people can care for two babies, for example. The supervision ratios are given in Table 2.1 below.

Supervision inside your home

It is essential that you can see and/or hear all the children all the time. There will be times when you may not be in the same room as them, for example, if you are in the kitchen preparing a meal or snack and the children are in the play room. Before you go into the kitchen or a different room, ask yourself:

● Are the children safe?
● How long am I going to be?
● Can I see and/or hear the children at all times?
● Could I organise my time differently so that I don't need to leave the room for long, perhaps by preparing the snack or meal before the children arrive?

Case study

Kim cares for a 13-month-old baby, a three year old during the day, and two six year olds after school and during school holidays. The baby has a nap after lunch in his buggy, which Kim puts in her front room. It often happens that the baby is asleep, the three year old is playing with toys on the carpet and the six year olds want to go outside. To make sure that all children are supervised properly, Kim uses a baby monitor and takes it with her if she goes outside so she can hear the baby. If the weather is suitable she encourages the three year old to take his toys outside. Kim can see all of her outside area from the glass doors of the play room so if the three year old doesn't want to go out, Kim can still see the older children in the garden. She uses a timer set for five minute intervals to make visual checks on the baby and also checks on the children outside by talking to them. By doing these things Kim believes that she is meeting her responsibilities for safe supervision of the children.

Discussion point

● Do you think Kim is meeting her responsibilities?
● How could you manage the supervision of the children differently?
● What would you do in Kim's situation if you needed to go to the toilet?

Links to the EYFS

Sections 3.41 to 3.43 in the 2014 EYFS (page 24) give you the statutory requirements for home-based childcarers with regard to adult-to-child ratios.

Table 2.1 Adult-to-child ratios in countries of the UK

Country	Total number	Under five years	Babies
England	Six under eight years	Three	One under 12 months
Wales	Six under eight years	Three	Two under 18 months
Scotland	Six under eight years	Three	One under 12 months
Northern Ireland	Six under 12 years	Three	One under 12 months

Discussion point

We all need to go to the toilet at some point during a working day. It is perfectly understandable that you want privacy at such times.

● How can you supervise children responsibly when you are not in the same room?
● How can you balance your need for privacy with your responsibility to supervise the children?

Supervision outside your home – the garden

The regulatory inspectors will check the outside areas of your home for safety. It is possible to become registered as a home-based childcarer without having access to a garden, provided you can prove that you can provide easy and regular access to other outside areas for play, such as a local park.

The same 'rules' apply in the garden as for inside your home when it comes to supervision. You must be able to see and/or hear the children at all times. It may be that for safety and to maintain correct supervision ratios you make decisions that mean all children are outside or all are inside at any one time. Ask yourself how you can guarantee safe supervision without being in several different places at the same time?

Checking your garden and outside areas for safety will be discussed later in this chapter under AC 2.4.

Supervision when out and about

Supervision requirements do not change just because you are not in your home or garden. In fact, supervision can often be more constant, for example, if you are crossing a road with a baby in a buggy and a three year old. Many home-based childcarers take and collect children from other settings and schools, and are out and about a lot. This can include transporting children in your car, on foot or sometimes on public transport, often in busy places with lots of people about.

Safe and effective supervision is essential in noisy, busy school playgrounds when there are lots of children running about. You do not want to be the red-faced, out-of-breath adult chasing their children – apart from anything else, it is unprofessional.

Tip

Don't forget you need written permission from parents to take children out of your premises. This applies not just to special trips, but to any off-site trip. Many home-based childcarers get a 'blanket' permission letter signed by parents to cover all trips out, and then get separate written permission for special events and trips.

Supervision in your car

You should never, under any circumstances, leave any child unsupervised in your car. All children travelling in your car must have their own seat, with their own secure restraints appropriate for their age, weight and size. Remember that you cannot give full and constant supervision while you are driving. Therefore it is essential that children are sitting in seats with appropriate secure restraints. The same adult-to-child ratios apply when travelling in your car as in your home.

Supervision when using public transport

Public transport is sometimes busy and noisy and it is relatively easy for you and children to become separated. Consider using personal restraints and/or safety harnesses for younger children. This means that the children are always close to you. Older children should be taught basic safety awareness, such as staying close or holding hands. All children will need very close and constant supervision.

Supervision when walking on roads

Walking along a road is potentially a dangerous situation and all children will need constant supervision. As with using public transport, personal restraints are a very good idea to keep children close. There are many different types on the market, including reins, harnesses and straps with wrist bands. You should also teach all children road safety awareness.

Reflective practice

It is a frightening fact but every day a child under five years is killed or seriously injured on our roads. This would suggest that we do not teach road safety well enough to our children, or to adults either. Supervision is about keeping children safe at all times and if we do not take this responsibility seriously when we are out on our roads and streets, we are failing in our duty of care. So make sure that you know how to cross a road safely before you venture out with children. Be a positive role model.

- How many times have you seen adults and children trying to cross a busy road when there is a light-controlled crossing within a short distance?
- How many times have you seen children and adults crossing a road between parked cars?

Figure 2.3 Are you aware of safe places to cross a road with children?

Useful resources

Website
BRAKE
BRAKE is a road safety charity for early years and schools. There is a wealth of very good resources on their website **www.brake.org.uk** to help children become aware of road safety.

Tip

If you are thinking about taking children on a special trip, it is a good idea to consider asking another adult to accompany you, as two pairs of eyes and ears are always better than one. If that other adult is neither a parent nor registered as your assistant, however, they must meet the suitable people requirement (EYFS Safeguarding and Welfare Requirements 3.9) (see page 9).

In your setting

Really study the areas that you plan to use when caring for children. Ask yourself:

- Are there areas where I can't actually see the children, such as hiding places in the garden?
- Can I see and/or hear the children when I am in the kitchen?
- How can I balance the need for safe supervision with a child's right to privacy?

AC 2.3 Describe procedures for the storage and administration of medication and record keeping in relation to medication

Key terms

Describe – write in detail about an idea, topic or subject, using language that is straightforward and does not contain jargon

Procedures – ways, practices, methods, systems to help carry out an action

In a perfect world, you would be caring only for children who are fit and well, and so the need to store and administer medication would not arise. Life is not like that, however. It may be that you are caring for a child who regularly uses an inhaler or injects insulin, or in an emergency requires an EpiPen. You may also have a parent's written permission to give a child a product such as Calpol when needed. All of these are classed as medication and procedures are needed to manage their storage and use safely.

Discussion point

A child has been unwell and away from your setting for a few days and is taking antibiotic medication. The parents want to return to work and think the child is much better; there are two more days of medication left, however. The parents ask you to care for the child and give the medication.

- Is this right?
- What should you do?

Procedures for the storage of medication

- All medicines and medications, such as cream and tablets, must be stored in the original container.
- All containers must be labelled with the child's name and the correct dosage to be given.
- All medicines and medication (except asthma inhalers) must be stored in a locked container that is inaccessible to children. If medicines have to be stored in the fridge you should put them, in their original packaging, in a separate container, away from foodstuffs if possible.
- Asthma inhalers should be kept nearby, so you can get them for the child if required quickly. They should still be out of reach of children and preferably in a cupboard, but quickly accessible for you.

Figure 2.4 It is important that you know how to store all medication

Procedures for administration of medication

- Medicines, both prescription and non-prescription, must be administered to a child only with the written permission of the child's parent or carer for that particular medicine. It is not good practice to have only one blanket permission form for administering medication. You should get a new signed form each time you need to administer a new medication.
- Medicines must not be given to a child unless they have been prescribed for that child by a doctor, dentist, nurse or pharmacist.
- Training from a qualified health professional must be undertaken if the administration of medication requires technical or medical knowledge, for example, for the use of an epi pen.
- Generally, no drugs should be given to a child while in your care; if the child has a long-term condition, however, such as eczema, you should discuss the child's care needs with the parents

or carers and obtain their written permission to administer their medication.
- You must give the child only the dosage as indicated on the original container.
- Read the instructions each time you give the medication. Check the dosage and whether the medication should be taken before or after eating, or with a drink, etc.
- After administering medicines make sure that you thoroughly wash the spoon or whatever the child has used to take the medicine, or dispose of the syringe. Place equipment out of reach of children.
- After administering the medication, return it to its original container and secure storage place.

Procedures for record keeping in relation to medication

- Have a record book with a sheet or page for each child, for each time you administer a new medication.

- Make sure that you fully understand how to give the medicine and the correct dose. If you are not sure about anything, ask the parents before they leave. Never guess or leave anything to chance.
- As an absolute minimum you must record:
  - the date
  - the time
  - the dosage
  - your signature
  - the parent's signature.
- It is good practice also to record if there are any problems giving the medication to the child. For example, you could record if the child refused to take it, or spat it out, or was sick shortly after having it. Make sure the parents or carers read this information.

Useful resources

Website
PACEY
The Professional Association for Childcare and Early Education (PACEY) has many very useful resources, such as medication record books, available to their members. You can get further information at **www.pacey.org.uk**

In your setting

- Check that you can store all medication appropriately.
- Check that you have procedures that are very clear about administering medicines, including information about individual children's needs for medicines.
- Make sure that all parents/carers understand your procedures.

Links to the EYFS

In Sections 3.44 to 3.46 of the EYFS on page 25, under the heading Health, you will find all the statutory information regarding medicines.

AC 2.4 Understand how to carry out risk assessments, both inside your home and outdoors

As mentioned earlier, you have a legal responsibility to keep the children for whom you care safe at all times. This means that the environment, both inside and out, and the equipment, toys and other resources that you use must be safe and fit for purpose. A very effective way to meet your responsibilities is to carry out risk assessments.

Key terms

Risk assessment – a check that is carried out to identify any hazards and find out the safest way to deal with the hazard

Hazard – a potential risk or something that could harm or damage a child

In your setting

There is no set way to carry out risk assessments. Whatever way you decide to do them, they must be thorough, accurate and work for you. Good and effective risk assessments have several parts:

1 **Identification** of the risk or hazard – what is it and where is it?
2 **Who** is at risk – is it you and other adults, only the children, only a certain age group?
3 **Evaluate** the risk – can you remove it completely? If not, can you control it?
4 Make a **note** of your decisions arising from points 1, 2 and 3.
5 **Do something** about the risks or hazards straightaway.
6 **Go back at a later date** and check that there are no further risks or hazards; there is a chance that in a busy working week you could forget to do this so put a reminder in your diary or calendar.

In your setting

If you decide to do a written risk assessment in, say, the form of a checklist, make sure that completing it is realistic. For example, you may decide to do a written checklist assessment of your outdoor area and equipment every day. To do this, however, you will need at least 45 minutes each day before children access that area. Ask yourself if you have actually got 45 minutes or more to complete a written checklist, or if you could walk around the outside area, make a mental note of potential hazards and remove them?

On the other hand, a written checklist completed once a month of all your electrical/technological equipment and resources may be achievable. This is not to suggest that written checklists are inappropriate, but merely to get you to think about other ways of carrying out good and valid risk assessments.

A possible risk assessment checklist is shown in Table 2.2.

Risk assessment of indoor rooms

You will need to do safety checks and risk assessments of every room that will be used by the children when in your care. Rooms that you do not use must be made inaccessible to children in safe ways. This could be with the use of stair gates, locks, bolts or security chains. It is recommended that you use gates with the safety standard number BSI 4125.

Tip

One effective way to check the safety of your rooms is to get down on your knees (in other words, at child height) and look around you. The chances are you will spot more potential hazards at this level than when you are at adult height. For every potential hazard, ask yourself:

- Why is this a danger?
- Who is at risk?
- What can I do about it?

Table 2.2 Example checklist for risk assessments

Date	Risk	Who is at risk	What to do	Action	Recheck
01/07/14	Broken wheel on scooter	Two to five year olds	Stop children playing with it	Remove from garden to recycling point	02/07/14
01/07/14	Spilt nuts at bird feeder	All children, but especially little ones who might try to eat the nuts	If time, pick up all the nuts or put a cover over the spilt ones and tell children to leave it alone	Pick up nuts, fix bird feeder securely	02/07/14
01/07/14	Parents not shutting gate	All children	Speak to all parents, make a 'shut the gate' sign	Put sign on both sides of the gate, speak to all parents as they leave	Visual check every time a parent leaves

The following bulleted lists are mental checklists for you, to prompt you to think about possible hazards in your rooms and consider what you are going to do about them.

Risk assessment of the kitchen

- No child should be ever allowed in your kitchen unsupervised, so how can you stop children having free access to this part of your house? If you have a kitchen door, consider using a stair gate across the doorway so you can see the children but they cannot get into the kitchen.
- Keep doors to washing machines and tumble driers closed at all times.
- Keep oven doors closed, and do not allow children to touch the door when it is hot.
- Make sure that pan handles on your oven top or hob are turned in. You can buy safety guard rails that will fit around the edge of your oven top or hob.
- Think about where and how you store knives and kitchen utensils.
- All cleaning materials should be kept in a locked cupboard. This includes dishwasher and washing machine tablets, powders, liquids and conditioners.
- Keep alcohol in a cupboard that children cannot open.
- Store plastic bags in a place that children cannot access.
- Don't have trailing cables and flexes (this applies to all rooms where electrical and technological equipment is used). You can get coiled flexes for kettles and toasters and the like, or use plastic clips to tie up flexes and cables.
- Have you got a fire blanket?
- Have you got a home fire extinguisher, and is it still in date?
- Does your smoke alarm work?

Risk assessment of other downstairs rooms

- Never leave any children, regardless of their age, unsupervised when eating or drinking. This includes babies with bottles.
- Don't use table cloths or mats that hang a long way over the sides of a table, as a toddler may try to pull herself up using the overhang.

Tip

Many home-based childcarers use plastic table covers to protect their furniture, which are very useful for messy play activities. You can also get clips that hold the cloth in place or you can make sure you don't have the cloth overhanging more than five centimetres.

- Look at the arrangement of furniture in your rooms.
  - Do you have sofas or chairs near windows that children could use to climb on to the sills?
  - Do you have low tables with glass tops or sharp edges?
  - Do you have rugs that move or could be a trip hazard?
  - Do you have uneven floor surfaces?
  - Could your television topple over if pushed?
  - Have you got trailing wires, cables and flexes?
  - Are table lamps safe?
- Are your doors and windows safe? Consider the use of window locks and door catches that prevent the window or door from fully closing.
- Is your fire, log burner or other heating appliance protected with a fireguard that is not free standing? Any fireguard should be fixed to the wall on either side of the fire and you should never put anything on top of or over the guard. Did you know it is an offence to leave a child under the age of 12 years in a room with an open fire?
- Does all furniture with glass in it or on it comply with British Safety Standards? Look for a label showing BS 73767 or BS 7449.8.
- Are toys and other equipment stored safely?
- Is the floor space free from trip hazards?
- Are there ornaments, pictures, candles, room diffusers or other items easily accessible with which children could hurt themselves?
- Have you checked your smoke alarm recently?
- Have you checked your carbon monoxide alarm recently?

Find out more

Many pieces of furniture, equipment and toys will have safety marks or symbols on them, for example, the British Standards Institution (BSI), which is often referred to as the Kitemark. Look at the marks and symbols below and find out what they mean.

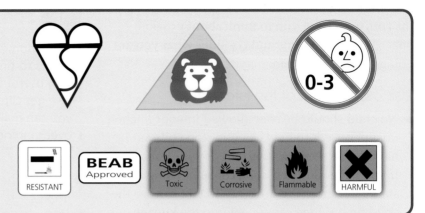

Reflective practice

Even though toys, equipment or a piece of furniture may have a safety mark or label, this does *not* mean that it is safe. The labels and signs are to give information that the item has been manufactured to certain safety standards.

Anything with a safety label can be a danger if used incorrectly. It is especially important that you thoroughly check any item that you buy or that is given to you. It may very well have a Kitemark, but it could, for example, have loose or worn fastenings and so not be safe.

Risk assessment of your hallway and stairs

- Is your main access door securely locked?
- Where do you keep the keys for your door?
- Would a security chain or spy hole be a good idea for you?
- Are children able to go upstairs or have you put up a stair gate (BSI 4125)?
- Are there toys or other items on the stairs?
- Is the flooring free from trip hazards?
- Are stair rails, bannisters and balustrades firm? Do they have any footholds for adventurous little persons to climb?

Risk assessment of your toilet and bathroom

- Where do you store cleaning materials?
- Where do you keep your shower gel, shampoo, conditioner and other cosmetics?
- Is your medicine cabinet locked and out of reach of children?

- Wet floors can be slippery, so check regularly and wipe and dry floors as needed.
- Check the temperature of hot water before children put their hands under the tap.
- It is reported that a piece of soggy soap sitting on a wash basin or sink contains millions of harmful bacteria, so are there other products you could use?
- Are toilet training seats and step stools firm?
- Are potties clean and disinfected?
- Have you got one hand towel per child?
- If the door locks, can it be opened from the outside in an emergency?

Risk assessment of toys and equipment

- Check the security fastening of high chairs and baby seats.
- Are high chairs and all seats used by children stable?
- Do not allow children to play on beds or in cots.
- Are the slide-down sides of cots secure and firm?
- Are mattresses flame retardant?
- Have you got separate bedding for each child?
- Have you got separate potties for each child?
- Have you got separate hand towels for each child?
- Are toilet trainer seats firm?
- Check that anything made from plastic is not split.
- Are your stair and safety gates firm?
- Are battery compartments on toys secure and not easy to open?
- Make sure all toys are age- and stage-appropriate for the child playing with them.
- Throw away any broken toys.
- Are toys with small pieces stored safely so that babies and young children cannot get them?

- Are you storing toys in safe ways? Don't pile up boxes of things on top of each other or just randomly put things in a shed or outside storage area.

Risk assessment of your outside areas

- Are all gates secured?
- Are all fences secure, with no 'escape holes'?
- Where do you store garden tools and equipment?
- Can children access your greenhouse, cold frame or shed?
- Are all surfaces trip free? Check for broken or cracked paving slabs; check patio and decking areas are trip free.
- Are your rubbish and recycling bins and boxes inaccessible to children?
- If you have a pond or water feature, is it accessible to children?
- Do you know which plants, shrubs and trees are potentially harmful to children?
- Are all large pieces of equipment safe, with no loose bits, frayed ropes, broken pieces or rust that might be hiding dangers?
- Are all outside toys safely stored?
- Have you checked for and removed pet faeces (either from your own pet or a neighbour's)?

Find out more

Use the internet, reference books or a local garden centre to check all the plants in your garden. Find out which ones have leaves, sap, flowers, seeds (or any other part) that could be toxic or cause skin irritations.

Discussion point

Discuss with other home-based childcarers what they do about potentially unsafe things in their gardens. Consider:

- Is it realistic to dig up all your plants and redesign your garden?
- Is this fair on your family and/or partner?
- What about neighbours' gardens? They could have a tree, such as a laburnum, which hangs over into your garden; what can you do about this?

Risk assessments when out and about

Your car

- Does each child have a seat in your car with appropriate restraints for their age, size and weight?
- Have you got valid road tax and MOT?
- Have you got fully comprehensive car insurance, and does your insurer know that you are transporting other people's children for business purposes?
- Are all car doors fitted with working child locks?
- When you park, make sure that children get out on the pavement side.

Public transport

- Have you checked the times of the buses or trains?
- Do you know where you are going?
- Have you done this trip before, without children?
- Can you manage a buggy and children easily?
- Make sure all children stand well back from bus stops and the edge of platforms.
- Have you got adequate and appropriate child harnesses or restraints?

Walking and road safety

- Do you know how to cross roads safely? Always use zebra or pelican crossings where possible.
- Have you taught children about road safety and awareness of possible dangers?
- Do you know where you are going?
- Have you checked that the buggy is in full working order?
- If you go to a park or other place where there is a risk that you may become separated, agree with the children an easily recognisable meeting point that you will all go to.

Useful resources

Websites

RoSPA
Look at **www.rospa.com** for more information on risk assessments and keeping children safe.

HSE
The Health and Safety Executive (HSE) also has a wealth of information about risk assessments in the home. Look at **www.hse.gov.uk**

Reflective practice

You must always remember that making your home and outside area safe is not just about doing risk assessments and checking for potential hazards and dangers. It is also about being aware at all times of possible dangers and hazards. You can never 'let your guard down'.

It is also about being a positive role model for the children. Don't ever take risks or behave in unsafe ways when you are with children.

And finally – teach children ways to keep themselves safe. Allow them to have challenge in their play so that they learn about risk. See AC 2.1.

Links to the EYFS

Details about risk assessments can be found on page 28 of the 2014 EYFS, in Sections 3.64 and 3.65.

AC 2.5 Summarise ways to maintain a safe and healthy environment for children in relation to preparation of formula feeds, sterilisation of feeding equipment, preparation and storage of food, safe disposal of waste and care of pets

In your setting

As a professional home-based childcarer your home is open to scrutiny. This could come from parents, other professionals such as local authority support workers, health visitors and regulatory body inspectors. It is very important that you have the highest possible standards of personal hygiene. You must also make sure that your home is a safe and hygienic environment for children. You must do everything possible to prevent the spread of infection.

Children will copy and learn from things that you do. Therefore it is very important that you are a positive role model and set the highest example. You will need to establish routines and procedures that encourage personal hygiene and help children learn safe ways to care for themselves. Routines for personal hygiene will be discussed in Chapter 5.

Key terms

Infection – disease, virus, illness

Routines – ways of doing things that follow a sequence or pattern, usually planned and carried out regularly

Washing your hands

Washing your hands and teaching children to do the same is one of the most effective ways of preventing the spread of infection. Any hand washing process should take no less than 30 seconds; in fact if you are doing it thoroughly it will take much longer.

In your setting

A routine for washing hands:

- Wet hands thoroughly in hot water before applying soap (ideally liquid soap should be used as a bar of soap retains bacteria, especially if it is left wet).
- Briskly massage both hands with the lather, paying special attention to fingers, thumbs, between fingers and under rings.
- Rinse hands well under running water.
- Dry on a clean dry cloth towel or paper towel.

Keeping your home clean

Keeping your home clean is essential if you are to prevent the spread of infection. Infections can be spread by transmission (such as by touch) and via droplets in the air (for example, from coughs and sneezes). Infections can also be carried on food, in water, on animals, on cuts and grazes, and on fingers and surfaces around your home. Children easily pick up infections and it is almost impossible to keep them completely infection-free. Keeping your home and work areas clean will stop germs from multiplying and so reduce the spread of infection.

In your setting

Cleaning products often claim to kill a high percentage of germs and bacteria. Remember, however, that most of these products are harmful to children and pets. All cleaning products must be stored out of reach of children or in a locked cupboard.

Activity

Make a list of when you wash your hands in any one day. Then check it against the following list:

● After handling money
● After wiping a child's nose
● After coughing or sneezing
● After using the toilet
● After playing outside or following messy play
● Before and after changing a nappy or helping a child with personal care/hygiene
● Before and after dealing with cuts and grazes
● After touching pets and their feeding bowls
● Before handling food
● Before you eat
● Before feeding babies.

Figure 2.5 Teaching children how to wash their hands helps prevent the spread of infection

Antiseptic cleaners and wipes are weak disinfectants. They do help prevent germs from multiplying, but they do not destroy germs or bacteria. They can also be harmful to children. Soap and water, fresh air and sunlight will destroy many germs.

- What do you use to make sure that surfaces are as germ-free as possible?

Links to the EYFS

The statutory requirement for all types of food and drink can be found under Sections 3.47–3.49 of the EYFS, on page 26.

Ways to maintain a safe and healthy environment for children in relation to preparation of formula feeds

The very first thing you should do is discuss formula feeding with the baby's parents. Some parents will make up all the feeds required before the baby is brought to you. Others may expect you to supply everything, including formula, bottles, teats, caps, covers and sterilising equipment.

It is good practice to establish a routine for preparing bottle feeds. This will mean that you follow a sequence or pattern of events and are less likely to forget to do something. If you have your own children you may be thinking that you have made up hundreds of feeds and don't need a routine. Caring for other people's children is a very different proposition to caring for your own, however. You do need a routine. If using commercially prepared baby milk, you must follow the manufacturer's instructions for storage and shelf life once opened.

Tip

It is good practice to record the date, time and amount of feed that a baby has had while in your care, so that you can give accurate information to the parents.

Ways to maintain a safe and healthy environment for children in relation to sterilisation of feeding equipment

There are several ways that you can sterilise feeding equipment: sterilising by boiling, steam sterilising or cold water sterilising.

In your setting

A routine for preparing formula feeds as adapted from the NHS website:

- Before you begin, wash your hands and dry them on a clean dry cloth towel or paper towel.
- Empty the kettle then fill with fresh water from the tap.
- Boil the kettle.
- Leave the water to cool for no more than 30 minutes. The water temperature should not be less than 70°C.
- Clean or disinfect the area or surface that you are planning to use to make up the feed.
- Wash your hands again.
- Take the bottle out of the steriliser and shake off excess water.

- Rinse the bottle with water from the kettle and place it on the clean surface.
- Follow the manufacturer's instructions and measure the correct amount of boiled water in the bottle.
- Use the scoop provided to measure out the formula and level it with a clean, dry knife.
- Take a teat out of the steriliser, shake off excess water and rinse it with boiled water.
- Put the teat on the bottle and shake the bottle until all the formula is dissolved.
- Cool the bottle by putting the lower half under a cold running tap, making sure that the tap water does not go on the teat.
- Test the temperature on the inside of your wrist. The feed should be at body temperature.
- Any left-over feed should be thrown away.

The method you choose is very much personal choice. A discussion between you and the baby's parents about sterilising bottles and other equipment is good practice, however, and helps to maintain a consistent approach to the baby's care and to develop partnership working.

Ways to maintain a safe and healthy environment for children in relation to preparation and storage of food

Many home-based childcarers provide meals and snacks for children. The ways that you prepare, cook and serve food will help the children to learn and develop healthy and sensible eating habits.

Links to the EYFS

It is a Safeguarding and Welfare Requirement of the EYFS (England) that where children are provided with meals and snacks, these must be healthy, balanced and nutritious. See Section 3.47 of the EYFS, page 26. Healthy diets will be covered in more detail in Chapter 5.

If you register as a home-based childcarer with Ofsted or a childminding agency (in England), and you plan to provide food as part of your normal home-based childcare service, the details you provide will also be used to register you as a food business. This means that your registration details will be available to your local authority, and you will not have to register separately as a food business with your local authority. This allows home-based

In your setting

A routine for **sterilising feeding equipment**:

- Before you begin any sterilising process, wash the used bottles, teats, caps and covers in hot, soapy water.
- Make sure that all milk deposits are removed. You can buy bottle brushes that are specifically designed to get into the awkward crevices and folds.
- Rinse under cold running water.
- Wash and dry your hands.
- Follow the manufacturer's instructions in full if you are using cold water sterilising solution or steam sterilising. The instructions detail how to put the bottles and other equipment in the steriliser; how long to leave the equipment in the steriliser; and whether you need to desterilise before using.
- If you are sterilising by boiling water you must take particular care with safety and do everything you can to prevent burns and scalds.
- Check on the other children, are they safe?
- Make sure that you do not leave any hot pans or liquids unattended.
- Check that the equipment to be sterilised is safe to be boiled.
- Wash your hands.
- Boil all items for at least ten minutes, making sure that all the equipment is covered with water.

Tip

Sterilising teats by the boiling water method reduces the life of the teat. So make sure that you check them for damage very carefully afterwards.

If using the boiling water method, remove bottles just before you are going to use them.

Whatever method you use, if bottles are not going to be used straightaway, put them together with the teat and lid in place. This will stop the inside of the bottle and the outside of the teat becoming contaminated.

childcarers who provide food to have their premises registered with the environmental health service of their local authority, which is a legal requirement.

After registering as a food business you may have a food safety inspection. This will be carried out by your local authority, as they are responsible for food safety in your local area. If your business does need an inspection, a food safety officer will contact you to arrange a suitable time to visit. The officer will talk about food hygiene and food safety to help make sure any food you give to the children is safely prepared, stored and handled.

In Scotland, the Food Standards Agency and the Scottish Food Enforcement Liaison Committee have produced guidance for home-based childcarers about whether they need to register as a food business operator. It is free of charge to register with your local authority if you do need to do this.

Useful resources

Food Standards Agency
More details can be found at: **www.food.gov. uk/enforcement/enforceessential/yourarea**

In Wales and Northern Ireland you will need to register with your local authority environmental health department. Further information about how to register and contact your local authority environmental health department (including a model registration form) is available at the Food Standards Agency website.

Tip

It is good practice to get a qualification in food handling. You will need to check with your local authority or training provider to see what courses are available for you. You are required to have a food handling qualification if you live in Wales and are planning to provide children with food.

When parents provide you with food for their children you should do everything possible to encourage them to supply only healthy, balanced and nutritious items, including drinks. It is your

responsibility to make sure that fresh drinking water is freely available all day to all the children.

Useful resources

Publication
'Safer food, better business'
The Food Standards Agency has produced a 'Safer food, better business' (SFBB) pack especially for home-based childcarers. The pack gives simple, straightforward advice on food safety, including information on feeding babies and children, cooking and chilling food, cleaning, and looking after a child with a food allergy.

Go to the Food Standards Agency website and search for the name of the publication.

Food hygiene is important for everyone. 'Food hygiene' includes all of the practices that need to be followed to make sure food is safe and healthy in all stages of production and right up to the point when it is eaten. Food poisoning happens when food has not been prepared or stored safely. Food poisoning is caused by bacteria multiplying on food and then being eaten. The first step in preventing food poisoning is to stop bacteria from coming into contact with food. Bacteria thrive in warm and damp conditions, so make sure that your hands and drying cloths are completely dry. Most food poisoning is preventable; it is not possible, however, to eliminate the risk entirely.

Tip

Don't forget: that soggy bit of soap on the kitchen sink is actually covered in bacteria, so think about using a soap dispenser.

Links to the EYFS

You must notify Ofsted or your childminder agency of any food poisoning outbreak that affects two or more children in your care. See Section 3.49 of the EYFS, page 26.

In your setting

When you are **preparing food** make sure that you:

- Know where all the children are and check that you are able to supervise them while you prepare the food.
- Thoroughly wash and dry your hands before you begin.
- Wear a clean apron.
- Cover any cuts on your hands; it is good practice to follow industry guidelines and use blue plasters.
- Tie back your hair.
- Check that the areas you plan to use to prepare foods are clean and safe.
- Check that the utensils, plates, dishes and beakers are clean and safe.
- Protect food from anything that could cause harm, for examples, use covers to keep flies off food.
- Never allow pets on to surfaces or in areas where you prepare food for children.
- Wash your hands after touching raw meat, poultry and fish.
- Keep raw food separate from cooked food.
- Avoid handling food if possible, use utensils instead.
- Use separate chopping boards, knives and dishes for raw meat, poultry and fish.
- Thaw food in a leak-proof container and make sure it is completely thawed before using.
- Make sure children wash their hands before helping you prepare food and before eating.

Tip

Some manufacturers produce colour-coded chopping boards with symbols on, so that you know which board to use for which foods.

Preventing bacteria that are already present on food from multiplying can be done by correct food storage. It might not completely eliminate all bacteria, but correct food storage should slow down the multiplying process. Bacteria thrive in warm conditions or in places that are warmed by the sun, such as your kitchen window sill. Bacteria can spread rapidly in temperatures between 5 and 63°C, so it is very important that you know the temperature inside your fridge and other places where you store foods. Harmful bacteria are not destroyed until food has been cooked to 71°C or more (boiling point is 100°C).

In your setting

When you are **storing food** make sure that:

- Your fridge is between 0°C and 5°C.
- Your freezer is between minus 18°C and minus 23°C.
- You do not overfill your fridge; air should be able to circulate around the inside.
- You do not refreeze anything that was previously frozen and has been thawed out.
- You do not store raw meat or fish next to other food. These foods should be in leak-proof containers at the bottom of your fridge.
- You store food in packets and cans in a cool dry place.
- You store salad foods in your fridge and wash before eating.
- You store fruit and vegetables in a cool dry place and always wash before eating.
- Once a tin or food container has been opened, leftover food is stored in the fridge in a different container with a well-fitting lid.
- Foods that are past their use-by date are not eaten.
- You read the labels on food to check how long they can be stored and where they should be stored.
- Children's lunch boxes are stored in a cool place, preferably a fridge.
- You do not store formula milk.
- Breast milk is stored in the main part of the fridge for no longer than five days, or up to two weeks in the freezer compartment of your fridge, or six months in your separate freezer.

Ways to maintain a safe and healthy environment for children in relation to safe disposal of waste

All waste material contains germs and bacteria. It is very important that any waste disposal is done hygienically and according to its type. All waste bins should be covered with a well-fitting lid and emptied frequently. Children should not have access to any waste bins.

Ways to maintain a safe and healthy environment for children in relation to care of pets

Caring for animals can be a very positive learning experience for children. It teaches them to take responsibility for their care and to understand the needs of other living things. For children who do not have pets at home, coming to your house and seeing your pet can be a rewarding experience.

Animals can be unpredictable in their behaviour, even your much loved dog! You must make sure that the children in your care are not in danger from any pets that you have in your household. You can teach children how to care for and treat animals, but you are responsible for keeping the children safe. You should never leave children alone with pets. If your pet is not tolerant of children, you must have an alternative place where the animal is safe but not accessible to children.

There are often horrific stories in the media about children being attacked by dogs, but remember that small pets, such as hamsters and rabbits, can bite too, especially if little fingers are pushed through cage bars. Cats may also scratch if handling becomes too boisterous.

In your setting

When dealing with **bodily waste** – that is, blood, urine, faeces and vomit – you should always:

- Wash your hands before putting on personal protective equipment (PPE), such as disposable gloves and a plastic apron.
- Put on disposable gloves before handling the waste.
- Use a dilute bleach (hypochlorite) solution to mop up any spillages.
- Put soiled nappies, dressings, disposable towels and gloves in a sealed bag before putting them in a plastic-lined covered bin that is not used for any other form of waste. You can buy specially designed covered containers that wrap and seal nappies separately in anti-bacterial film.
- If parents want their child to wear terry cloth or other reusable nappies, make sure that you have agreed with them how these nappies will be kept hygienically when soiled and how they will be washed and dried.
- Empty potties down the toilet, not the kitchen sink or wash basin, and then flush the toilet.
- Dispose of the gloves immediately afterwards.
- Wash hands after removing the gloves.

When dealing with **food waste** make sure:

- It is kept well away from bodily waste.
- Rubbish bins are emptied frequently and cleaned out.
- You have different waste bins for different types of rubbish; for example, if you are composting (or recycling) food waste make sure you have a covered container, preferably outside, where it can be stored until it is put in the compost bin.
- The food is covered when you are storing 'leftovers', preferably in a container with a lid, allowed to cool and put in the fridge. (Don't forget about it once it's in the fridge, either!)

Tip

It is good practice to provide children with paper tissues and teach them how to dispose of them hygienically. Consider having a separate covered bin for used tissues. Don't forget to teach children to wash their hands after blowing their nose. You should also wash your hands if you have wiped a child's nose.

Discussion point

Dogs, like children, need fresh air and exercise. You do need to think seriously about when you will fit in walking the dog while caring for children. Animals, like children, can also become sick and need special care and attention.

- Think carefully how you would manage a sick animal, which could perhaps require visits to a vet and isolating the animal from the children, around the children's needs.

In your setting

- Teach children to wash their hands after touching pets.
- Do not allow children to kiss pets.
- Do not allow animals to lick children's faces or hands.
- Keep animal food and water bowls separate from those used by children and other people.
- Wash animal food and water bowls separately.
- If you, or another family member, keep exotic pets, make sure that they are securely and appropriately housed so that children cannot gain access to them.
- Clean up any pet 'accidents' immediately, following the procedures for disposal of bodily waste.
- Check all your outside areas for animal faeces before children have access (this should be part of your risk assessment procedures). Even if you do not have a dog or cat, your garden could be visited during the night by neighbours' animals.

Case study

Oliver and Ahmed, both three years old, are cleaning out the hamster cage on the outside patio with their carer, Jules. This is something that they have all done many times before. Jules' mobile phone rings and she is momentarily distracted as she goes to answer it. In that short space of time, Oliver sticks his fingers through the cage bars and the hamster bites him.

Discussion point

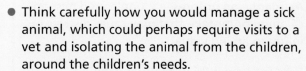

How could Jules have prevented Oliver being bitten?

AC 2.6 Explain procedures to follow in the event of accidents, incidents and emergencies

It is a fact of life that all children will at some point have accidents. Young children can trip and bump themselves. A baby can roll over and knock themselves on toys or the legs of furniture. Most of the time these are minor accidents, but occasionally something more serious may happen. It is essential that you know what to do in the case of a serious accident, incident or emergency – and that you do not unintentionally make the situation worse. It is a requirement of your registration as a home-based childcarer that you have a Paediatric First Aid qualification (remember that this must be renewed every three years). It is important, however, that you are aware of your limitations and in an emergency carry out only procedures that you are competent to do. It is good practice that private nannies also hold a First Aid qualification.

Key terms

Accident – an unforeseen, unplanned mishap, calamity or mistake that may cause distress or injury to an individual

Incident – something that happens, an occurrence, minor or serious

Emergency – a situation that is urgent; a crisis or real danger

Links to the EYFS

You must notify your regulatory body or childminder agency of any serious accident, illness or injury to, or death of, any child while in your care. You must also notify them of the action you took. Notification should be made as soon as possible, and must be made within 14 days of the incident occurring. You must notify your local child protection agencies of any serious accident, injury or death of a child while in your care, and act upon any advice given (Section 3.51).

In your setting

You must have a first aid box that is stored safely, but at the same time is accessible if needed. You can buy a first aid box and contents from a chemist, or make up your own contents. Every time you use your first aid kit, get into the habit of making a note of the items that you used and adding them to your shopping list. It is good practice to stick a list of the contents to the lid of your first aid box, and when you have finished using the kit to do a quick check to make sure that everything you need is there and usable.

Your first aid kit should be used only for your childcare business. You need a separate one for your family use.

Useful resources

Website
First aid kits
You can purchase an approved first aid kit from PACEY's website: **www.pacey.org.uk**

Procedures to follow in the event of accidents

If a child has an accident it is likely that they will initially be shocked. They may not cry immediately, but they will need calm reassurance. The correct action taken after an accident can often mean the difference between life and death.

- Stay calm.
- Deal first with the dangerous situation.
- Talk to the child to see if they respond.
- If possible, remove the child, other children and yourself from danger. You must not move the injured child if you suspect they are seriously injured, however; in this case, call the emergency services.
- Remember that some young children may not be able to explain their injuries so you will need to check the child very carefully. This includes checking their airway, breathing and circulation to see if they have a pulse.
- Put the child in the recovery position.

Many less serious accidents can be dealt with easily provided your first aid box is complete and you know what to do. Such accidents include:

- grazes
- nose bleeds
- bumps.
- minor burns
- bruises

Reporting accidents and incidents

You must follow the guidelines of Reporting of Injuries, Diseases and Dangerous Occurrences (RIDDOR) (1995) for reporting accidents and incidents. You are also required to have an accident report book. This book should be reviewed every few weeks to identify any potential or actual hazards in your home. Your accident book should have duplicate pages so that you can give a copy to the parents and keep one for yourself. Where there is an injury that requires a visit to a general practitioner or hospital, or where there is a death of a child, a report must be made to the Health and Safety Executive.

You should record:

- the name of the person injured
- the date and time of the injury
- where the accident happened
- exactly what happened
- what injuries resulted
- what treatment was given
- your signature
- the parent's signature.

Activity

Read the following research from the Royal Society for the Prevention of Accidents (RoSPA).

RoSPA research suggests that:

- Most accidents in the home occur in the living or dining rooms, and the most serious accidents happen in the kitchen and on the stairs.
- Children from birth to four years are most at risk from accidents in the home.
- Every year almost 70,000 children are involved in accidents in the kitchen. Sixty per cent of these involve children under four years.
- Most accidents happen between late afternoon and early evening in the summer and school holidays.
- Boys are more likely to have accidents than girls.

Useful resources

RoSPA

The Royal Society for the Prevention of Accidents (RoSPA) aims to save lives and reduce injuries by promoting safety at work, in the home, on the roads, in schools, at leisure, and on or near water. Their website, **www.rospa.com**, has much useful information to help you prevent accidents from occurring.

Procedures to follow in the event of incidents

Incidents could include any non-medical emergency, such as:

- A child going missing (this could also be classed as an emergency).
- A security issue, for example, threats of violence from a parent or other individual.
- A break-in.
- A flood, gas leak or electrical failure.
- An attack on you, a child or your assistant.
- Any racist incident involving you, a child or your assistant.

The procedures you should follow are clear:

- Stay calm, do not panic or make the situation worse.
- Assess the situation.
- Remove the children and yourself from any danger or harm.
- Seek help if necessary, such as by calling the police, emergency services or another trusted adult.
- In the case of a missing child:
  - Carry out a thorough search of your home and outside areas to make sure the child is not hiding or trapped somewhere.
  - Check doors and gates to make sure that they are still securely fastened.
  - Ask older children if they know where the missing child is.
  - Contact the child's parents and report the child as missing to the police.

Reporting incidents

All of the above incidents should be reported to the Health and Safety Executive as well as the child's parents. This means that you need to keep a reportable incident record book. Some home-based childcarers use their accident record book for this as some of the information required is the same. You must also record if the police or other emergency services were involved, and if so any crime number that you were given. If you later make an insurance claim, this also should be recorded.

Procedures to follow in the event of an emergency

Emergencies can include the serious illness of a child, a fire in your home or the need to evacuate your home very quickly.

Fire

In the case of a fire you must:

- Stay calm and reassure the children.
- Close all doors and windows.
- Get the children out of the house by the usual ways if possible, and go to your agreed safe assembly place, which should be well away from the source of the fire.
- Not leave the children unattended.
- Not stop to put out the fire (unless it is very small).
- Call the fire brigade as soon as possible.
- Make sure that you give your full address and do not hang up until your address has been repeated back to you correctly by the operator.

In your setting

It is very important that everyone in your home knows what to do in the event of a fire. The only way to ensure this is to carry out regular fire practices. Make sure that you carry out fire practices at different times of the day and week and from different points in your home. For example, pretend that there is a fire in the kitchen one time, the next time a fire in the play room or the bedrooms. Ideally your should carry out a fire practice at least every three months and also when you have a new child start at your setting. It is good practice to keep a record of your fire practices, recording the date, time of day and how long it took to evacuate your house. Record also any unusual events, such as difficulties getting through a doorway.

Explain to the children why you are doing a fire practice and reassure them. At the end of the practice praise the children for responding well and quickly.

Other reasons for emergency evacuation of your home could be a gas leak, a sudden flood or structural damage to your property. If you have established a fire practice routine with the children, you will be able to put this into practice for other emergencies and get all the children out of your home safely.

Serious illness

In the case of a serious illness of a child you will need to call for medical help or an ambulance if the child:

- has difficulty breathing
- is floppy or unresponsive
- is unconscious
- has used their normal medication for an asthma attack and five minutes later the symptoms have not been relieved
- shows signs of meningitis.

Illness

Young children can become ill quite quickly and with little warning. A child can arrive at your home in the morning apparently fit and well and by lunchtime be unwell. It is very important that you know the signs and symptoms of illness. You should also understand when you need to seek medical aid.

Babies and children who are unwell have additional needs and it is important that you know how to meet these needs. You must contact the child's parents (or emergency contact) as soon as possible. If the parents cannot collect their sick child from your home, they must make alternative arrangements. The decision not to care for a child rests with you, if doing so puts the well-being of the other children at risk.

The terms and conditions of your registration do not allow you to care for children who have infectious illnesses. If you find out that a child who became ill while in your setting subsequently developed an infectious illness you must inform all the other parents.

Useful resources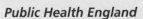

Public Health England

Ask at your local medical or health centre for any posters or leaflets that they have showing the signs and symptoms of common childhood illnesses.

Public Health England (formerly the Health Protection Agency) has useful information about illnesses: **www.gov.uk/government/ organisations/public-health-england**

Meningitis Now

There are many illnesses that give rise to a need for immediate and emergency action. The most common, however, is meningitis. There is an immunisation programme that offers some protection from the different strains of meningitis. If you think, however, that a child may have meningitis it is essential that you act quickly and get medical help. The signs of meningitis can be confused with other less serious illnesses, for example, a rash (one sign of meningitis is that the rash does not fade when under pressure; this is often referred to as the 'glass test'). Meningitis Now (formerly the Meningitis Trust) provides excellent information about the signs of this illness. Their website is **www.meningitisnow.org**

pacey says

As well as thinking about risk in terms of good and bad risks, it can also be very useful to explicitly note down the benefits or value of children experiencing the activity or situation. When the benefits as well as the risk are noted it is often known as a Risk Benefit Assessment or Risk Benefit Analysis.

Assessment links

This assessment task relates to Learning Outcome 2 and links to assessment criteria 2.1, 2.2, 2.3, 2.4, 2.5 and 2.6. This assessment task has four parts. You must successfully complete each part.

1 You are asked to design a leaflet for parents and carers that explains how you will promote a safe, healthy and secure environment for the children in your care. It must include information on risk management and how you take a balanced approach and how you ensure safe supervision of children, both in your home environment and off-site.

There is no set design for your leaflet; it can look any way that you find attractive and appealing.

Remember that your leaflet is aimed at parents and carers, so avoid using jargon or technical language with which they may not be familiar.

2 Carry out a risk assessment of all the areas that the children will access, both inside and outdoors. Again, there is no set format for your risk assessment, but it must be clear, identify possible hazards and risks, and have a section detailing what actions you plan to take and when those actions will be completed.

3 Procedures are ways that you carry out certain actions. For this part of the task you are asked to write six procedures. These must be clear, logical and realistic. The six procedures are those for:

● accidents
● incidents
● emergencies
● storage of medication
● administration of medication
● record keeping in relation to medication.

You may find it more logical to combine two or three of these procedures into one. This will be acceptable provided that you have covered all the required points.

4 This section of the task asks you to summarise ways that you can maintain a safe and healthy environment for children, relating to:

● preparing formula feeds
● sterilising feeding equipment
● preparing and storing food
● safely disposing of waste
● caring for pets.

Remember that this part of the task is a summary. Keep it concise and do not repeat yourself or 'waffle'!

Chapter 3

Understand how to support the safeguarding and welfare of children

Learning Outcome 3

By the end of this chapter you will be able to:

1 Explain the terms 'safeguarding', 'duty of care' and 'child protection'
2 Summarise the regulatory requirements for safeguarding children within a home-based setting
3 Identify your own local authority safeguarding procedures
4 Explain the roles and responsibilities of a lone worker in a home-based setting in relation to the safeguarding, protection and welfare of children

5 Describe the signs, symptoms, indicators and behaviours that may raise concerns relating to: domestic abuse, neglect, physical abuse, emotional abuse, sexual abuse
6 Describe the actions to take if harm or abuse is suspected and/or disclosed
7 Explain procedures to be followed by lone workers in home-based settings when harm or abuse is suspected or alleged against the lone worker or third parties
8 Write a policy and procedures for the safeguarding, protection and welfare of children in home-based settings

All children have the right to grow up in an environment where they are safe and protected from harm. All children may need to be protected from harm or ill treatment. This chapter will help you to understand how to safeguard and protect children.

AC 3.1 Explain the terms 'safeguarding', 'duty of care' and 'child protection'

Keeping children safe is the responsibility of everyone with whom a child could come into contact, not just their parents or carers. Keeping children safe must be your first priority in every aspect of your work and must underpin everything that you do at all times.

There is confusion between the terms 'safeguarding' and 'child protection', and many people use them interchangeably as if they mean the same thing. This is incorrect, however. They are quite different.

Safeguarding

Safeguarding is not just about protecting children from abuse. It encompasses everything to do with protecting children from any form of ill treatment that could impact on their health and development. This could mean working with the children's families as well as with the children themselves. It means making sure that children grow up in safe circumstances and receive effective care, and helping children to have the best life chances so that they can become successful adults. Safeguarding involves everyone in society, as we all have a responsibility to keep children safe and protected from harm.

Key term

Safeguarding – promoting children's well-being and welfare, and putting measures into place that will improve children's safety and prevent abuse

Duty of care

When human beings interact with each other, each has a duty of care towards the other. This means that we carry out actions that show a level of attention and caution to avoid negligence that could result in harm to other people. For example, if you break a glass bottle on a beach, there is a duty of care to other beach users to pick up the glass and dispose of it safely so that others will not be at risk of being cut and injured.

> ### Key term
>
> Duty of care – a requirement to exercise a reasonable amount of caution and attention to avoid negligence that could lead to the harm of others

Working with children brings a significant duty of care. The younger and more vulnerable the child, the greater the duty of care you have. You must have the ability to foresee and cope with potential dangers to children. This is why you undertake risk assessments of your home and outside areas, and when you go on trips and visits. This is why you practise what to do in an emergency or in the event of a fire in your home. Your duty of care towards children means that you must make sure that confidential information about any child is shared only when it is in the best interests of the child to do so. Issues around confidentiality will be discussed in more detail in Chapter 6.

You must develop good and effective communication skills so that you can help children to talk about things that frighten them or about harm that others may be doing to them. You have a duty of care to set boundaries for behaviour and to use strategies that help discourage behaviour in others that might harm or distress children. This will be discussed in greater detail in Chapter 7.

You have a duty of care to recognise the signs and symptoms of abuse. You do this by observing and assessing children's development, and by being aware of anything that indicates that their progress is not as expected for children of their age. Observing children will be discussed in greater detail in Chapter 9.

Child protection

Child protection is about what you actually do to keep children safe and protected from harm. It is about to whom you speak, what you record, whom you tell, what you tell, when you tell, and what you do before and after your suspicions have been aroused.

> ### Key term
>
>
> Child protection – part of the safeguarding process. This is about the actions that you take when you suspect a child is at risk of significant harm

> ### In your setting
>
> It is essential to access training, either online or face to face, on safeguarding and child protection. You should also make sure that you keep your knowledge, understanding and skills up to date. Many local authorities have a requirement that you must have this training before you start to care for children.

AC 3.2 Summarise the regulatory requirements for safeguarding children within a home-based setting

> ### Tip
>
> AC 1.2 in Chapter 1 looked at current legislation and guidelines in relation to safeguarding, protection and welfare of children. It is recommended that you look again at this section.

Links to the EYFS

Section 3 of the Statutory Framework for the EYFS sets out the Safeguarding and Welfare Requirements that you must follow. If you look at Section 3.3 you will see that it says that 'Childminders are not required to have written policies and procedures' (DfE, 2014). Many local authorities, however, do expect you to have a written policy for safeguarding and child protection – this is good practice. AC 3.8 relates to writing such a policy.

Key terms

Policy – a strategy, plan, course of action in given situations, or a set of guidelines

Procedures – ways, practices, methods, systems to help carry out an action or policy

Figure 3.1 Are you aware of behaviours that may be a cause for concern?

It is part of the Safeguarding and Welfare Requirements of the EYFS that you must do everything you can to keep the children in your care safe and well. This is your duty of care and you have very specific responsibilities. If you worked in a daycare nursery, a pre-school group or a school, there would be other members of staff who would share the responsibility with you. There would also be a designated person responsible for taking the lead in safeguarding children. As a home-based childcarer, often working alone, you have sole responsibility for meeting the Safeguarding and Welfare Requirements.

The regulatory requirements are as follows:

- You must have in place a policy and procedures to safeguard children, which are in line with your Local Safeguarding Children Board (LSCB).
- Your policy and procedures must include:
  - What to do if someone makes an allegation against you, your assistant or someone in your household.
  - Procedures relating to the use of mobile phones and cameras in your setting.

(See AC 3.8 for more details about policy and procedures.)

- You must have had up-to-date training so that you can identify, understand and respond appropriately to signs of abuse and neglect.
- You must be aware of the government's statutory guidance, 'Working together to safeguard children' (2013). The full PDF version of this guidance can be accessed in the resources section of www.workingtogetheronline.co.uk.
- You must notify Ofsted, or your childminder agency, of any allegations of serious harm or abuse by any person living, working or looking after children in your home. Allegations can relate to incidents outside of your home. You also need to tell Ofsted, or your agency, what actions have been taken.
- You, and anyone over the age of 16 years living or working in your house or having regular contact with children, must have checks to make sure that you and they meet the suitable people requirement.

- You must refer anyone in your household over the age of 16 years to the Disclosure and Barring Service if they have harmed a child or put a child at risk.

There are no 'ifs', 'buts', or 'maybes' with these requirements. They are regulatory and you must comply with them.

AC 3.3 Identify your own local authority safeguarding procedures

Your local authority has a statutory requirement to have clear safeguarding procedures. These will have been explained to you if you have attended local authority safeguarding and child protection training.

Local Safeguarding Children Board

Section 13 of the Children Act (2004) requires each local authority to establish a Local Safeguarding Children Board (LSCB) for their area. Each local authority must also state the organisations and individuals that should be represented on the LSCB. Membership of the LSCB is clearly set out in the Children Act (2004) and includes:

- the chief officer of police
- the Local Probation Trust
- the Youth Offending Team
- NHS Trusts whose hospitals and other facilities are in the local authority area
- representatives of the Children and Family Court Advisory and Support Service (Cafcass)
- the governors or directors of any prison or secure training centre in the local authority area that detains children
- two lay members, who represent the local community
- representatives from all types of school in the local area.

All of these members must be people who can speak with authority for their organisation. The LSCB can also get expertise and advice from other professionals, such as doctors, nurses, the Director of Public Health, and/or the Principal Child and Family Social Worker. The LSCB will have very close working links with the Children's Services department of your local authority.

There is a chairperson of the LSCB who must publish an annual report of the effectiveness of child safeguarding in your local authority area. The report must be shared with key professionals in the local authority. The LSCB chairperson has to work very closely with the Director for Children's Services in your area.

The key to effective working of the LSCB is that there is good information-sharing between professionals and relevant local agencies and organisations. The LSCB has a far-reaching range of roles and statutory purposes, and in order to achieve this it needs well-established lines of communication. Any barriers to information sharing must be addressed.

You should find out about your LSCB and take a look at their website.

Local Authority Designated Officer

The Local Authority Designated Officer (LADO) works within your local authority's Children's Services department. They must work within the statutory guidance set out in Chapter 2 (Organisational responsibilities) of 'Working together to safeguard children' (2013).

The LADO should be contacted in all cases where it is alleged that a person has behaved in a way that has harmed or may cause harm to a child. This can include if a person has committed a criminal offence against or related to children, for example, having pornographic images of children on a computer. You should also contact the LADO if you think that a person is not suitable to work with children. This could apply to an assistant or if you have concerns about people that you meet at drop-in groups, pre-school groups, nurseries and schools, or in the wider community.

The LADO will give you advice and information about what to do once the allegation has been made. They will then help to co-ordinate all of the information sharing with the right people. The LADO will monitor and track any investigations and try to resolve them as quickly as possible.

Tip

Store the telephone number for your LADO on your mobile phone. That way you will always have it easily accessible.

In your setting

Many home-based childcarers worry about the consequences of passing on information. They worry that it might lead to a family being split up and the effects this could have on the children. It is important to remember, however, that in the majority of cases the different agencies and services will work with a family to ensure a child's safety. Breaking up a family is often the last option.

Common Assessment Framework

The Children Act (2004) states that different organisations – such as health, education, children's social care and housing – must work together in the best interests of children. It can be quite difficult to get an overall assessment of the needs of a vulnerable child and their family as many professionals can be involved. The Common Assessment Framework (CAF), however, provides a structure to help information sharing and co-operation to take place.

Useful resources

Common Assessment Framework
For more information on the CAF process look at: **www.dcsf.gov.uk/everychildmatters/strategy/devliveringservices1/caf**

Team Around the Child (TAC)
For more information on TAC look at: **www.education.gov.uk/a0068944/team-around-the-child-tac**

Case study

Dylan's health visitor has noticed that he seems to have low energy levels at times and also seems susceptible to more infections than would normally be expected. Chris, Dylan's home-based childcarer, has noticed that he doesn't play with other children, that his social skills are not at the level expected for his age and that he prefers to play with the same toys over and over again. His two year progress check showed that his development was satisfactory in relation to the number of words that he knew and his physical development. Chris decided to raise her concerns about Dylan's social skills with his parents, who agreed to ask for a meeting with the health visitor and Chris.

The health visitor took the lead at the meeting and followed a pre-assessment checklist from the CAF. The checklist looked at Dylan's health, whether he was safe from harm, his learning and development, and any significant effects of poverty. This type of meeting is called a Team Around the Child (TAC).

Following the TAC meeting all the information was brought together using CAF forms, and an assessment of needs was made in relation to Dylan's development, his parents and the family environment.

AC 3.4 Explain the roles and responsibilities of a lone worker in a home-based setting in relation to the safeguarding, protection and welfare of children

You are quite possibly working on your own or with an assistant. Caring for children in this way can be quite lonely and it is not unusual for home-based childcarers to feel isolated. Many people find dealing with any issue about child protection and safeguarding very difficult, so it is important that you know where to get help and support and also what your roles and responsibilities are.

Every childcare professional, in whatever role, has a duty of care and a responsibility to put a child's needs and welfare first. It follows, therefore, that if you have a concern about a child you must do something about it. Rather than thinking that safeguarding and child protection are the responsibility of someone else, they must be part of your everyday practice.

You will establish relationships and partnerships with the parents and families of children in your care. Because of this some home-based childcarers find it very difficult to report parents or other family members if they have concerns. They may feel that they are betraying a trust, and jeopardising the partnership and their relationship with the parents. This is not the case. You have a legal responsibility to report all concerns and suspicions. The well-being of the child is paramount.

Your first responsibility is always to the children in your care. Your most important role is to ensure their well-being and protect them from harm. When you suspect or have a concern that a child may be at risk you *must* report your suspicions.

In your setting

If you have a concern that a child may be at risk:

- Take your cues from the child, do not question or probe.
- Allow the child to talk to you and give them your full, undivided attention.
- Sensitively and gently encourage the child to continue talking to you.
- Never ask the child to keep the conversations secret.
- Never promise to do anything that you are not 100 per cent confident you can do.
- Make a written record of what the child has said, date and sign it. Be factual and objective in recording exactly what the child has said.
- Make a note of any obvious signs or symptoms, date and sign it.
- Don't make assumptions.
- Contact LADO.

Reflective practice

- If you have a concern about a child, would you talk to the parents of that child before you spoke to LADO?
- What could happen if you asked a parent about unusual bruises on a child's arms, or a black eye?

Links to the EYFS

One of the prime areas of learning is personal, social and emotional development. Aspects of this area of learning include helping children to talk about how they feel and understanding that some forms of behaviour are unacceptable. If children have developed a good relationship with you, they are more likely to talk about their feelings and things that concern them.

AC 3.5 Describe the signs, symptoms, indicators and behaviours that may raise concerns relating to domestic abuse, neglect and physical, emotional and sexual abuse

Domestic abuse

Domestic violence is officially classified as 'any incident of threatening behaviour, violence or abuse between adults who are or have been in a relationship together, or between family members, regardless of gender or sexuality'.

We think of domestic violence as hitting, slapping and beating, but it can also include emotional abuse, as well as forced marriage and so called honour crimes. It is abuse if a partner or a family member:

- makes threats
- shoves or pushes the other partner
- makes the other partner fear for their physical safety
- puts the other partner down, or attempts to undermine their self-esteem
- exerts controls, for example, by stopping the partner from seeing their friends and family
- is jealous and possessive, such as being suspicious of friendships and conversations
- frightens the other partner.

Reflective practice

It is a frightening statistic that one in four women and one in six men in the UK will suffer domestic abuse during their lifetime. Equally frightening is that two women a week are killed by a current or former male partner.

How could you support someone who may be experiencing domestic abuse?

Do you know how to access support and guidance for yourself and the victims of domestic abuse?

Witnessing domestic violence, where one of their parents is abusing the other parent, has a significant effect on children's well-being and development. Children who witness domestic abuse in the home often believe that they are to blame. They can live in a constant state of fear and are 15 times more likely to be victims of child abuse.

The physical effects of domestic abuse on children can start when they are a foetus in their mother's womb. These effects can include low infant birth weights, premature birth, excessive bleeding, and foetal death, due to the mother's physical and emotional stress.

In general, children who witness domestic abuse in the home can suffer a tremendous number of physical symptoms as well as emotional and behavioural ones. These children may complain of general aches and pain, such as headaches and stomach aches. They may also have irritable and irregular bowel habits, cold sores, and they may have problems with bedwetting. They may be inconsolable and irritable, have a lack of responsiveness, suffer from developmental delays, and have excessive diarrhoea from both trauma and stress. They may appear neglected and nervous, and have a short attention span.

Such children may show symptoms of fatigue and constant tiredness. They may fall asleep in school due to the lack of sleep at home. Much of their night could have been spent listening to or witnessing violence within the home. Children who are experiencing domestic abuse are frequently ill and can suffer from poor personal hygiene. They also have a tendency to partake in high-risk play activities, self-abuse and suicide.

Young children who live in a home where domestic violence occurs are often caught in the middle. They may suffer physical injuries from unintentional actions as their parent is abused. Children may not have the ability to express their feelings verbally and so their emotions can cause behavioural problems. They can become withdrawn from those around them and become non-verbal, or exhibit regressed behaviours such as clinging, whining and bedwetting. They may startle at the smallest things, such as a car door slamming or a cup accidentally falling to the floor.

Useful resources

National Domestic Violence Helpline
0808 2000 247 – a free helpline for anyone who is a victim of domestic abuse, open 24 hours a day, seven days a week. Or online at www. nationaldomesticviolencehelpline.org.uk

Women's Aid
Women's Aid works to help women and children stay safe: www.womensaid.org.uk

Neglect

Neglect is the persistent failure to meet a child's basic or essential needs, or both. All children need adequate food, water, shelter, warmth, protection and health care. Children need their carers to be attentive, dependable and kind.

Reflective practice

According to the NSPCC, nearly one in ten children is neglected by their parents, causing serious and long-term damage. As with other forms of abuse, however, this statistic can only be an estimate as we know only about the cases of abuse and neglect that have been reported. It is a dreadful fact that some abuse and neglect stays hidden.

There are many signs that may indicate neglect. If your instincts tell you that something is wrong then you should take action and report your concerns.

Tip

If you believe a child is in immediate danger, call the police on 999 or the NSPCC on 0808 800 5000.

There are many reasons why child neglect happens. Some parents find it difficult to organise their lives, possibly due to drug or alcohol abuse, or mental health issues. These situations often lead to a chaotic home life for children. Some parents may not have received adequate parenting themselves and so do not understand how to meet the needs of their children. A child's emotional needs can be neglected if their parents have difficulty themselves in showing feelings and emotions. Some children are more vulnerable to neglect, such as children who are in care or seeking asylum.

Neglect can have a debilitating and long-lasting effect on a child's physical well-being, and on their mental, emotional and behavioural development. In some cases the effects can cause permanent disabilities and, in severe cases, death.

Signs that a child could be suffering from neglect include:

- living in an inadequate home environment
- being left alone for long periods
- being persistently ignored by parents or carers
- displaying an unkempt appearance and delayed development
- taking on the role of carer for other family members.

Physical effects of neglect may include:

- poor muscle tone and prominent joints
- poor skin: sores, rashes, flea bites
- thin or swollen tummy
- poor hygiene: for example, being dirty or smelly
- untreated health problems, such as bad teeth
- unwashed clothing
- inadequate clothing: for example, not having a coat in winter.

Emotional and behavioural effects may include:

- difficulties with school work
- missing school
- being anxious about, or avoiding, people
- difficulty in making friends
- being withdrawn
- anti-social behaviour
- early sexual activity
- drug or alcohol misuse.

None of the signs outlined here would indicate for certain that a child is being neglected – busy family homes are often untidy or in need of a good clean; children get nits, and their clothes become dirty as part of day-to-day activity. But children who frequently and persistently have some of these signs may be at risk of neglect.

In your setting

Deciding if a child is neglected can be very hard – even for a trained social worker. It is natural to worry that you may be mistaken. Some parents and carers simply need more resources and support to properly care for their children, but some have more complex problems. In both cases they need help from professionals. If your instincts tell you something is wrong, do something about it. Do not put yourself at risk. If you think that you may make matters worse, contact the LADO or NSPCC first to get advice.

Useful resources

NSPCC
www.nspcc.org.uk, telephone 0808 800 5000

Childline
www.childline.org.uk, telephone 0800 1111

Physical abuse

Physical abuse is the most obvious form of abuse. You can actually see bruises, burns or unusual marks on a child's body. Physical abuse can include any kind of deliberate physical harm to a child, such as cuts, broken bones, hitting, shaking, throwing, poisoning, burning and scaling, drowning and suffocating. Physical abuse during childhood can affect a person later in life as an adult and can cause conditions such as post-traumatic stress disorder and other mental health issues.

It is very difficult to know if an injury or behaviour is the result of physical abuse, as children often get some injuries through genuine accidents or play. All children have accidents, like bumps and falls. Injuries that can be genuine for children include:

● Bruising on the shins, knees, elbows, and backs of the hands.
● Bruising on children who are crawling or walking (especially older children).

However, if a child persistently has bruises, burns or other unusual marks that cannot be reasonably explained, you should report your concerns. You should also be alert to the possibility of abuse if you notice suspicious bruises on young children and babies who are not yet mobile.

Reflective practice

Physical abuse remains a problem in the UK.

One child is killed every ten days in England and Wales, according to Home Office figures. It is only the horrific cases that hit the media headlines, however; many cases we simply don't know about.

Case study

Keanu Williams was two years old when he was murdered by his mother in 2011. He had been seen at hospital A&E departments with a range of physical symptoms, such as cuts to his head and burns to his feet. Nursery staff had noticed bruises on his body, but did not report their concerns. Only days before he died he was seen by medical staff with bruising, burns and unusual marks. He was beaten to death by his mother after two years of constant abuse. The horrific catalogue of injuries was revealed at the Serious Case Review in September 2013. This also showed that professionals working with Keanu and his family had failed in their duty of care to protect him.

There are many reasons why parents or other family members physically abuse children. They may be unable to cope with the stress and frustration of parenting; for example, coping with a baby who doesn't sleep and constantly cries, as well as with a lively toddler. The parent may feel isolated. They may not have friends or other family members living nearby who could offer support. Adults who have experienced physical abuse from a violent parent can become abusers themselves. Some parents have unrealistic expectations of how a child should behave, and when their child fails to live up to their expectations they can become abusive.

Physical harm can also mean that a parent makes up symptoms of an illness by giving a child something or doing something to them that makes the child ill, for example, feeding them excessive amounts of salt. This is referred to as fabricated or induced illness and is a serious mental illness that requires trained medical help. Whatever the situation or cause, however, there is never a good reason to deliberately harm a child.

Physical abuse can happen in any family, but some children are more at risk than others. Children who live in families with complex problems such as domestic violence or substance abuse, or with parents who have mental health problems, are at increased risk.

The NSPCC states that:

Children born prematurely and disabled children are also more vulnerable to physical abuse. No one knows why this is the case, but the increased demands and stress of caring for a child with special needs could be a possible reason.

The signs of physical abuse can be very wide-ranging, from minor injuries to major trauma. These can include:

- bruising:
    - on the cheeks, ears, palms, arms and feet
    - on the back, buttocks, tummy, hips and backs of legs
    - on babies who are not yet crawling or walking
    - multiple bruises in clusters, usually on the upper arms or outer thighs

- bruises that look like they have been caused by fingers, a hand or an object
- a history of bruising
- burns or scalds:
    - burns on the backs of the hands, feet, legs, genitals or buttocks
    - burns that have a clear shape, e.g. a circular cigarette burn
- large oval-shaped bite marks
- fractures
- scarring
- poisoning
- drowning or suffocating
- head injuries caused by a blow or by shaking
- fabricated or induced illnesses.

As well as the physical signs of abuse, children may also suffer mental health or behavioural concerns. These include:

- depression and anxiety
- aggression and violence
- problems with relationships and socialising
- trying to hide injuries under clothing
- running away from home
- being distant and withdrawn.

Emotional abuse

Emotional abuse can be very difficult to detect or define. Emotional abuse is the severe and persistent ill treatment of a child. Emotional abuse may be the only form of abuse suffered by a child, or it may be an element of other abuse and neglect. Emotional abuse can affect a child from infancy, through adolescence and into adulthood. It can have long-lasting and devastating effects on a child's emotional health and development.

Emotional abuse includes:

- humiliating or criticising a child
- disciplining a child with degrading punishments
- not recognising a child's own individuality and limitations
- pushing a child too hard
- being too controlling
- exposing a child to distressing events or interactions

- domestic abuse
- substance misuse
- failing to promote a child's social development
- not allowing a child to have friends
- persistently ignoring a child
- being absent
- never expressing positive feelings towards a child
- never showing any emotions in interactions with a child (this is emotional neglect).

Case study

Jake was a lively 13 year old, who appeared confident and had some friends at school. He had behavioural problems, however, and had great difficulty in controlling his temper. His form tutor found him one morning before school started, sitting on a corridor floor, crying. When asked what the matter was, Jake said that he had had an argument with his mother that morning. She had said that she wished he had never been born and that she should have had an abortion when she found out she was pregnant.

Emotional abuse of children occurs in all kinds of families. No parent or carer gets it right every time, and an isolated act of poor parenting does not amount to emotional abuse. Babies are not like washing machines – they do not arrive with an instruction book. Continued ill treatment, however, can seriously harm a child's emotional health and development, as the above case study shows.

There are many complex reasons which may lead to a parent emotionally abusing their child. It could be because they feel anger towards themselves that they misdirect on to their child. Or it could be because the parent feels worthless, lacks self-confidence or has low self-esteem. The parent may have experienced emotional abuse as a child as a result of poor parenting and so not know anything different. It is possible that the parent misunderstands their child's behaviour, for example, believing that their baby cries intentionally to annoy them.

Some children are more at risk, particularly where there are additional stresses on the family. These can leave a parent unable to behave or respond appropriately to their child's emotional needs. Risk factors include:

- adult mental health problems
- domestic abuse
- drug or alcohol addiction
- marital break-up
- family disputes.

Signs that a child may be suffering emotional abuse include:

- a parent's constant negative and harsh behaviour towards their child
- a fearful, distant or unaffectionate relationship.

Signs of emotional abuse may also be present in a child's actions, or in their physical, mental and emotional development.

A child's physical development can be delayed; stressful mealtimes, for example, can affect a child's eating.

Emotional abuse can hold back a child's cognitive development, such as their intelligence and memory. It can also increase the risk of a child developing mental health problems, such as eating disorders and self-harm.

A child should be able to understand and express a range of emotions and feelings as they grow older. Emotional abuse can limit a child's emotional development, including their ability to feel and express a full range of emotions appropriately, and to control their emotions.

Emotional abuse can put a child at greater risk of developing one or more behavioural problems, such as:

- learning difficulties
- problems with relationships
- rebellious, aggressive and violent behaviour
- anti-social behaviour and criminality
- self-isolating behaviour (making people dislike you)
- negative impulsive behaviour (not caring what happens to you).

A word of caution, however: the signs outlined above do not necessarily mean a child is being emotionally abused. There is no such thing as a perfect parent and a child's development may be delayed for a number of different reasons. If you think a child's emotions, mental capacities or behaviour seem very different from other children of the same age, however, then this may indicate they have an emotionally abusive relationship with a parent and you should report your concerns.

Sexual abuse

Child sexual abuse involves persuading or forcing a child to take part in sexual activities, or encouraging a child to behave in sexually inappropriate ways. Sexual abuse can be very difficult to identify. Often the people who carry out sexual abuse are very plausible, sometimes very well qualified and outwardly appear to be very sociable and likeable. Acts of child sexual abuse are committed by men, women, teenagers, and other children. Sex offenders are found in all areas of society and come from a variety of backgrounds.

The sexual abuse of children is more than just physical sexual contact. It includes:

- Sexual touching of any part of the body, clothed or unclothed, including using an object.
- All penetrative sex, including penetration of the mouth with an object or part of the body.
- Encouraging a child to engage in any sexual activity, including:
  - sexual acts with someone else
  - making a child strip or masturbate.
- Intentionally engaging in sexual activity in front of a child.
- Not taking proper measures to prevent a child being exposed to the sexual activity of others.
- Meeting a child following sexual 'grooming', or preparation, with the intention of abusing them.
- Taking, making, permitting to take, distributing, showing or advertising indecent images of children.
- Paying for the sexual services of a child, or encouraging them into prostitution or pornography.

- Showing a child images of sexual activity, including photographs, videos or via webcams.

The causes of sexually abusive behaviour towards children are not fully understood, although abusers may have unusual sexual urges and a willingness to act on these. They may also have power and control issues. Some sexual offenders themselves had traumatic childhood experiences, or come from troubled families.

Child sexual abuse can also be motivated by money, for example, with child prostitution and pornography. Significantly more men than women sexually abuse children; however, sexual abuse committed by women does exist and is sometimes not recognised as abuse.

The NSPCC estimates that nine out of ten abused children know their abuser. Their abuser is more likely to be a relative, family friend or a person in a position of trust, than to be a stranger. Also, it is believed that an abused child may not say anything because they think it is their fault, that no one will believe them, or that they will be teased or punished. The child may even care for the abusing adult. They almost certainly will want the abuse to stop, but they may fear the adult will go to prison or that their family will break up if they say anything.

Very young children and children with additional needs are particularly vulnerable because they may not have the words or the ability to communicate what is happening to them to someone they trust. Sometimes children are sexually abused by other children and young people. Two-thirds of sexual abuse involving physical contact is committed by peers.

Children and young people who abuse other children, or who develop harmful sexual behaviours, have often experienced abuse and neglect themselves. A child who is being abused by other children and young people may be very confused about their feelings and rationalise, or be persuaded, that what is happening is 'normal'.

Children who have been sexually abused may show a variety of signs. They may try to tell you about the abuse through hints or clues. They may also describe behaviour by an adult that suggests they are being 'groomed' for future abuse. Other signs include:

- aggressive behaviour
- sexually inappropriate behaviour, becoming sexually active at a young age and using sexual language that you would not expect them to know.
- promiscuity
- suddenly starting to behave differently
- staying away from certain adults, or avoiding being alone with them; showing fear of an adult
- problems with school or poor attendance
- sleep problems
- bedwetting or soiling
- risk-taking behaviour during adolescence
- negative thoughts
- not looking after themselves
- missing school, or other problems with school.

Physical symptoms of sexual abuse can include:

- anal or vaginal soreness
- unusual discharge
- pregnancy.

You should also be alert to any adults who pay an unusual amount of attention to children; this is usually referred to as 'grooming'. For example, adults who give children gifts, toys or do favours for them for no apparent reason. Children who are being groomed may also be offered trips, outings and holidays, again for no apparent reason other than that the adult is looking for opportunities to be alone with the child.

Useful resources

National Society for the Prevention of Cruelty to Children (NSPCC)
The NSPCC has a campaign to help children be aware of sexual abuse called the 'Underwear rule'. The information is aimed at children and parents. Details can be found at **www.nspcc.org.uk**

AC 3.6 Describe the actions to take if harm or abuse is suspected and/or disclosed

Sometimes a child may tell you something that leads you to think that they may be being abused. This is sometimes called a disclosure.

Key term

Disclosure – when a child has told an adult or another child what has been happening to them. This can include evidence of abuse or neglect

A child can disclose information in many ways. They can tell you directly or can use their play situations to communicate. For example, a child might say, 'Mum went shopping last night and left me on my own in the car. I didn't like it as I was scared.' Or you may see a child hitting and punching dolls in a role play area and using aggressive language.

In your setting

- In all cases, you must listen to the child and take your cues from them.
- Reassure the child that they are doing the right thing in talking to you.
- Say that you believe them.
- Ask for clarification if you do not understand what the child has said, to make sure you get the facts correct.
- Do not question or probe.
- Do not put words into the child's mouth.
- Make a written record of what has been said and also record if there are any obvious signs, symptoms or indicators. Don't forget to sign and date the record.
- Seek advice and/or report your concerns as soon as possible.
- Do not attempt to investigate any allegation or disclosure yourself.

Tip

It is always better to report a concern and find that there is no need for any action, than to do nothing and the child subsequently be subjected to more serious harm.

AC 3.7 Explain procedures to be followed by lone workers in home-based settings when harm or abuse is suspected or alleged against the lone worker or third parties

Protecting yourself from allegations of abuse

All childcare professionals in all settings are in positions of trust and have great responsibilities in caring for other people's children. In such positions they are vulnerable to allegations of mistreating children and accusations of abuse. In many ways lone workers in home-based settings are even more vulnerable due to the fact that they are alone. You do not have the support of co-workers and colleagues in your setting, nor do you have much legal protection.

For people working in an organisation with several employees there is a process whereby they can air their concerns about bad practice, usually called 'whistleblowing'. The Public Interest Disclosure Act (1998) protects staff from unfair practices and victimisation provided they make their claim in good faith. The European Court of Human Rights ruled in 2008 that whistleblowing was protected as freedom of expression. Home-based childcarers do not have such protection, however, and therefore are vulnerable to accusations.

It is essential that you remain calm and professional at all times – but do make sure you have a support mechanism in place for yourself. You may wish to talk about how you feel with a close friend or family member, but remember that you must not breach confidentiality. There is also a range of organisations and professionals that you could turn to. These include:

- Professional Association for Childcare and Early Years (PACEY)
- National Society for the Prevention of Cruelty to Children (NSPCC)
- Local authority designated office (LADO)
- social workers
- health visitors
- Ofsted or your childminder agency staff.

In your setting

- Be professional.
- Maintain confidentiality at all times.
- Make sure that all accident and incident records and registers are kept up to date at all times.
- Make sure that all information about children is stored securely.
- Tell parents about every accident, event or incident that has happened to their child while in your care and that could result in a mark or injury on the child's body.
- Record existing injuries.
- Keep a written record of every accident, event or incident and make sure that parents read and sign it.
- Note if a parent refuses to sign anything.
- Never leave children unsupervised or in the care of unauthorised people.
- Encourage personal hygiene in children as soon as they are able.
- Always use appropriate language with children.
- Never handle a child roughly.
- Never ask a child to keep a secret.
- Keep yourself up to date by attending relevant training.

Allegations against third parties

Third parties could be members of your family or household, your friends or neighbours; in other words anyone to whom you are close. Allegations can be made by the parents of children in your care or by the children themselves. This can be very distressing for all concerned, but especially for you. You may have feelings of guilt that you have failed in your duty of care and responsibilities to the child. You may also have to deal with angry and distressed parents and children. You may lose business because of this. Above all you must remain professional and calm at all times.

In your setting

- Stay professional.
- Keep calm.
- Make sure that all of the children in your care are correctly supervised and not at risk of any further or potential harm.
- Try to get the facts of the allegations. Speak calmly to the people concerned, one at a time.
- Make a written record of what has been said, and get it signed by all parties concerned, and sign it yourself.
- Tell the people what you are going to do, but do not attempt to investigate the allegation yourself.
- Get advice and/or report the allegations to LADO, Ofsted or your agency. If the allegation is really serious, call the police or NSPCC.

AC 3.8 Write a policy and procedures for the safeguarding, protection and welfare of children in home-based settings

Any policy and procedures that you write should be individual to you and your setting. Every home-based childcare setting is different but your statutory responsibilities are the same.

Tip

When writing any policy and set of procedures it is important to keep the language simple and avoid jargon. Think about who is going to read the document – whom is it for? Keep the sentences short and to the point.

1 It is always good practice to start your policy with a statement that stems from the statutory requirements.

For example:

Sample policy statement

The Early Years Foundation Stage Statutory Framework (2014) Safeguarding and Welfare Requirements state that providers must take all necessary steps to keep children safe and well. I have a duty of care for all children in my care. If I have any cause for concern I will report it, following the Local Safeguarding Children Board procedures. I have a copy of these procedures and they are available to you on request.

I understand that child abuse can be physical, sexual, emotional and neglectful, or a mixture of these.

I understand that children can also be bullied in many different ways.

I understand that children can be at risk from technology, mobile phone and camera misuse.

I understand that I must notify Ofsted (or my childminder agency) of any allegations of abuse that are alleged to have occurred while the child was in my care.

2 After the statement you can then write about what you will actually do if allegations are made. These are the procedures. For example, you could include:

- Training that you have had, when you did the training and when you plan to update it.
- How often you plan to review your policy and procedures, and why. For example, you may review your policy and procedures every time a new child starts at your setting, when legislation is updated, and when new guidance is issued as a result of any training you have had.
- The impact of your training on developing your awareness and knowledge.
- What you will do if you have concerns about a child, including whom you will contact.

- Issues of confidentiality and sharing information on a 'need to know' basis.
- How your policy and procedures for working in partnership with parents influence this policy and procedures.
- What you expect from parents – for example, that they must tell you of any concerns, accidents, injuries – and how you will record this information.
- Under what situations and circumstances you will begin the LSCB procedures, for example, if you see sudden and significant changes in a child's behaviour, or unusual and unexplained bruises.
- Details of what you will do if a child tells you about abuse suffered by them or another child.
- Ways in which you will make sure children are safe when online.
- When and how mobile phones, cameras and other mobile technology may (or may not) be used in your setting.
- What you will do if an allegation is made against you.
- What you will do if an allegation is made against a third party, such as a member of your family or household, a friend or neighbour.

- That it is not your responsibility to investigate allegations yourself.

3 Put a page at the end of the procedures that includes a list of useful telephone numbers and contact details. These could include:

- LADO
- Ofsted or your childminder agency
- PACEY's information line
- PACEY's legal helpline
- NSPCC.

4 At the end of the above page put:

- your signature and date
- the parent's signature and date to show that they have read the document
- when the policy and procedures were written
- the date that they will be reviewed.

> **Tip**
>
> Some home-based childcarers do not ask each parent to sign each policy and set of procedures. They have one form that lists all their written policies and procedures, and parents sign once to say that they have read all of them.

pacey says

It is important to access local safeguarding children's board training wherever possible. You can access further information about online safeguarding training via the PACEY website.

Assessment links

This assessment task relates to Learning Outcome 3 and links to assessment criteria 3.1, 3.2, 3.3, 3.4, 3.5, 3.6, 3.7 and 3.8. This assessment task has four parts.

1 Safeguarding children is an essential part of your role and responsibilities. It is also important that parents understand how you will do this. You are asked to produce a leaflet for parents and carers to explain safeguarding, duty of care and child protection.

   Your leaflet should also include a summary of the regulatory requirements that impact on you as a home-based childcarer. You should include the local authority safeguarding procedures for your area, information on your role and responsibilities, and what actions you will take if harm is suspected and/or disclosed.

   Remember that you are producing your leaflet for parents/carers, meaning:

   ● You should avoid jargon and abbreviations that may not make sense to them.
   ● The language used must be straightforward and clear.
   ● You should think of different ways to present information, such as flow charts, to make it more appealing and interesting.
   ● If you are not using a computer to produce your leaflet, you must make sure your handwriting is legible.

2 You are asked to describe the symptoms, indicators and behaviours that may cause concern relating to:

   ● domestic abuse
   ● neglect
   ● physical abuse
   ● emotional abuse
   ● sexual abuse.

   This is quite a lot of information to describe so think carefully how you will present it. You could develop a series of charts, or produce written information. There is no set format for this task, nor a word limit. Your information should be clear, however, and should also be of use to you in the future, should the need arise.

3 As you work through the course you will develop a portfolio of evidence, work pieces and information. As part of your portfolio you should write a policy that identifies the procedures for safeguarding, protection and welfare of children in a home-based childcare setting. It is good practice to try to reference this policy to the relevant legislation and regulatory requirements. Look again at the section of this chapter that discusses writing a policy and procedures (see page 55).

4 Include in your portfolio an explanation of the procedures that you as a home-based childcarer must follow when harm or abuse is suspected or alleged against yourself and third parties.

Chapter 4

Understand how to promote equality, diversity and inclusion

Learning Outcome 4

By the end of this chapter you will be able to:

1 Explain the role and responsibilities of the home-based childcarer in supporting equality, diversity and inclusive practice

2 Evaluate the impact of your own attitudes, values and behaviour when supporting equality, diversity and inclusive practice

All the work that you do with children, or indeed adults, must be underpinned by the values of equality, diversity and inclusion. These must be evident in every aspect of your professional practice. Upholding the values of equality, diversity and inclusion will help every child to reach their full potential and give them fair chances in their lives.

Key terms

Equality – being fair or impartial, and making sure that all people are treated appropriately

Diversity – the variety of values, beliefs, cultures, life experiences, knowledge and skills in any group of people

Inclusion – making sure that every person has the opportunity to access education and care, to participate in activities and to belong

AC 4.1 Explain the role and responsibilities of the home-based childcarer in supporting equality, diversity and inclusive practice

When children spend time in a setting, such as home-based childcare, that promotes equality, diversity and inclusion, they are more able to make progress in all areas of their development and learning. We all want to do what is best for the children for whom we care. We want them to be happy, healthy and reach their full potential. For these things to happen we must see every child as a unique and individual person, with rights and needs. This is a key responsibility.

We live in a diverse society, which includes a wealth of different backgrounds, lifestyles and characteristics. It is this diversity that can give strength to a society. It enriches our experiences and helps to break down barriers.

The experiences of children will inform their views as adults. These views are influenced by the adults in their lives, and this is where you can have a huge and significant role.

Links to the EYFS

The EYFS places a great emphasis on the unique child. It recognises that children develop and learn in different ways and that they deserve the best possible start in life. Read the introduction to the EYFS (2014) document (pages 5 and 6) and you should begin to understand why equality, diversity and inclusive practice are so important.

During your time as a home-based childcarer, you will work with children and families from a variety of cultural backgrounds. You have a responsibility to treat each child, and their family, uniquely and to respect their needs, values, lifestyle and culture. Seeing every child as an individual will make it possible for you to support their right to be treated with equal concern and help them make progress in their learning and development.

The structure of the family has changed in recent times and is now more complex. The actual word 'family' means different things to different people, depending on their experiences and beliefs.

Different types include:

- families with married or unmarried parents
- nuclear families
- extended families, with grandparents, uncles, aunts, cousins and other relations
- step-parents and step-children
- blended families
- foster parents
- single parents
- parents of the same sex.

A family is usually a mix of children and adults who live together and are related in some way, either biologically or legally.

There is no 'correct' or 'better' family structure. But there is no doubt that parents know their children better than anyone else, and you must respect and acknowledge that fact. Whatever the structure of the family, their needs are the same. Sometimes parents' views as to what they want for their children may be different from your views. So you need to talk openly and honestly about the needs of the children and respect those needs.

Children could live in families with a wide range of lifestyles. You must respect the lifestyle choices of the parents. You must talk to the parents and come to an agreement on the care of their child. It is vital to be non-judgemental, and you must avoid giving

Figure 4.1 A family is usually a mixture of children and adults who live together

the parents the impression that you disapprove in some way of their lifestyle choices. You have a responsibility to treat all children and their families equally, to be fair and not to discriminate.

You have a responsibility to promote inclusion by looking at the barriers that prevent children from fully participating and belonging. Discrimination and prejudice are significant barriers to inclusion.

Prejudice can be very damaging and its effects can be long lasting. Prejudicial views often lead to discriminatory behaviour. When children are subject to discrimination they are harmed because they may be denied the opportunities or advantages offered to others. This could mean that they do not have the chances or opportunities that would help them to reach their full potential.

Key terms

Discrimination – treating someone less favourably than others because of their race, gender, religion, sexual orientation or disability, or because they belong to a different group in society

Prejudice – a judgement that is made without careful consideration of accurate, relevant information, which can lead to narrow-mindedness, bigotry and unfairness

Activity

Read the following scenarios and think about the impact on the children's well-being.

- Janie is told she can't play football as it is a boys' game.
- Amir is told he can't play football because he wears glasses, and they may get broken.
- Casey is stopped from playing football because he isn't big enough.
- The children won't let Oliver play football because his shirt is the wrong colour.

Figure 4.2 These children enjoy playing together

Their progress and opportunities to develop skills and talents can be restricted. This could lead to damage to their self-esteem, self-confidence and self-image, not to mention the impact on their learning and development.

Prejudice and discrimination impact on children's rights and well-being because inclusive practices are hampered. Children are not treated with equal concern or do not experience the positive effects of diversity. Consequently, there is no place in any early years setting for any practice that promotes prejudice or discrimination. You have a responsibility to work in an inclusive way. This means that you have to be aware of barriers – whether real or perceived – and do everything that you can to break them down.

Part of your role in promoting inclusive practice is to help children develop positive attitudes. This means it is less likely that they will develop prejudiced views. You can do this in several ways:

- Develop children's understanding and knowledge of people. Give them opportunities to talk about similarities and contrasts.
- Help children to value diversity as interesting and enriching in our lives. Provide factual information when answering their questions.
- Help children develop respectful and positive attitudes towards everyone.
- Be a positive role model at all times.

In your setting

You have a responsibility to challenge discrimination and prejudice. You should have strategies in place to help you do this. With **children**:

- Never ignore or excuse any form of discrimination. You would not ignore a child causing physical pain to another, so do not ignore discriminatory behaviour.
- Intervene, but do not make the situation worse by drawing attention to what has been said or done. If you do nothing, you give the impression that you condone the behaviour.
- Intervene straightaway. Point out to the child who has behaved in the discriminatory way that what was said or done is hurtful, unfair and cruel, and that the behaviour is not acceptable.
- Support the child who was the focus of the discriminatory behaviour. Reassure them and help to support their self-esteem.
- Be patient and consistent.
- Point out anything that is incorrect or untrue and give correct information. Use new words to help the child learn new vocabulary for the future.

- Help the child learn from the situation, to see the consequences of their actions and understand why their behaviour is unacceptable.
- Make it very clear that you will not tolerate what the child said or did, but do not leave the child feeling that you do not like them.

With **adults**:

- Be assertive, not aggressive.
- Be polite when you challenge the remark or behaviour, but be firm.
- Stay calm.
- Offer support to the person who was the focus of the discrimination.
- Be aware of your surroundings; you may not feel it is appropriate to challenge another adult in front of children, but you should respond as soon as you can.
- Make it clear that you find the behaviour or remark offensive. Remember: if you let the incident pass, you are condoning it.
- Make sure that your information is factual and accurate, and offer correct information if you believe the remark or behaviour has arisen from ignorance or from being unaware of the implications.

Case study

Mira started to go to her local Children's Centre for drop-in sessions with her minded children. She noticed that while there were several languages spoken by both the adults and children attending, the information leaflet about the drop-in sessions was written only in English. Mira felt that this gave the message to home-based childcarers who had English as an additional language that they were not as welcome as English-speaking home-based childcarers.

Discussion point

- Do you think Mira was right?
- What could be done to promote inclusive practice?
- Can all staff say at least 'good morning' and 'goodbye' in all or some of the spoken languages?

In your setting

Children learn from copying the people around them. This means that they will learn from you, so you have a great responsibility to be a positive role model at all times. If they see you being discriminatory towards people, they, in turn, will learn to discriminate against others. If they see you treating some children unfairly, they will learn that is all right not to treat everyone with equal concern. Being a positive role model does not mean that you will be perfect all of the time – you are human and we all make mistakes. Acknowledge your mistakes, however, and learn from them. Make sure that the children see and hear you being open-minded and treating all people with respect and care.

A truly inclusive setting does not treat all children in the same way. Treating all children in exactly the same way is the opposite of inclusive in many ways, as it shows that you do not respect individual needs. An inclusive setting treats all children with equal value, which may mean embracing a variety of needs and behaviors. Children of different ages and at different stages in their development should be treated taking that into account. For example, a two year old at the meal table will need very different help and support to a seven year old.

In order to respect individuality and be inclusive, you may have to adapt the way you work with a child according to their individual needs and characteristics. Adapting your practice will mean that all children have access to opportunities that will help them get the most out of the experiences and activities offered.

Useful resources

Equality and Human Rights Commission
The website of the Equality and Human Rights Commission (EHRC): **www. equalityhumanrights.com**

The Children's Commissioner for England
For information on children's rights go to **www.rights4me.org**

AC 4.2 Evaluate the impact of your own attitudes, values and behaviour when supporting equality, diversity and inclusive practice

Key term

Evaluate – look at information or opinions from different views and make a reasoned conclusion or judgement

Your attitudes, values and behavioural standards are formed when you are young. They come about as a result of the way you were brought up, how you were parented, and where and with whom you lived. As a result of your education and life experiences, however, your attitudes, values and behavioural standards will develop, adapt and quite possibly change.

You cannot, however, blame all your negative views and attitudes on your parents, or on the way you were brought up, or on where you lived. There is no doubt that these factors will have influenced what you believe; but you will have had many experiences since you lived at home that will also have contributed to your attitudes, values and behaviour. We learn all through our lives, and that learning changes our outlook on life. We must also take into consideration that the attitudes, values and behavioural standards of society develop and change.

Your attitudes, values and behavioural standards in relation to supporting equality, diversity and inclusive practice are now, hopefully, positive. They should be based on current standards, legislation, and your personal knowledge,

learning and good practices. You should organise your work setting so that all children are treated with equal concern, so that you challenge all discriminatory behaviour, and are at all times a positive role model.

Prejudice and prejudicial opinions are often based on incorrect assumptions and in many cases lead to stereotypical assumptions. For example, saying that all football supporters are hooligans does not take into consideration that many families and children regard supporting their local football team as a great way to spend time together. Stereotypical attitudes, labelling of individuals and prejudice will all lead to discrimination and have negative effects on children and their families.

Key term

Stereotype – to label, put into artificial categories, typecast

Reflective practice

Jenna, a home-based childcarer, was waiting for her children in the school playground when another parent came over to her. They exchanged pleasantries and then the parent asked Jenna when she was going to get a 'proper' job now that her youngest child had started school. One of the children with Jenna overheard this remark and later asked her why Jenna wasn't doing a proper job. The child was quite upset about it.

Think about the following:

● Is this how you view working as a home-based childcarer?

● Do you think of it as a 'fill-in job' while your children are small and you want to be at home with them, but want to earn a bit of money as well?
● If this is your view, are you not guilty of reinforcing stereotypical and negative attitudes about home-based childcarers?
● What is stopping you from seeing home-based childcare as a real profession, where you can make a really significant difference to children's lives?

In your setting

Think about your understanding of equality, inclusion and awareness of diversity as you start to work with children.

● What are your strengths? What do you think you do well?

● How can you make sure that your strengths continue to grow?
● What are you weaknesses?
● What do you think you could improve? What are you going to do to develop your practice?

pacey says

- Introduce books and puzzles in your setting which show a diverse society e.g. children of different ethnic groups, children with SEND, adults in a range of professions e.g. female doctors, male nurses.
- Acknowledge a range of festivals – Eid, Diwali, Chinese New Year as well as Christmas.
- Have welcome signs in two or three languages.
- Make sure that children and families feel that they are valued in your setting whether or not you share the same beliefs.
- If you have dressing-up clothes, try to have clothes that represent the diversity of our society. E.g. a sari, some African print fabrics.
- Allow boys and girls to play equally with the dolls and footballs and bikes.

Assessment links

This assessment task relates to Learning Outcome 4 and links to assessment criteria 4.1 and 4.2.

In your portfolio of evidence you should include an explanation of the role and responsibility of the home-based childcarer in supporting equality, diversity and inclusive practice. You may find it helpful to include actual practical examples of your own work or things that you have observed in other settings.

You also need to evaluate the impact of your own attitudes, values and behaviour when supporting equality, diversity and inclusive practice. You might find it helpful to talk to others and share views and opinions to help you evaluate your own attitudes, values and behaviour.

Although both parts of this assessment task are specifically linked to Learning Outcome 4, it is very important that you remember that the principles of equality, diversity and inclusive practice must be evident in everything that you do and in all aspects of your portfolio as a whole.

Chapter 5

Understand how day-to-day care routines promote children's well-being

Learning Outcome 5

By the end of this chapter you will be able to:

1 Discuss children's well-being in relation to current frameworks
2 Plan to meet the needs of a child between birth and seven years in relation to: diet, personal care needs, rest and sleep provision, personal hygiene routines

3 Plan to meet the needs of a child aged seven years or older in relation to: diet, personal care needs, rest and sleep provision, personal hygiene routines
4 Explain strategies to encourage healthy eating
5 Identify reasons for special dietary requirements

Day-to-day routines are unique to you and the children for whom you care, but there is a common factor. Your routines will be planned to make sure that children's well-being is supported. One way that you can promote well-being is to develop and establish routines that help all children create a secure foundation for the future.

Key term

Well-being – safety, comfort, security, happiness

AC 5.1 Discuss children's well-being in relation to current frameworks

All the frameworks of the UK stress the importance of children's well-being. It is recognised that just like keeping them healthy and safe, children's emotional well-being is key to their overall development and learning. Routines provide children with continuity and emotional security and are therefore essential to their well-being.

England

In England you are required to follow the Statutory Framework for the EYFS. The EYFS is for all children from birth to five years old. The introduction to Section 3 of the Safeguarding and Welfare Requirements (page 16, DfE, September 2014) makes very clear your responsibilities to create an environment where children's well-being is given the highest priority. When you are inspected by Ofsted or an agency, one of the sections of the report is on the contribution of the setting to the children's well-being. This will include how the children develop relationships, their levels of independence, and if they are happy and enjoy being in your home. The section also covers how you care for the children, how healthy the diet is, the opportunities you provide for physical exercise, how children manage their personal hygiene, and how you help children prepare for transitions in their lives. All of the items in the well-being section are usually met by routine events – for example, you will have routines for mealtimes, and to help children settle and develop relationships.

Wales

The Foundation Phase is an approach in Wales to learning for children aged from three to seven years. It is the statutory curriculum for all children in Wales between these ages in both maintained and non-maintained settings that are funded for education by the Local Education Authority (LEA). This framework sets out the curriculum and outcomes under seven areas of learning. One of these areas of learning is 'Personal and social well-being and cultural diversity'. Registered home-based childcarers who are not funded for education by the LEA can still support children's learning and development by understanding the philosophy and ethos of the Foundation Phase and linking this to the care they provide. This is now a requirement under the National Minimum Standards for Regulated Child Care in Wales, as Standard 7:10 states:

The principles of the Foundation Phase and its seven areas of learning are understood and applied in a way appropriate to the age, abilities and stage of development of children in their care and the nature of the provision.

Useful resources

Foundation Phase
For more information on the Foundation Phase and for publications to download visit the Welsh Government's Foundation Phase webpages: **http://wales.gov.uk/topics/educationandskills/earlyyearshome/foundation_phase/?lang=en**

Scotland

In Scotland, all home-based childcarers must comply with the national care standards for childcare. These cover services for children and young people up to the age of 16 years

and are regulated under the Regulation of Care (Scotland) Act 2001. The national care standards for childcare apply equally to services operating in the public, private and voluntary sectors, and in domestic and non-domestic premises that provide services for more than two hours a day and for six or more days each year. The standards reflect the rights of children and young people, as set down in the UN Convention on the Rights of the Child. They also reflect the general principles applying to all the standards developed by the National Care Standards Committee. The principles themselves are not standards but reflect the recognised rights that children, young people, parents and carers enjoy. The main principles are dignity, privacy, choice, safety, realising potential, and equality and diversity. All of these are aspects of well-being.

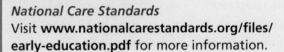

Useful resources

National Care Standards
Visit **www.nationalcarestandards.org/files/early-education.pdf** for more information.

Northern Ireland

In Northern Ireland all home-based childcarers must comply with the Minimum Standards for Childminding and Day Care for Children Under Age 12 (July 2012). The standards are used by Health and Social Care Trusts to register and inspect childminding and day care services for children under the age of 12. Standard 3 focuses on children's health and well-being. In many ways these standards have very similar content to the EYFS, in that children's well-being is given high significance.

Useful resources

Northern Irish Minimum Standards
For more information on the Northern Irish Minimum Standards visit:
www.nicma.org/cms/docs/ChildmindingandDayCareMinimumStandardsJuly12.pdf

Common Core of Skills and Knowledge for the Children's Workforce

The Common Core of Skills and Knowledge for the Children's Workforce was introduced in 2011. The aim was to provide a shared language and a set of common areas of expertise across all sectors and professions providing care for children. The areas of expertise are:

- effective communication and engagement with children and their families
- child and young person development
- safeguarding and promoting the welfare of the child and young person
- supporting transitions
- multi-agency and integrated working
- information sharing.

You will see that all of these areas of the Common Core are covered by this qualification, and indeed all qualifications for the childcare profession are underpinned by this framework.

AC 5.2 Plan to meet the needs of a child between birth and seven years

This AC relates to meeting the needs of a child between birth and seven years with regard to:

- diet
- personal care needs
- rest and sleep provision
- personal hygiene routines.

Plan to meet the needs of a child between birth and seven years in relation to diet

There are several factors that you need to consider when planning a diet for children, in order to make sure it contains sufficient nutrients and calories. These are shown in Figure 5.1. Young children need to have a range of nutrients to satisfy the body's need for growth, energy and maintenance. This can be done through offering a range and variety of different foods. When planning the diet it is important to look at a child's food and liquid intake across a whole day.

You also need to take into consideration any special dietary requirements resulting from allergies or food intolerances, such as intolerance to dairy products or nut allergies. You must also be aware of any medical conditions, such as diabetes or coeliac disease, that may affect or restrict a child's diet. You must get this information from the parents before you begin caring for a child. You should make sure that you are aware of any dietary restrictions of religious and cultural groups. A table outlining common dietary habits can be found on page 174.

Two very important factors are the age of the child and their stage of development. If you care for young babies you may be involved in weaning them. Look again at Chapter 2, AC 2.5 to remind yourself about preparing formula feeds and sterilising feeding equipment. You must work with the parents and respect their wishes in relation to which solid foods to offer to their baby. Older babies and young children will want to feed themselves so you should be prepared for mealtimes to be messy and possibly to take longer than you planned. But remember that this is developing the children's independence and self-help skills, which are vital to a child's overall development.

Young children, especially those under three years, need a wide range of nutrients to ensure that the body grows and develops. Toddlers grow rapidly and are extremely active, and so need a diet that is higher in fat and lower in fibre than that recommended for adults and children over five years. In relation to their size, a toddler's daily energy requirement is high. Young children do not need as much milk as in the first year of life, but they do need plenty of fluids. Young children should have six to eight drinks of water or milk a day to prevent constipation and make sure they stay adequately hydrated. Encourage young children to pour their own drinks to develop their independence and physical skills.

Meal and snack times should be regarded as social events and opportunities for learning. Babies who can sit up unaided can participate in mealtimes.

You must make sure that a harness in the high chair is used every time to prevent the baby falling or climbing out. Toddlers and young children can help to set the table for a meal and so develop learning concepts including counting, matching and sorting. You can use mealtimes to develop the communication and language skills of all the children.

 Tip

Some parents will choose to provide their child with a packed lunch or meal while in your care. You should encourage the parents to provide foods that are healthy and balanced. For ideas for healthy lunchboxes go to www.eatwell.gov.uk or www.childrensfoodtrust.org.uk.

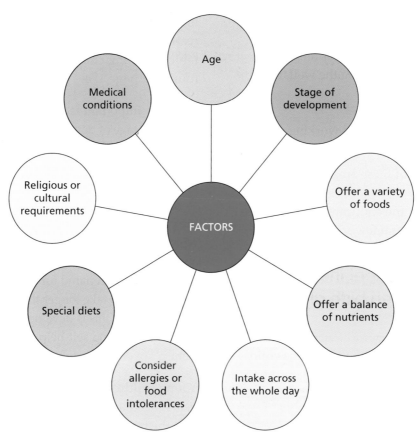

Figure 5.1 Factors to consider when planning a diet to meet children's needs

Figure 5.2 Make sure that you offer healthy and nutritious foods

Links to the EYFS

The Safeguarding and Welfare Requirement 3.47 clearly states that meals, snacks and drinks must be healthy and nutritious. It also states that fresh drinking water must be available and accessible at all times.

How do you make sure that drinking water is available and accessible for all children at all times?

Figure 5.3 How do you make sure that drinking water is available and accessible for all children?

Useful resources

Publication
'Birth to five'
'Birth to five' is a guide to parenting in the early years and contains 150 pages of NHS-accredited information, videos and interactive tools: www.nhs.uk/Planners/birthtofive

Plan to meet the needs of a child between birth and seven years in relation to personal care needs

Personal care includes a range of needs to support children's well-being. These are shown in the figure below. Personal care needs are part of a child's overall health and well-being. If these needs are not met then children may become unwell; for example, if the nappy area of a baby is not thoroughly cleaned it is possible that cross infection could happen, resulting in illness. It is very important that you take into account the wishes of the child's parents, particularly with regard to differences arising from ethnicity or culture.

Care of hair will depend on the child's hair type and the preferences of their parents. By the age of around two years many parents will style their child's hair at home, but you may need to do this occasionally. It is important to follow parents' preferences and use the same hair tools as they do, for example, a soft brush, a wide tooth comb or oil rather than shampoo. All children should have their own hair tools and should not share them. It is important that you look out for head lice. This is necessary especially when a young child is attending a nursery class or pre-school group or mixing with other children generally.

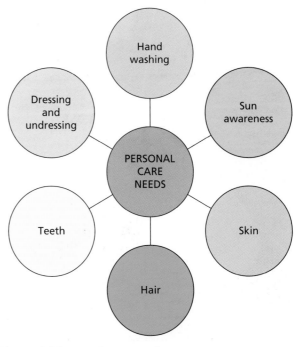

Figure 5.4 Personal care needs

As soon as babies have their first teeth, parents and carers should begin to brush them. This will help to prevent dental decay. A child's first teeth, or milk teeth, are as important as their second (adult) teeth, and need as much care. Each child and baby should have their own small, soft toothbrush. Teeth should be brushed in the morning and at the end of the day before bed at the minimum; some parents like to clean their child's teeth after meals or each time they have eaten, however. Sugary drinks, sweets and snacks should be avoided.

Keeping babies' and young children's skin clean is a basic way of reducing the risk of cross infection. Babies and toddlers will need to have their hands and faces wiped and washed many times during the day. They often dislike having their faces washed and so it is important that it is not rushed. It is more respectful to face a child when washing their face and not to approach from behind. Children should have their own towels or use disposable paper ones. The skin of young children is very sensitive and should never be exposed to strong sunlight. They should be kept in the shade, wear sunhats and keep their bodies covered up.

Useful resources

SunSmart
For the latest advice about care of the skin in the sun: **www.sunsmart.org.uk**

Hand washing is one of the most significant factors in preventing the spread of infections. All children should be encouraged to wash their hands after using the toilet or potty, after a nappy change, before eating, after coughing, sneezing and blowing noses, after handling or touching pets, and after being outside. Independence can be promoted by having appropriate steps so that young children can reach the water and soap dispenser themselves. Even babies can be encouraged to wipe their hands

Figure 5.5 Hand washing is one of the most significant factors in preventing the spread of infections

by copying your actions. They probably think of this as a game, but it is an important way of learning.

An important self-help skill for young children is to be able to undress and dress themselves. Doing this as independently as possible will help with their physical development, confidence and independence levels. Babies as young as eight or nine months old can be encouraged to push their arms through sleeves – and they are often very adept at pulling off hats! You must give toddlers and other young children plenty of time to dress or undress themselves. Yes, it will take a lot longer than if you do it for them, but they won't learn self-help skills if you always put on their shoes or socks or fasten their coat. It is a great confidence booster for children just starting school if they can dress and undress themselves with minimal help.

In your setting

Don't forget to praise all young children's efforts to become independent in personal care, even if they have put their shoes on the wrong feet!

Plan to meet the needs of a child between birth and seven years in relation to rest and sleep provision

Sleep is essential for good health and well-being. Scientists believe that sleep has an important function in allowing the brain to develop and consolidate learning and experiences. This means that babies, especially, need large amounts of sleep – usually around 12 hours per day – as they are constantly learning new things. The amount of sleep does vary between individual babies and children, however. Sleep does not have to be taken all in one go, and many babies and young children benefit from naps during the day. Contrary to what some parents think, having a nap during the day does not stop a young child from sleeping at night. Sometimes not allowing a young child to nap when they are tired can lead to sleep deprivation, which can be harmful. It is important that you do everything possible to keep to the sleep routines of a baby that have been established by the parents.

Key term

Sudden infant death syndrome (SIDS) – also known as cot death, the sudden and unexplained death of an infant

The places where babies and young children sleep should be safe, well ventilated and easy for you to supervise adequately. If the baby or young child is sleeping in a different room, you should use a baby monitor and check on them frequently and regularly. Although sudden infant death syndrome is very rare, it is important that you are aware of the risk factors and avoid these. This means not smoking near the baby, not letting the baby become overheated, and putting them in the correct position for sleeping. Babies should sleep on their backs, with their feet to the foot of the cot and without a pillow.

Useful resources

Foundation for the Study of Infant Deaths The Foundation for the Study of Infant Deaths produces the latest research on sudden infant death syndrome: **www.lullabytrust.org.uk**

In your setting

Going to nursery or pre-school, or just generally playing with others, can be very tiring for young children. Quite often when you pick them up from these places, they just want to rest or nap. Think about how you plan your daily routine and make sure that you can accommodate a tired three or four year old at a time when some of the others are having lunch. Your routines should match a child's needs. If a young child needs to sleep before lunch, then if at all possible you should let them do so and give them their lunch later.

Babies and young children do not require constant stimulation throughout the day. They need some quiet times with activities that allow them to rest. Ideal activities are reading a book together, doing a simple jigsaw puzzle or watching a DVD; taking

Figure 5.6 Some school-aged children may need to have quiet moments when they arrive in your setting

a baby out in a buggy for a walk can be a restful activity. While rest is important for babies and toddlers, however, it does not replace sleep.

Children coming in from school, especially in their first term, are often very tired. You need to plan routines to allow them to rest and re-energise. This could involve looking at a book in a comfy chair, just sitting and talking about their day, or sometimes playing with children younger than themselves as this does not challenge them and is 'easy'. Children may also be hungry and need a healthy snack and drink.

Plan to meet the needs of a child between birth and seven years in relation to personal hygiene routines

All toileting and nappy changing should be regarded as private activities and children should be encouraged to do as much as they can independently. Obviously a baby cannot change its

own nappy, but it can be involved by you talking to them, perhaps letting them hold the clean nappy or pot of barrier cream if it is used. Children who are gaining bladder and bowel control can develop independence by fetching the potty.

 Tip

Don't forget that it is good practice to always wear disposable gloves when changing a baby's nappy and dealing with body fluids.

Children vary considerably as to when they are ready to be toilet trained. You must work with the child's parents in deciding that a young child is ready to move out of nappies. Toilet training should be approached in a relaxed and unhurried way, and can take a few days or a few weeks. You must respect a child's privacy and, regardless of how convenient it may seem, having a child sitting on a potty in the middle of your play room while other children are playing around them is not appropriate or respectful. You should also ask young children before you start personal care routines, for example, ask a child if you can help to pull their pants down, rather than just going ahead and doing it.

Encourage good personal hygiene routines when they are very young, supporting independence appropriately, so they become an automatic part of going to the toilet. Teach children to wipe their bottoms themselves; teach girls to wipe from front to back. Teach boys to aim carefully and not to sprinkle all over the floor. Teach them to dispose of toilet paper down the toilet, always to flush the toilet when they have finished, and then to wash their hands.

As children become older and more independent they will want to go to the toilet on their own. You must respect their need for privacy, but that does not mean that you do not have to supervise them. It is not a good idea to have locks that children can reach on toilet doors. This is in case you need to get in quickly. Agree with children that they can close the door and that you will talk to them and check on them with the door closed.

AC 5.3 Plan to meet the needs of a child aged seven years or older

This AC relates to meeting the needs of a child aged seven years and older with regard to:

- diet
- personal care needs
- rest and sleep provision
- personal hygiene routines.

Plan to meet the needs of a child aged seven years or older in relation to diet

Look again at the figure of factors to consider when planning to meet dietary needs (page 68). These needs are common to all children and babies regardless of their age.

School-aged children are also growing rapidly and often becoming very active. They have a high energy requirement comparative to their size. They need foods that are high in energy and rich in nutrients. It is better for children to have small, frequent meals, rather than just three main meals a day; although with a busy school day this is not always possible. This means that any snacks that they have should be healthy and provide energy.

Despite the fact that children aged seven years and older are active and growing rapidly, it is thought that between 5 and 15 per cent of school-aged children are overweight. This is partly due to the fact that they did not develop an understanding of a healthy diet when younger. This reinforces the importance of teaching children as young as possible about healthy eating and having a balanced diet. This will be discussed further in AC 5.4.

It is also recognised that some children become less active as they grow older and may not willingly participate in sport activities in or out of school. Girls and boys can become very self-conscious when expected to wear sports kit and will avoid doing so if possible. Inactivity will impact on a child's level of health and fitness, however.

Case study

Libby enjoyed playing games and doing sport at primary school and was picked for the school rounders team. When she went to secondary school, however, rounders was not offered on the PE choices. Libby was also expected to wear shorts and a polo shirt for all PE activities, whereas at primary school she had worn tracksuit bottoms. Libby was very self-conscious of her body shape and invented all kinds of excuses to avoid doing PE activities.

Discussion point

How could you help Libby?

As children enter puberty, their dietary needs may change. Girls will need to make sure that they have plenty of iron in their diet to make sure that they do not become anaemic. During this time they may become very conscious of their body image and want to diet and lose weight. Their bodies are still growing, however, and there is the need for a balanced and healthy diet with sufficient protein and iron to support growth and development. During puberty boys frequently have voracious appetites to satisfy their growth needs. A snack when they come in from school may not be enough and you may have to offer other filling and healthy foods, such as brown bread sandwiches, cereals and milk, rather than quick fixes like crisps and fizzy drinks.

Find out more

School children in the UK spend more than £1.3 billion a year on food. Almost a third of their pocket money goes on snacks eaten while travelling to and from school. Ask the older children for whom you care how much they spend each week on food and what they buy.

Plan to meet the needs of a child aged seven years or older in relation to personal care needs

By the age of seven years children should be fully independent in their personal care routines, providing that there has not been any reason to hinder their development, such as a serious accident, illness or medical condition.

If you are caring for an older child with a disability you will need to talk to their parents/carers about developing an intimate care policy that respects the child's needs and maintains their dignity and privacy.

Older children will know when they should wash their hands, but they will frequently need reminders. Older children can be encouraged to wash their hands thoroughly if you teach them about some of the bacteria that may be present on their hands. A science experiment in which bacteria from supposedly washed and clean hands are cultured on plates can show them the results of poor hygiene.

As with younger children, hair tools, hand towels and toothbrushes should never be shared. All children should have their own personal care kit. As part of your on-going care routines you should watch out for signs of head lice. Signs that a child has head lice include scratching, small red marks on the scalp and white eggs on the hair shaft. If you suspect that a child has head lice you must talk to all the parents as all the children will need to be treated.

Older children will have greater independence levels than younger ones and should be able to care for their hair, skin and teeth themselves. You still need to be vigilant, however, and aware of possible changes. For example, children whose feet are exposed to moist and warm conditions, such as changing rooms, can develop fungal infections like athlete's foot. Any concerns must be reported to the child's parents and action taken to prevent the spread of infection to others.

Plan to meet the needs of a child aged seven years or older in relation to rest and sleep provision

Older children coming in from school or during hot weather may need to rest during the day; some may actually fall asleep and nap. As part of planning your environment you should think about having an area where children can rest and still be supervised adequately. This could be a corner of the room with big cushions, a soft sofa or a comfy chair. Older children who are tired may not be tolerant of younger ones so try to arrange your routines so that younger children are actively engaged while older ones rest.

Children who do not have sufficient rest and sleep may display the symptoms of hyperactive behaviour. They can be irritable and find it hard to concentrate or settle. Sleep-deprived children may find that feelings of anxiety are pacified by eating food high in calories such as sugary foods, which in turn affect their general health and well-being.

A short nap or time of rest can be beneficial, although this will not solve the problem. You should talk to the child about why they are sleep deprived and try to see if there is an underlying emotional cause. You may not be able to solve the problem but you may know of someone who could help the child.

If an older child, or indeed a baby or young child, seems especially drowsy or tired, it may be a sign of illness. You should take their temperature with a child-friendly thermometer. Normal body temperature as taught in first aid courses is 37°C, depending on the child. If the child has a fever you should reassure them, keep the child cool and contact the parents.

In your setting

- Make sure that you are familiar with the common signs of illness.
- Keep up to date with what infectious diseases are currently affecting your area. Make sure you know what to look out for.
- Make sure that your first aid box is complete.

Plan to meet the needs of a child aged seven years or older in relation to personal hygiene routines

All children have a right to privacy in relation to personal hygiene routines. Most children are fully independent and take care of their own hygiene routines, however, you may have to remind them to wash their hands after using the toilet. Some children with SEND may need support and help specific to their needs, but you must respect their privacy, while at the same time being aware of safeguarding issues for the child and yourself. Some girls are reaching puberty and menstruating earlier and so you must be prepared to support such children. Make sure that you have appropriate sanitary protection available and that the child understands how to dispose of used products hygienically.

AC 5.4 Explain strategies to encourage healthy eating

Every child, regardless of their age, needs to have a balanced and nutritious diet. A healthy diet ideally consists of a variety of different foods, but not everyone likes every food that is offered to them. Everyone will have their favourite foods and those that they really dislike. Every child is unique, and as they grow and develop they will develop strong likes and dislikes. These likes and dislikes can change, however, so it is important to keep offering a range of foods. Just because a child rejects broccoli one day shouldn't mean that you never offer it again. No eating experience should be a time of stress or become a battle of wills between you and the child.

Increasing rates of childhood obesity and diet-related disorders, such as dental decay, anaemia and rickets, seem frequently to be media headlines. All of these conditions occur because children are not offered a healthy and balanced diet. Sometimes socio-economic factors can be the reason for poor diet. You must, however, provide the children that you care for with a healthy and balanced diet.

The key to encouraging healthy eating in children is to get them involved as soon as they show an interest in food. Childhood experiences of eating will set the pattern for their future life. Let babies and young children try to feed themselves, even if it does make a mess. Offer a range of finger foods, and those that can easily be put on a spoon. Try to vary the foods that you offer. You do not always have to provide pieces of apple or carrots at snack time; be adventurous and encourage children to try small pieces of different foods, such as sweet peppers, raw cauliflower and broccoli. Babies and young children are often more willing than older children to try out new foods and experiment.

Healthy eating can be encouraged by having foods with lots of different colours, textures, smells and tastes – eating should be a total sensory experience. Foods that look attractive are more appealing to children. Let children arrange their own food on their plates, making patterns or faces, for example. Some children are quite particular

Case study

Jan began caring for Lily when she was nearly three years old. Lily was a very fussy eater and Jan often despaired of what she could give her at lunchtime. Lily would not eat fruit or vegetables, apart from potatoes, specifically chips. She refused pasta and rice and seemed to get by on tuna sandwiches. Jan discussed Lily's diet and her concerns with Lily's mum, who was finding mealtimes very stressful and said that it was like a battleground at home. As the school holidays were coming up, Jan decided to plan a series of picnics in different places, including the local park, another home-based childcarer's house and her own garden. All of the children were asked to choose food to take, with the condition that it had to be finger foods, such as cheese cubes, strips of cooked chicken, pieces of fruit and vegetables. At the first picnic Lily ate very little apart from a bread stick. The next time, she watched the others eating slices of peach and very tentatively took a piece and liked it. Gradually over the course of four or five picnics, Lily began to try different foods, some of which she liked and some she didn't. While Jan knew that Lily was still a fussy eater, she did feel that by taking a very relaxed approach and varying the location, she had managed to get Lily to start to eat a more varied and healthy diet.

about how their food is arranged and may like each different food type to be separate and spaced out on the plate. Brightly coloured foods are always more appealing.

Older children can be encouraged to develop healthy eating habits by being involved in planning their own menus. This could involve researching different food types, costing out meals, and actually shopping and cooking the foods. Not all children have the opportunity to cook at school or at home, and doing a cooking activity with you can be a very positive way of learning about diet, nutrition and many other concepts. Even young children can be involved in food preparation; they can stir, mix, and roll out pastry and dough.

Eating should be a social experience and so it is good practice to eat as a group as much as possible. If children enjoy mealtimes they will be relaxed and more willing to try new things. Another strategy that you could use is to vary where you actually eat. It is obviously good practice to sit at a table but 'variety is the spice of life', so why not plan to have a snack in the garden, or in a den that the children have made? Try taking a picnic to a park or other local facility, or eating it in your garden. Eating in different locations will often encourage a fussy eater to be a bit more adventurous.

AC 5.5 Identify reasons for special dietary requirements

Dietary requirements can be related to culture, religious beliefs, ethnicity, or medical conditions and illness. The UK has a multi-ethnic and multi-cultural society that has a diverse range of foods and diets. You do not have to belong to one particular cultural or religious group to enjoy and appreciate the food of that community.

At the back of this book you will find a chart that sets out some common dietary habits for specific cultural and religious groups (see page 174). The importance of diversity (see Chapter 4) extends to a child's dietary requirements. It is very important, however, that you do not make assumptions about a child's diet; you should always discuss it with their parents.

Tip

Particular foods are associated with special festivals, celebrations or traditions. For example, you could provide pancakes on Shrove Tuesday, poori at Diwali and jiaozi at Chinese New Year. Providing foods from different cultures is a very good way of teaching children about different celebrations. Parents of children from different cultural or religious groups will often be very pleased to share their traditional foods.

Food allergies are abnormal responses to usually harmless foods. It is estimated that up to 5 per cent of children have a food allergy. Some allergies will disappear as the child grows; however, an allergy to peanuts and some other nuts can be for life. Eight foods cause nearly all allergic reactions. These are:

- peanuts, some tree nuts, such as almonds, pecans, walnuts
- cereals, such as wheat, rye and barley including some flours made from cereals
- milk
- fish, shellfish and molluscs
- eggs
- soy
- sesame seeds
- celery/lupin seeds, mustard seeds
- sulphur dioxide (used in the preparation of some products).

Food intolerances are not the same as food allergies and are much more common. Babies sometimes develop an intolerance to cows' milk, or specifically lactose, the protein in the milk. This can cause vomiting and diarrhoea. Sometimes food intolerances can be a temporary thing, such as after an illness. The offending food should always be removed from the child's diet, however.

Coeliac disease is a condition where the individual cannot tolerate gluten. Gluten is found in wheat and rye. Coeliac disease is often not diagnosed in babies until weaning, but some children do not show any adverse effects until they are older. Coeliac disease can be controlled and managed by offering a gluten-free diet.

Diabetes is caused by a difficulty in converting carbohydrates into energy due to the body not producing insulin. Additional insulin is usually given by daily injections. As part of a normal healthy diet children with diabetes, like all children, should avoid foods that are high in sugar, such as sweets, cakes, biscuits and carbonated drinks. Dieticians advise that a normal healthy and balanced diet is ideal for people with diabetes.

A **vegetarian** diet is one where the individual does not eat meat or fish. Vegetarian children need an alternative to meat, fish and chicken in order to get sufficient protein for growth and development. This could include cheese, eggs, milk and pulses. A vegetarian diet should include additional sources of iron, such as leafy green vegetables.

A **vegan** diet is one where the individual does not eat any foods of animal origin. This means that a vegan would not eat any meat, fish, eggs, dairy produce, honey or any food additives based on animal products, such as gelatine. Children who follow a vegan diet will eat cereals, pulses, fruits, vegetables, seeds and nuts. Vegan babies would normally be breastfed.

Some families will follow diets that are **ethical and environmentally aware**. This means that they will buy only food that is organic or has been ethically produced, such as those approved by Fairtrade or the Soil Association.

Case study

Anga and her partner live on a smallholding where they raise chickens, a few pigs and two cows. Part of the smallholding is given over to vegetable growing and there are several fruit bushes and trees. Anga is a home-based childcarer and the children she cares for are actively involved in the smallholding; for example, they feed the chickens and collect the eggs, harvest the vegetables and pick the fruit. Anga's unique selling point for families is that she knows exactly from where all the food she provides for the children has come.

 says

You must be aware of the Food Information for Consumers Regulation (Regulation (EU) 1169/2011). From 13 December 2014, new rules on allergen labelling are being applied. As a result you are required to declare the allergens in any food that you provide in your setting.

There are 14 allergens on the European list. These represent the most common and potent allergens across the EU and these foods are responsible for the majority of the allergic reactions occurring within the food allergic population.

Things to consider:

- Look at the allergens contained in any food that you currently provide and make a record
- Tell parents about the regulation and discuss with them how you will provide allergen information, this could be by displaying information on your menus, writing in the daily diary, telling them directly.
- Consider any craft materials or baking activities you do – are there any ingredients that contain allergens?
- If you have a child with an allergy in your setting how might you risk assess for outings and eating outside the setting?

The food standards agency have updated their childminder page to incorporate some detail around allergens at www.food.gov.uk/business-industry/caterers/startingup/childminders.

Assessment links

This assessment task relates to Learning Outcome 5 and links to assessment criteria 5.1, 5.2, 5.3, 5.4 and 5.5. This assessment task has three parts.

1 You are asked to produce an information sheet that considers children's well-being in relation to current frameworks.
  You must consider the different and diverse needs of children and make sure that your information sheet considers different ages of children.
  There is no set format for your information sheet, but try to make all of the information clear and precise. Try not to repeat yourself. You may find it helpful to make a plan before you begin of what you intend to include.

2 This part of the assessment task can be thought of as being in two parts, as you must look separately at children from birth to seven years and those older than seven years. You are asked to produce a plan that will meet the needs of both age groups in relation to:

  ● diet
  ● physical care needs
  ● rest and sleep provision
  ● personal hygiene routines.

  Although the task only asks for 'a plan' you may find it easier actually to do two plans, one for each age group.
  There is no set format for the plan, so you can do it as a chart, a table, or a written piece.

3 You are asked to produce a poster encouraging healthy eating and detailing special dietary requirements.
  Making a poster can be fun, as you can let your imagination run riot! Try to make your poster colourful and attractive. Use clear lettering and be as neat as possible. Posters do not have to be all text, but can be a mixture of illustrations, charts, tables, diagrams and text.
  It is intended that you could display your poster on a noticeboard for your parents/carers so that they can become aware of healthy eating and dietary requirements.
  Make sure that your poster includes information on strategies to encourage healthy eating and identifies reasons for special dietary requirements.

Chapter 6

Understand how to work in partnership to support children's outcomes

Learning Outcome 6

By the end of this chapter you will be able to:

1 Identify typical partnerships established by a home-based childcarer
2 Discuss the benefits of working in partnership
3 Describe how partnerships with parents/carers are established and maintained
4 Explain how working in partnership with parents/carers supports the home learning environment
5 Explain the boundaries of confidentiality

Working in partnership with parents and other professionals gives you greater opportunities to share knowledge and expertise. Partnership working, particularly with parents, is highly beneficial for children. Children are more likely to reach their full potential if effective lines of communication and sound working partnerships have been established.

AC 6.1 Identify typical partnerships established by a home-based childcarer

Partnership working allows the different professionals working with or supporting children and their families to come together. This means that knowledge and expertise can be shared. It also often means that problems can be identified earlier, or even prevented from occurring in the first place. Partnership working is extremely beneficial and supportive for you, the home-based childcarer, too. So, with whom could you work in partnership?

Key term

Partnership – a collaboration or relationship based on trust and respect in the best interests of the child

Parents/carers

First and foremost you will work in partnership with the parents/carers of the children. Parents and primary carers – such as grandparents, foster parents – are the most important people in young children's lives. They are the first educators of their child. It is from them that children will learn about their family's culture, religious beliefs and traditions. Parents/carers know their child better than anyone else. They can powerfully influence the child's development.

Links to the EYFS

Partnership with parents/carers is a requirement of the EYFS (see Section 3.73). You have to provide information for parents/carers about how you deliver the EYFS and the types of activities and experiences that you make available to the children so that learning can be continued at home. You have to tell parents about the food and drinks that you provide. Parents also have to share information with you about their child, such as their full name, date of birth and who has parental responsibility. Ideas for how you can meet this requirement will be discussed later in the chapter.

Other home-based childcarers

You may also work in partnership with other home-based childcarers. It is possible that you will go to drop-in groups or meetings where you can meet up with other home-based childcarers, share ideas, get support and socialise. You may also meet up at school or nursery playgrounds as you drop off and collect children.

Staff in other childcare provisions

It is always good practice to try to work in partnership with the other professionals at settings attended by the children. This could include staff in other childcare provisions, pre-school staff, nursery staff, teachers, teaching assistants and other people in schools. You are all working in the best interests of the child first and foremost and can share appropriate knowledge and offer continuity.

Health and medical professionals

Partnership working can be with health and medical professionals, particularly if you are caring for a child with special educational needs or disabilities. This could include health visitors, portage workers, speech therapists, and physiotherapists. Sometimes, if a child has a specific need or disability, you can work in partnership with voluntary organisations or support groups. When groups of professionals work together to support children and their families they may follow the Common Assessment Framework (this is explained in greater detail in Chapter 3).

Activity

Make a list of all of the other professionals with whom you could work in partnership if you were caring for a child with cystic fibrosis.

It is possible that you could be involved with a family that has been identified as needing additional support. This could then involve you working in partnership with social workers, early intervention teams and family support workers.

Voluntary organisations or support groups have already been identified in relation to health and medical issues, but you can also work in partnership with many other such groups to support yourself and the children. Such groups could include PACEY, NSPCC and Barnardo's, for example.

Useful resources

Websites
PACEY
www.pacey.org.uk

NSPCC
www.nspcc.org.uk

Barnardo's
www.barnardos.org.uk

AC 6.2 Discuss the benefits of working in partnership

We know that the best outcomes for children can be achieved when everyone involved with the child works together, including the parents/carers. Parents, as the first educators of their child, know the needs of their child, know their preferences in terms of food and have the best understanding of their personality.

Working with parents/carers

The partnerships that you develop with the parents of the children for whom you care are crucial to the children's overall well-being. The partnership should begin the first time you meet the parents, even before you begin to settle the child. They will probably be more nervous than you about leaving their child, and the quality of the partnership at the start will set the tone for your future relationship with them. You must value, respect and consider their wishes and views on how they want you to care for their child. You will need to share information about the child's care, likes, dislikes and interests. This will help you to meet the child's needs and offer appropriate care, while at the same time being consistent with what the child is used to at home.

The benefits of working in partnership with parents are immense. The child will be emotionally secure if they see that your relationship with their parents is strong and caring. The child will develop a greater sense of trust in you if they know that their parents also trust you. You are more likely to have good, open lines of communication if you work in partnership. Children will benefit from the partnership as you and the parents develop your relationship and share the child's achievements and progress. A partnership with all parents will be very beneficial in helping you have a better understanding of the needs of all children in your care. A good partnership will also help to support the child's learning when at home.

Partnerships with parents are often strong: they regularly come into your home; they may get to know your family members. It is really important, however, that you maintain professional boundaries and do not let the partnership change into a friendship. This will be discussed in more detail later in this chapter (see page 86).

Figure 6.1 It is important to have a professional relationship with parents

Working with other professionals

A partnership will help everyone involved with the child to maintain their focus on the child. It ensures that the child is central and also means that everyone will communicate and share knowledge about the 'whole' child, rather than just one aspect of the child's life. This will give continuity and consistency of care in any decisions that are made.

Partnership working enables all professionals to share their knowledge and expertise about a child. We all see different aspects of a child, depending on where and with whom they are. A child who is quiet and shy in large groups, such as at pre-school, may be chatty and confident when with you and one or two others. The pre-school staff could learn from you how to encourage the child to engage more. You could learn from the pre-school about situations where the child is less confident, meaning you could both support the child more effectively.

Partnership working with other settings that a child attends can help with transitions. These can be difficult times for some children. If all the adults involved can share relevant information about the key things that happen to the child, it will help to make the child's experiences more positive. Of course, all such information must be shared with the child's parents.

Key term

Transition – a time of change; can mean big experiences, such as starting school, or small, for example, moving from one activity or another

It is essential that you are professional at all times and show respect for the roles and responsibilities of all professionals and parents.

Sharing knowledge and expertise is vital if you are caring for a child with a specific condition. You may need to understand how to carry out certain procedures or have specific knowledge about diet. For example, you may be caring for a child with diabetes and need to know how to check their blood glucose levels and administer insulin. Partnership working helps to meet the child's specific needs and offer continuity and consistency of care.

A child who is going into hospital, even if it is a planned stay, can be anxious and concerned, just as an adult might be. Working in partnership with the child's parents and medical professionals can help the child emotionally as everyone will be giving the same supportive messages.

You could care for a child who has difficulties at school, for example, with behaviour issues. The child will be helped and supported far more effectively if you, the school and the child's parents all work together and offer consistent approaches and strategies to help the child.

It is highly likely that you will take and collect children from different settings. You can be a very important link between that setting and the child's parents. The better partnerships you have with these settings, the better the outcomes for the children. With the written permission of the parents, information can be shared with you and passed on to the parents – for many parents this can be a great time saver. They know that you have information and that they do not need to make another call to the school, for example, to find out dates of parents' meetings.

Case study

Zakia cared for the twins of a single working mother, who worked long hours. Zakia had the mother's written permission to get information about the boys from the school. Information and messages were put into a shared three-way communication book, which everyone wrote in. For example, the teacher wrote reminders for special events, such as special assemblies or incidents that had happened at school. Zakia added comments about the boys; for example, she wrote about one boy telling her he didn't like school lunches but hadn't told anyone at school. The mother sometimes added comments about activities the boys had been involved with at weekends and in the evenings. As a result everyone involved had a good overall knowledge of the boys.

Links to the EYFS

At some point between the ages of two and three years you are required to carry out a progress check on a child. You have to provide parents/carers with a short written summary of their child's development and progress in the prime areas and discuss with them how they can support the child's learning at home. This partnership is further extended as you should encourage the parents/carers to share the progress check with other relevant professionals, such as their health visitor and staff at any other provision the child may attend. In the same way, if a child spends more time at a day nursery, for example, than with you, you can ask to see the progress check that the day nursery has done. You may also be asked to share information, with the parents' permission, with the day nursery, so that a better overall insight into the child's progress can be gained.

Apart from checking progress in the prime areas of learning, the check also serves as a very useful tool for identifying any possible problems. If this is the case early intervention can be made and in some cases prevent the problems from developing into anything significant.

Figure 6.2 Sharing observations with parents keeps them informed of their child's progress and development

AC 6.3 Describe how partnerships with parents/carers are established and maintained

The first meeting

In an ideal world your first meeting with parents/carers would be a well-planned and unhurried event, where you could share information and get to know both the parents and the child. This first meeting will set the tone for the rest of your relationship with the parents and so it is very important that you are professional and welcoming. Hopefully an atmosphere of trust and mutual respect will be initiated at the first meeting. The meeting can be in the parents'/carers' home, but ideally it is better if it is in the place in which the child will be cared.

The first meeting should include the parents/carers and the child. Agree a time when you know that

you can give the child and their parents your full attention. This may have to be an evening or even a weekend. If that is not possible, it is a good idea to tell the other children, including your own, that someone is coming to have a look around.

Some parents, however, may be less understanding about the need for a first meeting. They may be happier with a quick phone call, email or even text message to agree times and costs. This is not good practice. You cannot meet the needs of the child without a first meeting, and meeting the child's needs should be your first priority.

A first meeting can be a bit strained to begin with, so start by talking about everyday things and give yourself, the parents and the child the chance to relax. Remember to show them all the rooms and areas that you use when looking after children. A tour sounds a bit grand perhaps, but it does help people relax. The parents will have a lot of questions for you and you will have information that you want to get from them. Make sure that you have any paperwork needed ready to hand, including your welcome pack or sample policy and procedures. It doesn't look very professional if you have to go hunting around to find things. Don't forget to discuss with the parents how you plan to settle their child into your home and how it should be a shared process between you and them.

Tip

You should **never** agree to care for a child after just a hurried conversation in the school playground, the supermarket or after a telephone call the day before. In an emergency, however, you may have to care for a child with little or no notice; for example, if you have signed up to a local authority scheme for short-term or respite care. In such situations you should be as calm and welcoming as possible and offer the child plenty of reassurance.

In your setting

You may need to offer anxious parents lots of reassurance, especially if they are feeling guilty about leaving their child. If you are new to home-based childcare you may be feeling nervous yourself, as well as a whole range of other emotions. Take a deep breath and remind yourself of the reasons you decided to become a home-based childcarer in the first place. Hold your head up high and be professional.

Activity

Think about the questions that you will need to ask the parents/carers about the child. It is a good idea to write down your questions beforehand so that you do not forget anything.

Write down the answers to your questions during the meeting as well, as this will help to avoid any misunderstandings.

Develop a welcome pack

A welcome pack does not have to be a big file of information; that can come later, after the first meeting. A welcome pack could simply be an information leaflet that parents can take away with them. It should include:

- Obvious details, such as your name and phone number or email address.
- A brief résumé of your experience, including details of your own children and your qualifications.
- How much you charge: sessional, daily, hourly and late charges; costs in the event of a child being ill or on holiday.
- What parents will get for their money; for example, whether you will provide food, nappies.
- Days and hours that you work, including details of your holidays.
- A brief overview of activities that you can offer.
- An outline of your day so that if a parent needs to contact you they have an idea where you might be.
- If you take to and pick up from other settings.
- Any other unique selling points you think you have.

After the first meeting, give parents any child record forms and other information forms you may have, for them to take away and complete if they want you to care for their child. It may not be after the very first meeting, but at some point soon after you will also need to give parents a detailed registration document; this will probably be your contract. Try not to overload the parents at this time. You want to establish a professional partnership with them, so make sure you give plenty of time and opportunity for them to give you information and to ask questions. Remember that a partnership is a two-way process from the beginning.

Tip

You must not start to care for a child without having a signed contract between you and the parents/carers.

After the first meeting, and assuming that the parents/carers want you to care for their child, you can give them more information. Some home-based childcarers keep a file of information for parents, such as:

● Your First Aid certificate.
● Certificates, such as from this course, from local authority training on EYFS, safeguarding and food hygiene, and other courses you have attended or completed.
● Your inspection report.
● Any written policies you may have produced.
● Details of how to contact Ofsted or your childminding agency.
● How to make a complaint about your service.

This file should be available for parents to read and it is a good idea to have a form for them to sign to say that they have read it.

In your setting

Your registration document and details of your public liability should be displayed in your home, not kept in your welcome file.

After the first meeting

Make sure that you have agreed with the parents how they want to be addressed and what they should call you. Names are important and it shows that you respect and value the parents if you make every effort to address them correctly. Also make sure that you get the name of the child right and are aware of any special words that they use, such as for needing to go to the toilet.

Remember to talk to the other children for whom you care about the new child. Introduce the new child and their parents to the other children and your own family members if they are around. Don't rush introductions; your aim is to make both the child and their parents/carers feel welcome and valued.

You should have agreed with the parents/carers a settling in process and when the child will start. You should try to be flexible in settling the child, so that you meet their needs and those of the

parents/carers. The settling in process is crucial for the child's well-being and should not be hurried. Some parents do not understand that they should not just arrive on the first morning, leave their child and go. We all have busy lives and time restraints, but it is really important that you make it very clear at the first meeting that you place a great deal of importance on settling their child into your setting. You must work with the parents/carers, however, not against them.

In the early days of a partnership you are establishing a professional partnership. You must remember that this is a professional partnership, not a friendship. Keeping this in mind will make it easier if there are problems. For example, dealing with a parent who owes you money can be less difficult if it is on a professional level, not personal. This does not mean that you cannot be friendly and sociable, but be aware of your responsibilities.

Reflective practice

A friendship happens when two people share a common interest and choose to share it. A professional relationship occurs because of work, and the people concerned do not necessarily choose to be with each other. You do not have to like someone to have a professional partnership with them.

● Think about the differences between a professional partnership and a friendly relationship with parents/carers. You might find it helpful to think about, or list, the key features of a professional partnership and the key features of a friendship.

Developing and maintaining your partnership with parents

Developing and maintaining any partnership has two main features of equal importance. These are:

● exchanges of information
● two-way communication.

Problems can arise when either the parent or the home-based childcarer fails to exchange information or communicate effectively.

Sharing and exchanging information

Sharing and exchanging information is vital for every aspect of your partnership with parents/carers. It is a good idea to agree very early on the best way to do this. A quick chat as the child is dropped off may work, but if the parent/carer is in a hurry, they could easily forget something. In the same way, you could be distracted with other children who are also arriving or needing your attention. The same is true at the end of the day. Both parents and child could be tired and want to get home or to the shops. You may want a few moments of peace to relax after a busy day and not feel that you can give your full attention. So what can you do?

A face-to-face chat is good, but so is a text message, phone call or email. Some home-based childcarers have home-to-setting diaries, in which they write about the child, and the parent/carer does the same when at home. Then, in a less busy moment, the information can be read fully. You do need to know first thing in the morning, however, if, for example, a child has not slept well the night before, as that could impact on your working day. In the same way a parent/carer needs to know if their child has not eaten very well during the day. This kind of information should really be shared face to face.

Many home-based childcarers take digital photographs of the children engaged in activities and send them to the parents/carers so they can see what their child is doing. While this is a way of sharing information, you must remember to get written permission from parents/carers before you take any photographs of their children.

Social media sites are designed to share information, but you should use these only with caution and great care. Once a message and photograph is on Facebook, for example, you have

Figure 6.3 The progress check at two not only shows a child's progress and development, but can also highlight any areas of concern

lost 'ownership' of it, even with privacy settings. There is also the possibility that some information may be shared that is wholly inappropriate. For example, if you post that you have had a 'rubbish' day with children, do you really want all the parents to know? Furthermore, that type of 'information' will not help build a partnership between you.

Some home-based childcarers produce newsletters for parents to let them know what activities the children have done, or what their plans are for the future, or to pass on information. This doesn't have to be paper-based, an email can be just as effective. You could have an open day for parents/carers, but do plan this carefully if you hold it in your own home.

The way you exchange information is a matter of personal choice. The main point is that you do exchange information in appropriate ways with parents/carers. Remember, one size does not fit all and offering a variety of methods will ensure you meet parents' preferred ways of receiving information about their child.

In your setting

- How do you plan to share information with parents/carers?
- Will you have the same method for everyone or different ways for each parent/carer?

Two-way communication

A partnership will only develop well if there is effective two-way communication. You can try to exchange information with parents/carers, but you are not communicating if they just receive it and do not respond. The same is true if a parent/carer tells you something and you do not act upon it.

Communication is just as much about listening as it is about speaking and getting your message across. Listening properly means you give the person who is speaking your full attention and if possible make eye contact. Listening also includes

all the other ways that we give messages, apart from talking, such as eye contact, body language, facial expression and gestures.

Communication is a two-way process with a giver and a receiver. Look at the following text conversation, for example:

Parent/carer (giver): *is Josh ok cos cried when I left?*

You (receiver): *yes he's fine, playing in garden at the mo.*

Parent/carer (giver): *ok tks*

You (receiver): *don't worry*

Effective communication requires time and effort from both the giver and the receiver, but it is the foundation of your partnership. Lack of communication leads to misunderstandings, misinformation and, ultimately, the breakdown of the partnership.

Activity

There are skills that you can learn to help you become a more effective communicator, not just with parents, but with children and other professionals. Find out how you could develop your skills.

AC 6.4 Explain how working in partnership with parents/carers supports the home learning environment

Parents/carers are the first educators of their child. This is a huge responsibility and by working in partnership you can build on and strengthen this learning. This will help parents/carers get more enjoyment from and understanding of their child. It will also improve the parents'/carers' self-image and views of themselves as parents. You can share information about progress, achievements and milestones in the child's development, such as potty training, trying new foods. This type of information helps strengthen your relationship, but it also encourages the parents to continue aspects of the child's learning at home.

Children are learning from the second they are born. They learn wherever they are and their learning never stops. They learn in their own home, at the shops and in the car; from siblings, from other family members; at other settings, at your home. They will learn from everything that you say and do, from all the activities available to them and the experiences that they have while in your care. (How children learn will be discussed more in Chapter 7.)

To maximise a child's learning when with you, ideally there should be continuity and consistency between you and the parents/carers. This is where an effective and strong partnership can be highly beneficial. You are not trying to tell parents/carers how they should bring up their child or that your way of doing things is better than theirs. You must respect parents'/carers' views and help them to build on what they already know about and want for their child.

When in your home, children are not learning in isolation. They take experiences from home, such as self-feeding or dressing themselves, and build on them when with you. You need to have shared information from parents/carers about their home learning experiences, and a good partnership will enable this. But these are also personal experiences for parents/carers and they are not likely to share them with you unless they trust and respect you.

Sharing children's learning with parents/carers, telling them what their child has achieved and encouraging them to continue at home will show the child that you and their parents/carers are working together. This will help the child's overall well-being and can extend and develop activities that a child has been involved in at home.

Useful resources

Website
Parents, Early Years and Learning
Parents, Early Years and Learning (PEAL) is a body that has identified good practice in engaging parents with their children's learning. The website has some good resources on the subject: **www.peal.org.uk/resources.aspx**

There will be times when the partnership with the parents/carers is not as effective as you would like. This will impact on the child's learning when in your care. Barriers to effective partnerships could be:

- You may have concerns about the welfare of the child. You may believe that the child is being neglected or not in good health. You will have to pass on your concerns to other professionals and while you do not have to tell the parents/carers that you have taken this action, it will impact on your partnership with them.

- The parent/carer may work very long hours or away from home; they may often pick their child up late, never have time to talk to you and always be in a rush. Over time this may begin to affect your partnership with them. You have to accept, however, that not all parents/carers behave in the same way. Provided the child is well cared for and developing well, and provided the parent/carer pays the late pick-up fees, there is not a lot that you can do. You could terminate their contract and break the partnership completely. But ask yourself: is that in the best interests of the child, and what will they learn from you if you do this?

- Parents/carers may have different expectations for their child than you have. Hopefully this will have come to light early on in your partnership, or even at the first meeting. For example, parents may think that their child is ready to be potty trained, but you may disagree. Expectations can change, however.

- Sometimes parents/carers can become angry or upset with you. This might be over something that you regard as quite trivial, such as paint on clothing, which will wash out. At the end of a tiring day for a parent/carer, however, this could just be the last straw. This is distressing for the child and could mean that they don't want to take part in messy play activities in the future because they are frightened of their parents'/carers' reaction if they get dirty. This in turn will affect the child's learning opportunities.

- Children learn from you and their parents/carers. If a child behaves in a discriminatory way towards another child, you must challenge it. You also have a responsibility to discuss it with the parents/carers. This can be difficult and could impact on the quality of your partnership with them.

AC 6.5 Explain the boundaries of confidentiality

You will acquire a lot of personal information about the children and families with whom you work. Some of this will have come from the parents/carers; some will have come from the children as you observe their learning. The source of the information is immaterial. You have a legal responsibility to keep it confidential.

> ### Key term
>
> Confidential – keeping things private, not disclosing any personal information about children or their families

You must regard all forms of information as confidential. If information is freely available, parents/carers can feel very vulnerable and may stop giving you information altogether. This will have a very negative impact on your partnership and on the outcomes for the children.

There are only two circumstances when information should be shared:

1 If the parents give you written permission to share information, such as with another professional.
2 If you have concerns about the welfare and safeguarding of the child. You do not need the parents'/carers' permission to share this information and report your concerns.

Children and their families have a legal right to privacy. The Data Protection Act (1998) was designed to prevent personal and confidential information being shared without the individual's agreement. Information includes anything stored

Figure 6.4 Use a variety of ways to keep parents informed

on a computer or other electronic device, or written, photographic or observation records. You also have a responsibility to make sure that any information that you store is accurate and relevant. If something is not relevant, do not keep it.

Tip

Remember that it is good practice to get into the habit of shredding any paper-based information about a child and their family if it is no longer relevant.

Look on PACEY's website (www.pacey.org.uk) for details of how long you must keep confidential information.

There may be times when another professional may wish to discuss information with you about a child. This could happen, for example, as you collect a child from another setting. If you do not have written permission from the parents/carers to share information about the child you should not do so. It may also happen when another setting is completing the two year progress check. They may want to see the child's learning journey or ask you about any observations you have made. Again, you must not share any information without the written consent of the parents/carers.

You should not take any information – such as personal records, medical details, observations or printed photographs – out of your home. All information must be securely stored at all times. Completing observations of children while sitting in your car outside school is unprofessional and not acceptable.

In your setting

- Never discuss one set of parents/carers with another.
- Do not gossip or chat idly to friends and family about children in your care or their families.
- Password protect your computer and other electronic devices.
- Report lost and stolen mobile phones as soon as possible and make sure that they are deactivated.
- Have a secure, locked cupboard or cabinet where you store paperwork.
- Remember that if you are preparing coursework and assessments you should not refer to any child or parents/carers by name. It is good practice to use their initials, or child X, parent/carer A.
- Register with ICO, the Information Commissioner's Office.

pacey says

Working effectively with other professionals, both within your setting and externally, is key to providing a good service to families. It supports the individual development of children, ensures continuity of care and supports the sustainability of your business.

As a childcare professional you play a key role in early identification as you are well placed to recognise a child's individual needs and work closely with their family. If a child has additional needs the sooner these are spotted the better as plans can be put in place to help address these needs and provide support. Many childcare professionals will be able to seek advice from their Special Educational Needs Coordinator (SENCO). Find out more about the support available locally by contacting your Local Authority.

Assessment links

This assessment task relates to Learning Outcome 6 and links to assessment criteria 6.1, 6.2, 6.3, 6.4 and 6.5.

You are asked to produce a written piece of work that can be shared with parents and carers.

Remember that you should not use jargon or abbreviations that may not be understood.

Your writing should be clear and use straightforward language.

It is also a good idea to be very aware of the length of sentences. Generally, a sentence should express one idea and be about 20 words in length. Your written work for this task has no set word limit or format, but must include and explain:

● How partnerships are established and maintained with parents and carers.
● How working in partnership supports the child's home learning environment.
● Boundaries of confidentiality.
● The typical partnerships that home-based childcarers can establish.
● The benefits of partnership working.

Chapter 7

Understand children's learning and behaviour in relation to sequence, rate and stage of development

Learning Outcome 7

By the end of this chapter you will be able to:

1 Identify areas of learning and development in relation to current frameworks
2 Explain factors that influence children's development
3 Explain the difference between sequence of development and rate of development
4 Describe key milestones in development for children from birth to 12 years, in relation to:

physical development; cognitive development; speech, language and communication development; social and emotional development
5 Explain how children's learning is influenced by positive relationships and environment
6 Describe factors that influence children's behaviour
7 Outline strategies for managing children's behaviour

Keeping children safe and well cared for is a fundamental requirement of your role as a home-based childcarer. Equally important is helping children to achieve their full potential. In order to do this you need to have a good understanding of how children develop and learn.

AC 7.1 Identify areas of learning and development in relation to current frameworks

All four countries of the UK have focused and specific frameworks for their youngest children. As you will see below, there are slight differences in the names of the areas of learning, but fundamentally they all have a common theme – that children learn best through play. As this CACHE qualification is for England only, you only need to know about the framework in England. Information for the other three countries of the UK is included to widen your awareness.

England

In England all providers of early years care and education must work to the Statutory Framework for the EYFS. This framework sets the standards for learning, development and care for children from birth to five years.

Useful resources

Early Years Foundation Stage
You can download copies of the Early Years Foundation Stage (EYFS) from this website: **www.gov.uk/government/publications**, reference DFE-00337-2014.

There are seven areas of learning and development, which are divided into prime and specific areas. All areas of learning and development are important, however, and inter-connected.

The prime areas are:

● Communication and language
● Physical development
● Personal, social and emotional development.

The prime areas are regarded as being crucial for developing children's interest, curiosity and enthusiasm to learn. These areas are highly significant in helping children to build relationships and thrive overall.

The specific areas are:

● Literacy
● Mathematics
● Understanding the world
● Expressive arts and design.

The specific areas strengthen and support the prime areas. For example, learning about other people in the community (understanding the world) will help children develop relationships with others (personal, social and emotional development).

Wales

Settings in Wales follow the Foundation Phase. This is the statutory curriculum for all three- to seven-year-old children in both maintained and non-maintained settings. A maintained setting is part of a school, such as a nursery class or early years unit. A non-maintained setting could be a Welsh- or English-medium pre-school group or a day nursery.

There are seven areas of learning:

● Personal and social development, well-being and cultural diversity
● Language, literacy and communication skills
● Mathematical development
● Welsh language development
● Knowledge and understanding of the world
● Physical development
● Creative development.

Scotland

Scotland has very recently reviewed its provision for its youngest children. This has resulted in the Provision of Early Learning and Childcare Order (2014). The curriculum that is offered to children between three and five years covers eight areas.

These are:

● Health and well-being
● Language and literacy
● Mathematics and numeracy
● Expressive arts
● Religious and moral education
● Science
● Social studies
● Technology.

Northern Ireland

Northern Ireland has a pre-school educational programme, Learning to Learn, which was developed in October 2013. There are six areas of learning:

● The arts
● Language development
● Early mathematical experiences
● Personal, social and emotional development
● Physical development and movement
● The world around us.

AC 7.2 Explain factors that influence children's development

Many factors can influence children's development. Some can be short term, such as a temporary hearing loss after a cold. Some can be more long lasting and in some cases permanent, such as food intolerances, allergies or medical conditions. It is almost an impossible task to list all of the factors that could influence a child's development, however.

All children are unique, and some things may influence one child's development whereas for another child may not have any lasting impact at all. For example, having a new baby in a family could influence a child's emotional development. They could regress in their behaviour as well as in other aspects of their holistic development, become clingy or attention seeking, and display signs of jealousy; another child may easily accept their new sibling and carry on as before!

In most cases factors cannot be isolated as to their influence on one particular area of development. A factor that influences physical development could also influence other areas. For example, a child with a medical condition that affects their physical development may spend periods of time in hospital or at home. Opportunities to develop social relationships could be influenced by this, which in turn could affect their emotional development, meaning they may become anxious, shy, withdrawn, or frustrated.

Some researchers of children's development have attempted to look at the influencing factors under three categories:

1 **Antenatal** – from conception to birth.
2 **Perinatal** – birth itself.
3 **Postnatal** – after birth.

Reflective practice

It is important to take a balanced approach to factors that could influence a child's development. Not all influences will be negative or adversely affect development. Some factors, such as a child's home life, can positively influence their development. The family could have many activities to stimulate overall development, such as trips and walks; there could be lots of books to encourage reading, a balanced and healthy lifestyle and diet, and firm and consistent boundaries for behaviour. On the other hand a family may face a range of challenges, meaning the activities engaged in at home do not stimulate overall development as well as they might; alternatively, diet could be limited, or boundaries for behaviour not consistently applied.

Links to the EYFS

The EYFS clearly outlines the areas of learning and development. Development is holistic but the EYFS does break it down into separate areas, to help make accurate assessment and measurements. There are generally accepted to be five areas of development (some people also include spiritual and moral development, but for the purposes of this book this will be included within personal, social and emotional; see page 104).

The table below shows how the areas of learning can be loosely cross-matched to the EYFS areas of learning.

Table 7.1 Areas of learning cross-matched to the EYFS areas of learning

Area of development	EYFS
Physical	Physical development
	Expressive arts and design
Intellectual (or cognitive)	Mathematical development
	Understanding the world
	Expressive arts and design
Language	Communication and language
	Literacy
Emotional	Personal, social and emotional development
Social	Personal, social and emotional development

Antenatal influences

Antenatal influences focus on the condition of the mother before the birth. It includes such things as smoking, drug use and alcohol; for instance, it is well documented that mothers who smoke during pregnancy often give birth to babies with low birth weights.

Any infections or illnesses that the mother picks up can affect the baby's development, such as rubella. Maternal anxiety and stress can also influence development.

Research published in the *American Journal of Psychiatry*, and information on the NHS website, state that our genetic code, formed at the moment of conception, can produce a pre-disposition to certain conditions later in life, such as depression or addiction. However a pre-disposition does not mean these conditions are inevitable as environmental factors also play a large role.

A child's health status is determined by their genetic inheritance, as well as other factors such as diet and health care. Some children are born with a condition that could adversely affect their development, for example, Down's syndrome, heart defects or cystic fibrosis.

Perinatal influences

Perinatal influences focus on the birth itself. Birth difficulties can significantly influence a child's future development. The main danger during birth is lack of oxygen (anoxia); however, this is relatively rare. If the oxygen supply to the baby is disrupted during birth it can result in brain damage or in extreme cases can be fatal. Brain damage may impact on learning and children can experience learning difficulties in all areas of development. They may be slow to walk and talk, or have difficulties at school and in making relationships.

Prematurity and multiple births can influence a child's future development. The extent of the influence varies considerably between babies. The medical advances in recent years have significantly increased and almost 90 per cent of babies born with a birth weight of 800 grams now survive. For some, however, there can be effects on their later development.

Postnatal influences

Postnatal influences are numerous and can be both positive and negative. Influences can be loosely divided into:

- poverty and deprivation
- family environment and background
- personal choices
- being a looked-after child
- education
- accident, illness and disability.

These are each discussed below.

Poverty and deprivation

Many of the influences that adversely impact on development are closely inter-related. For example, families in receipt of a very low income tend to live in poorer housing conditions and may also have an inadequate diet. Poor diet can lead to increased susceptibility to infections and diseases. Eating habits established in childhood are likely to be continued into adulthood, which can lead to health issues in later life. There is also a higher rate of accident and illness for children living in poverty, which impacts on their development. Poor quality housing may influence children's development as they may have limited spaces to play and live. Children living in poverty may have poorer school attendance records and do less well at school.

Family environment and background

Children's holistic development is strongly influenced by their family and culture. Parents are the first educators of their children and are very important in children's lives. All children need love and affection, need to feel safe and secure, and need to be stimulated and have opportunities and spaces to play. Parents/carers can be supportive as their child progresses through school and have consistent boundaries for behaviour. They can provide a healthy diet and encourage healthy lifestyles. The majority of parents/carers provide a nurturing environment, regardless of their financial position, in which their children thrive.

> ## Key term 🔑
>
> Holistic – all-inclusive, whole, overall

Some children, however, can appear to be physically thriving and healthy, but their social and emotional development is not progressing in the expected way. They may be miserable or unhappy and not be able to express their feelings or needs. This can be due to influences within the family over which the child has little or no control. Factors that impact on children's social and emotional development include mental health issues, drug or alcohol misuse, depression, marital conflict or domestic violence.

Breakdown in family relationships can influence a child's development. They may suffer not only emotionally, but if the breakdown results in house and school moves their social relationships could be affected as well.

Personal choices

The personal lifestyle choices that children can make as they grow will influence their development. It can be argued that the choices made are influenced by their parents/carers and family, but as children develop more independence they are influenced by things outside of the family, such as the media or their peers. Children can make choices about every aspect of their lives, such as what they eat and wear, what music to listen to. Some choices may not influence their development, but others will. For example, food choices can impact on physical and cognitive development; not having a breakfast affects concentration levels, or cutting out certain foods can lead to an unbalanced diet.

Being a looked-after child

Children in the care of local authorities are one of the most vulnerable groups in society. Children who are looked-after are in that situation because their family has not been able to offer a consistent and secure environment; these children may have been abused or neglected. Their social and emotional development may be affected. Some may find stability and security with foster or adoptive families and may then begin to thrive.

Education

Education is important and sets the tone for the rest of a child's life. Education is not just the learning that takes place in school but includes learning in every aspect of a child's life. Education includes experiences with family and carers, as well as wider social experiences such as schools, clubs, religious groups and places of worship, cultural networks and society.

> ## In your setting
>
> As you are probably aware, you carry your school experiences with you throughout your life; for example, if you couldn't do maths at school you may believe many years later that you are no good at maths, or if you disliked school because of one particular teacher this may influence how you view all teachers now. You must be very careful not to adversely influence the opinions of your own children and those for whom you care if you had negative experiences of school.

Children may not benefit from a quality education for many reasons. They may have poor attendance at school and so fall behind academically. Children may have limited opportunities to join clubs or groups, which impacts on their social development.

Accident, illness and disability

All children have accidents as they grow and develop, the majority of which are relatively minor and the impact often small. Sometimes, however, a child can have an accident that will have a life-changing impact. For example, a serious car accident could result in head and body injuries that may impact on intellectual development and mobility.

Reflective practice

In England there have been moves by the government to offer nursery education to all children of two years. The thought behind this is that early years' experiences are crucial to future learning. All children over three years are offered 15 hours' free nursery education, and compulsory education in school begins at five years. England, however, is one of only a few countries in the world that has young children in some form of education by the age of five years. Many European countries, Australia and America do not have formal schooling until children reach the age of six or seven years of age. The achievements of older children in these countries often compare favourably with England, especially in mathematics and science.

● What is your view? Do you think we begin formal education too early? Should there be a greater focus on play for longer and less on reaching an early learning goal? Have we got our system right or should we be looking at a different approach to support our youngest children's learning?

The overall health of a child will influence their development. A child who is healthy, has a balanced diet and takes regular exercise can be expected to have the best chance to thrive and develop well. Ill health can be due to many things. Food allergies and intolerances that are not detected early can influence physical development as the child's diet will be restricted. The impact on the child's holistic development of being born with a disability may or may not be significant as they grow and develop. Sometimes a disability happens later in life, perhaps as a result of an accident or illness. Complications from childhood illnesses and disease may influence development in many ways, for example, due to long-term absence from school, prolonged hospital stays and disruption to usual family life or social groups. This can impact on intellectual and social development. Meningitis can result in limb amputations, which could impact on physical development, balance, co-ordination and

mobility. Severe asthma can limit physical activity. Sensory impairments, such as hearing or sight loss, may influence a child's language development, but this does not mean that the child will not thrive. The impact of these influences will vary, however, as all children are different.

AC 7.3 Explain the difference between sequence of development and rate of development

Regardless of where in the world a child is born, lives and is educated they all will pass through very similar sequences of development. For example, most very young babies will develop strength in their neck muscles that allows them to lift and turn their heads before they can sit themselves up; mobile babies can walk before they can run.

Key term

Sequence – order, succession of actions or skills

The speed or rate at which children develop varies, depending on the individual child and the factors influencing their holistic development. For example, some babies may smile at five weeks, others may smile at seven weeks; some babies may walk at 11 months, others at 14 months. These are all examples of normal development. Some parents/carers worry that their child is slow at developing certain skills, and while their fears may be justified, sometimes they are not as all children develop at different rates or speeds.

Key term

Rate of development – the speed or time it takes for a child to develop

Most children will pass through the same sequences of development, but the rate of development will be different for each child. This is why measurements of development such as the EYFS 'Early years outcomes' have a broad range of ages.

AC 7.4 Describe key milestones in development for children from birth to 12 years

This assessment criteria relates to meeting the needs of a child from birth to 12 years with regard to:

- physical development
- social and emotional development
- cognitive development
- speech, language and communication development.

Tip

While it can be very useful to categorise development into different areas, it is very important to remember that all development is inter-related and interconnected. For example, a baby cannot start to make vocal sounds (language development) until the muscles of the mouth, face and tongue strengthen (physical development); a young child who cannot communicate effectively (language development) may consequently not be able to make friends easily (social development).

Physical development

Physical development is about how children gain control of their bodies. It includes:

- **Balance** – a skill that requires co-ordination. The ability to balance is developed by the body's central nervous system using information received from the movements made.
- **Co-ordination skills** – control of the eyes, hands and feet, and the ability to combine more than one skill or movement at the same time. For example, a child may use their eyes to guide their feet when going upstairs or when using a climbing frame.

- **Gross motor skills** – large body movements involving an arm or leg, or both, such as throwing a ball, kicking or swimming.
- **Fine motor skills** – small movements of the whole hand.

Table 7.2 shows the key milestones in physical development from birth to 12 years, but you must bear in mind that these are *approximate age bands only*. All children are different and develop at different rates.

Figure 7.1 Provide opportunities for children to develop balance, control and co-ordination

Key term

Primitive reflexes – actions that originate from the central nervous system that new-born babies present, but which disappear as the baby develops

Table 7.2 Key milestones of physical development from birth to 12 years

Approximate age of child	Key milestones of physical development
New-born	Primitive reflexes present. Sucks vigorously. More leg than arm movements. Sleeps about 21 hours a day.
6 weeks	Can lift head. Will follow a moving object with eyes for a few seconds. Stares into space when awake.
3–5 months	Holds head steadily. Waves arms in a more controlled way. Kicks and pushes feet against a firm surface. Rolls on to side from back. Watches hands and fingers, clasps hands. Lifts head and pushes up with arms when lying on stomach. Awake for about eight hours.
6–8 months	Sits with support for long periods, and without support for short periods. Grasps using whole hand (palmar grasp), may try to hold a bottle. All objects go to the mouth. Moves arms purposefully. Rolls from back to stomach. Hands and eyes are co-ordinated. Practises making different sounds. First tooth may appear. Pulls self into a standing position with help. May try to feed themselves.
9–12 months	Very active, may begin to crawl, shuffle, or take first steps. Sits without help. Picks objects up using finger and thumb (pincer grasp). Top lateral incisor teeth appear. Competently feeds independently with finger food.
13–15 months	Pulls self to feet, walks holding on to furniture. May walk without help. Crawls and shuffles quickly. Holds a cup. Points to objects and can put small items into containers. Uses hands and eyes to explore objects as well as mouth. →

Table 7.2 Key milestones of physical development from birth to 12 years   (*Continued*)

Approximate age of child	Key milestones of physical development
16–21 months	Restless and active, stands alone, walks unaided, knee walks backwards. Goes upstairs on hands and knees, comes down with adult support. Builds a tower of two or three blocks. Canine teeth erupt. Makes marks with crayons. Feeds self, using a spoon.
24 months	Shows a preferred hand. Can run, kick a ball from standing, climb. Begins to show bladder and bowel control. Builds a tower of five or six blocks. Draws circles and dots. Attempts to dress self.
36 months	Confidently runs, jumps, kicks a ball, walks on tiptoe. Pedals and steers wheeled toys. Washes and dries hands. Uses scissors. Dresses and undresses with minimal help. Usually has full set of milk teeth.
48 months	Developing skills such as hopping, balancing on a line or low beam, changing direction when running. Cuts out shapes.
60 months	Forms letters and writes own name. Begins to lose milk teeth. Hits ball with bat. Independently dresses and undresses.
6–7 years	Full of energy and active, enjoys large play apparatus. Moves in meaningful ways to music. Handwriting is controlled and evenly spaced. Catches and throws balls using one hand. Uses small construction toys skilfully to make models. Rides a two-wheeled bicycle without stabilisers.
8–11 years	Increased strength and co-ordination, agility and control. Girls can begin to show first signs of puberty. Body proportions resemble those of an adult. Energy levels usually high, good appetite and enjoys food, but may need short rests to maintain energy.
12 years	Rapid growth, sexual characteristics develop in both boys and girls. Oil-secreting glands may become overactive. Sweat is produced in response to stress, emotion or sexual excitement.

Links to the EYFS

In the document 'Early years outcomes' (2013) from the Department of Education, physical development is divided into two sections – moving and handling, and health and self-care. Physical development is one of the prime areas of learning. There are two early learning goals that children are expected to have reached by five years. These are:

- **Moving and handling:** Children show good control and co-ordination in large and small movements. They move confidently in a range of ways, safely negotiating space. They handle equipment and tools effectively, including pencils for writing.
- **Health and self-care:** Children know the importance of physical exercise for good health, and a healthy diet, and talk about ways to keep healthy and safe. They manage their own basic hygiene and personal needs successfully, including dressing and going to the toilet independently.

Intellectual or cognitive development

Intellectual development or cognitive development is about how children learn. It includes:

- **The different ways that children can learn** – learning is an individual process for everyone and takes place throughout life; in fact we never stop learning. There are many theories about how children learn; some appear to be contradictory, while others complement each other. They all make very valid points, however, that are worth considering.
- **Sensory development** – this is very important for the way that babies learn, through sight, sound, taste, touch and smell. For example, the mouth is very sensitive and can send numerous messages to the brain about how an object a baby puts into its mouth not only tastes but feels.
- **Imagination and creativity** – this is about making mental pictures or images. It is an important part of developing the ability to become a symbol user and to understand how to represent things, such as using letters to represent sounds. We need to be able to understand symbols in order to read and write.

- **Memory skills** – these are crucial to any form of learning. We all have short-term and long-term memory. The span of short-term memory is estimated to be about 15 seconds, but this can be extended by rehearsal or repeating things several times. Young children are not capable of rehearsal, which explains why they quickly forget things such as instructions.
- **Attention and concentration** – these are used by the brain to focus on specific information and filter out distractions such as smell or noise. Humans, however, are quite skilled at multi-tasking and can do more than one thing at the same time. For example, a baby having its nappy changed can concentrate on the face of the adult, enjoy the sense of freedom of not wearing a nappy, and exchange verbal interactions – all at the same time.
- **Perception** – this is quite different from seeing or vision. Our eyes see and send our brain an upside-down flat image, yet what our brain perceives is a three-dimensional meaningful picture. Perception is developed through stimulation of the senses.

Figure 7.2 Doing jigsaw puzzles together is a good way to help support the development of a child's intellectual skills

Key term

Theory – a well-researched and unique idea or perspective on a particular subject or topic

Table 7.3 shows the key milestones of cognitive or intellectual development. Note that the age bands are very wide as all children develop at different rates.

Table 7.3 Key milestones of cognitive or intellectual development from birth to 12 years

Approximate age of child	Key milestones of cognitive or intellectual development
New-born	Learning is linked very closely to the senses; for example, recognises mother's smell, sound of mother's voice, taste of milk.
	Is very sensitive to light.
6 weeks	Stops crying when hears a familiar voice and can be soothed.
	Recognises different voices and smells.
3 months	Aware of mobiles and other objects around them, follows moving objects with eyes.
	Begins to imitate high or low pitched sounds.
4–6 months	Recognises different foods by taste.
	Explores objects with their mouth.
	Reaches for objects, so may be able to judge distance.
	Knows that they have one mother.
	Enjoys bright colours and looking at complicated things.
7–9 months	Explores objects with hands, fingers and mouth.
	Co-ordinates movements; for example, can reach for and grasp a rattle, move it to the mouth, suck it and then drop it.
	Develops preferences for certain tastes.
12 months	Aware of the routines of the day; for example, gets excited when placed in a high chair prior to feeding, showing they can anticipate the future.
	Imitates actions, gestures and sounds.
18 months	Enjoys toys such as posting boxes, pop ups.
	Shows beginnings of problem solving.
	Follows simple instructions.
	Learns by trial and error.
24 months	Engages in pretend play with small scale toys.
	Often talks to self when playing.
	Engages in symbolic play; for example, a big cardboard box could be a car, a boat or a bed.
36 months	Begins to show interest in purposeful mark-making, painting.
	Memory skills are developing rapidly, can understand concepts such as colours, numbers.
	Understands cause and effect; for example, that if something is dropped it could break. →

Table 7.3 Key milestones of cognitive or intellectual development from birth to 12 years   (*Continued*)

Approximate age of child	Key milestones of cognitive or intellectual development
48 months	Concentrates for quite long periods of time if an activity or object captures their interest.
	Counts, usually up to 20, and begins to do simple calculations, understands mathematical language such as bigger, smaller, more, less, fewer.
	Begins to understand someone else's point of view.
60 months	Begins to understand games with rules and fair play.
	Recognises own name and can usually write it.
	Uses voices to be different characters in pretend play, can communicate using gestures and body language.
	Begins to differentiate between reality and fantasy.
6–7 years	Reads books silently.
	Understands concepts of height, weight, length, time, volume.
	Plays out stories and supports younger children to do the same, often returning to the same story several times.
7–9 years	Understands how to problem solve.
	Expresses own thoughts and ideas.
	Plans ahead and evaluates actions.
	Begins to deal with abstract ideas.
9–12 years	Understands more abstract concepts, such as morality, politics, religion.
	Uses reasoning and logical approaches to problem solve, may hypothesise.
	Understands the motives of others.
	Devises memory strategies.
	Thinks and plans ahead.
	Curious about drugs, sex, alcohol, smoking.

Useful resources

Book
How Children Learn by Linda Pound

All of the above aspects of cognitive or intellectual development are huge topics and this book is not the place to explore them further. If you want to research how children's intellectual capabilities develop, however, there are many resources available, both online and printed publications. The book *How Children Learn* by Linda Pound is a good starting point.

Ways in which you can encourage learning will be discussed in Chapter 8.

Links to the EYFS

The document 'Early years outcomes' does not have a specific section assigned to intellectual or cognitive development. Intellectual or cognitive development may be covered more typically in mathematical development, understanding the world and expressive arts and design.

- Mathematical development has two sections, which cover numbers and shape, and space and measurements.
- Understanding the world includes people and communities, the world and technology.
- Expressive arts and design covers exploring and using media and materials, and being imaginative.

Aspects of intellectual or cognitive development can be found in all of the EYFS areas of learning and development.

Language and communication development

Language and communication development is not just about talking. It is about all of the different ways that we communicate with one another. We all use language in different ways. We know how to make our needs known, express feelings, describe events, find out information, give directions, and get reassurance and confirmation from others. There is a clear sequence to language development and adults play a crucial part in this development. It is through hearing language that babies learn to differentiate between different sounds and are encouraged to repeat them. Table 7.4 outlines the key milestones of language development.

Key terms

Motherese (or **fatherese**) – high pitched 'sing song' tone of voice, describing what is going on

Holophrase – one word that is used to express more than one meaning

Echolalia – echoing the last part of what others say

Social and emotional development

Social development and emotional development are the building blocks of future success in life. Social development is learning to be with and relate to other people. It is about how we make friends, build relationships and develop an

Links to the EYFS

Communication and language is a prime area of the EYFS; literacy is a specific area.

In the document 'Early years outcomes', communication and language is broken down into listening and attention, and understanding and speaking. You should be able to make direct links to cognitive (intellectual) development, for example, to attention.

Literacy includes reading and writing. Writing, of course, has direct links to physical development.

understanding of whom we are. Self-help skills, such as dressing and feeding, are often included in social development, although these also have clear links to physical development.

Emotional development is how children learn to express and deal with their feelings. It also includes how children bond and develop relationships with their parents/carers. Emotional development also includes how we develop self-esteem, self-confidence, self-control and self-image.

It is quite difficult to try to separate out emotional and social development, as aspects of each affect the other. Sometimes problems with emotional and/or social development have very far-reaching and long-lasting effects, often well into adulthood.

Table 7.5 outlines the key milestones of social and emotional development.

Table 7.4 Key milestones of speech, language and communication from birth to 12 years

Approximate age of child	Key milestones of speech, language and communication
New-born to 6 weeks (pre-linguistic stage)	Cries to communicate needs. Coos to show pleasure. Moves head in the direction of sounds.
2–4 months	Makes non-crying noises. Cries become more expressive. Recognises familiar voices and sounds, responds to 'motherese' with babbling and coos. Can become distressed by loud and sudden noises.
4–6 months	More aware of others so tries to communicate more. Listens and tries to imitate sounds heard. Can be upset by an angry tone of voice. Starts to use vowel sounds. Laughs and squeals with pleasure.
6–12 months	Babbles, blends consonants and vowels to make strings of sounds. Later, uses intonation to copy the sound of adult speech. Recognises about 15 to 20 words. Follows simple instructions, such as 'wave bye-bye'. Understands that words stand for people, objects, actions and events.
12–24 months (linguistic stage)	Repeats words that have the most meaning for them (first words). One word can be used to express several meanings (holophrase). Puts two words together to communicate meaning, for example, 'me up'. Echoes the last part of what others say (echolalia). Uses gestures alongside words. Knows the names of objects, people and things.
24–36 months	Becomes a competent user of their home language: uses plurals and negatives, but can make mistakes; for example, 'I've doned it'. Follows instructions. Asks lots of questions: how, why, what, where, who. Enjoys complicated stories and asks for favourites over and over.
36–48 months	Still asks lots of question to satisfy growing interest in the world around them. Understands that language can be written symbolically. Uses different tenses: past, present and future. Makes up words and jokes that the child finds hilarious. →

Table 7.4 Key milestones of speech, language and communication from birth to 12 years   (*Continued*)

Approximate age of child	Key milestones of speech, language and communication
60 months to 7 years	Speaks with confidence and fluency.
	Defines objects by their function, for example, 'What is a banana?' 'It is a fruit that I eat.'
	Understands book characters, story plots and structure, beginning, middle and end of the story.
	Uses different forms of language in different situations.
7–12 years	Competently uses spoken and written language.
	Enjoys making up stories and telling jokes.
	Understands the purpose of reference books and materials, and uses them efficiently to find out more.
	Written stories show imagination.

Figure 7.3 Playing alongside another child is an important part of social development

Table 7.5 Key milestones of social and emotional development from birth to 12 years

Approximate age of child	Key milestones of social and emotional development
New-born	Is most content when in close contact with main carer. Needs to develop a strong bond or attachment.
6 weeks	Senses the presence of main carer and may appear to smile. Responds to human voices. Watches main carer's face. Swings from contentment to unhappiness very quickly.
3–5 months	Smiles and shows pleasure. Enjoys being held and cuddled. Has rapid and sudden mood swings.
6–8 months	Can show anxiety towards strangers. Interested in what is going on around them. Generally friendly, laughs and chuckles. Easily distracted.
8–11 months	Knows the difference between familiar people and strangers. Shows feelings such as anger and frustration through body movements. Begins to play games such as peek-a-boo. Waits for attention.
12–14 months	Shows affection towards familiar people and family members. Plays simple games. Can have angry outbursts when independence is thwarted. Mood swings less rapid and shows more curiosity than fear.
15–17 months	Shows jealousy and emotionally less stable than at one year old. Swings between being independent and dependent. Has temper tantrums due to frustration.
18–24 months	May be obstinate and refuse to follow adult directions. Very short attention span but very curious. Displays quite rapid mood swings, with temper tantrums, nightmares and irrational fears. Has very strong emotions. Tries to be independent. No understanding of right and wrong.
36 months	Seeks adult approval, wants to do the 'right thing'. Begins to understand right and wrong and can follow simple rules. Asks lots of questions. Shows concern for others and begins to share playthings. Develops friendships, but these can be quite short and transient. →

Table 7.5 Key milestones of social and emotional development from birth to 12 years (*Continued*)

Approximate age of child	Key milestones of social and emotional development
48 months	Has control over most emotions.
	Displays the standards of behaviour of their family and/or groups.
	Develops stronger friendships with both sexes.
	Shows consideration of others but still seeks adult approval.
60 months	Is self-confident but still wants to please adults.
	Plays co-operatively and often has a best friend.
	Has good control over emotions.
	Understands right and wrong and can follow rules.
6–7 years	Can be more moody than at five years.
	Peers become very important.
	Enjoys own company.
	Father or male authority is not questioned, and teacher's standards are often accepted over those of their mother.
	Has a strong sense of justice and will tell others when rules have been broken.
8–10 years	Emotionally independent of adults and intolerant of weak adults.
	Seeks approval of peers, usually of same sex.
	Enjoys team games and social events.
	Understands consequences of own behaviour and shows increased thoughtfulness.
11–12 years	A period of great change as puberty and adolescence begin.
	Emotions can become heightened and be very strong, reacts badly to criticism.
	Friendships away from the home are very important, peer pressure very strong.
	Shows interest in moral issues and abstract standards or concepts.

Links to the EYFS

Personal, social and emotional development is one of the prime areas of learning. In the EYFS this is divided into self-confidence and self-awareness, managing feelings and behaviour and making relationships. The focus is on helping children to develop skills that will not only help them build a positive sense of themselves and confidence in their own abilities, but will also teach them to respect others and understand appropriate behaviour. It is a very important area of development and underpins successful learning and development in the specific areas.

Useful resources

Publication
'Early years outcomes'
The document 'Early years outcomes', from **www.gov.uk/government/publications**, reference DFE-00167-2013, is non-statutory guidance to help you understand more about children's development through the early years, up to the age of five years. Children's development is divided into six overlapping stages. These are: birth to 11 months, 8 to 20 months, 16 to 26 months, 22 to 36 months, 30 to 50 months and 40 to 60+ months.

AC 7.5 Explain how children's learning is influenced by positive relationships and environment

How children's learning is influenced by positive relationships

Children become confident and independent learners when they are secure in the relationships around them. Relationships do not just happen, they take time and effort to develop and become established. The basis of any relationship with children is consideration of what their needs may be and ways that you can meet those needs. Children whose needs are considered feel valued and will respond better to you, and so are likely to have better learning experiences.

Babies need to establish a consistent and responsive relationship, often referred to as an attachment. The quality of this special relationship has an impact on how the baby will form relationships in later life. If this attachment is not made, the effects can be long lasting and can impact not just on social and emotional development, but on other aspects of their learning and development as well. Children who are happy, content and secure are more willing to try out new experiences. They are more confident and willing to take risks and challenge themselves.

A positive relationship provides a child with:

● **Emotional security** – this arises when children know that they have a caring person to whom they can turn for support with all aspects of their lives. This could be their play, moving to different settings (transitions) or just when they need someone to talk to or to comfort them.
● **Ways in which to express their feelings** – children need someone to talk to, to share ideas with, and to encourage their self-confidence and resilience.
● **A sense of well-being and self-esteem** – we need to accept children for whom they are, so that they in turn learn to value themselves. If children are happy with themselves they are less likely to show unacceptable behaviour.
● **Responsive care** – built on a sound understanding of the child's needs, respecting differences, and being fair and consistent.

The ways in which we build and develop relationships with children are based on how we communicate with them showing respect and courtesy. One way to build a strong relationship with a baby is through physical contact – just holding and cuddling a baby will help the child to feel wanted and reassured. Older babies, toddlers and young children also benefit from physical contact. Physical contact is a form of communication.

We should aim to be a play and language partner to develop a positive relationship. Children need other people, both children and adults, with whom to play. As we play with them, we can model their language and develop vocabulary by introducing new words and correct grammar. We can introduce different forms of language and communication, such as questioning, giving information, recall and description.

We also need to be a positive role model; if we enjoy and are enthusiastic about learning, children will learn from us. If you shy away from anything mathematical, because you believe that you are no good at maths, children will pick up the same message.

How children's learning is influenced by the environment

The influence of the learning environment is crucial and should never be under-estimated. The learning environment that you offer the children in your care directly influences all areas of their development. This does not mean that you have to provide worksheets with letters and numbers, endless plans of activities with an 'educational' theme, or trips to museums and art galleries. All of these have their place but do not on their own make a quality learning environment.

A quality learning environment includes how you talk, listen and communicate with the children, the opportunities that you provide for them to play and exercise in different ways, the way you develop your relationships with the children, and the consistent and warm care that you provide.

You have limited control over the environment outside of your home and the social factors that impact on it. You do, however, have greater control over the learning environment actually in your own home. It is important to plan and

organise an environment where children and their families feel valued, respected and welcome. This will help develop children's emotional security and well-being.

Your environment should be organised in such a way that you can meet children's needs according to their age and stage of development. For example, is your home appropriate and free of hazards for crawling babies or children with limited mobility? Think about how you store toys and resources. Ask yourself if they are stored in such a way as to encourage independence and help children learn how to make choices.

The physical environment where learning takes place must be safe. You have a responsibility to make sure that it meets the regulatory health and safety requirements.

> **Tip**
>
> Chapter 2 covers ways to make a safe and healthy environment and you may want to look at it again, especially AC 2.2 and AC 2.4.

Language and communication development can be supported by a stimulating environment. This means not just having books around, but creating an atmosphere where talking and listening are given high priority and valued. Clearly and correctly printed labels on resources will help children to recognise the printed word and develop literacy skills. Labelling, incorporating letters and pictures, can help to develop children's independence skills as they can freely make choices about with what they want to play. You can talk to children about how they would like to organise their environment, perhaps suggesting a different place to paint or have water play, or asking whether they want to play with cars inside or outdoors.

Your learning environment can be extended, not just by accessing parks, outdoor play areas and drop-in groups, but also by using toy libraries and other equipment loan schemes. You cannot be expected to have every piece of equipment or toy to meet all children's needs. You can use toy libraries and loan schemes to temporarily extend learning opportunities. For example, you can borrow story sacks to stimulate language development, different role play equipment to encourage expressive arts and design, specialist equipment to meet the additional needs of a child, or books to help support a child who is experiencing a transition or traumatic event in their lives. The possibilities are endless, but the benefits to your environment are also endless.

AC 7.6 Describe factors that influence children's behaviour

There are many factors that can influence a child's behaviour. Some influences can be short term, such as not feeling well or being very tired. Other influences, such as abuse, can be long term and have far-reaching effects. Most behaviours are learned and if reinforced will become stronger. A child is not born able to use offensive language,

for example. The child will learn this vocabulary from others and may also learn that when they use offensive language they will get attention; it may not be positive attention but it is attention. Therefore, if a child swears, you may respond and give them attention, so the child learns that if they swear they will get attention.

Figure 7.4 shows some of the main factors that can influence behaviour.

Overall development

A child may behave in a certain way due to emotional difficulties or because some aspect of their development is delayed. It can be very frustrating for a child if they cannot verbally express or communicate their needs effectively, what they want or how they feel. For example, a child new to your home may miss some instructions and as a result not achieve in the way you had expected. This could lead to the child feeling disappointed and perhaps to an angry outburst.

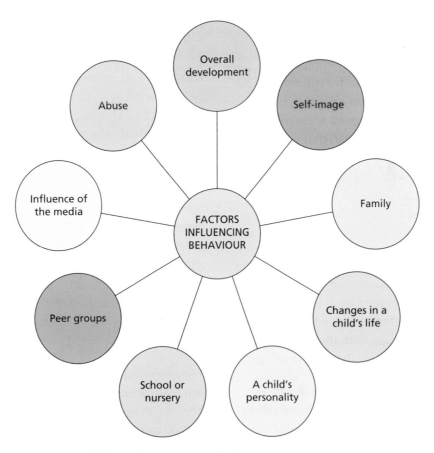

Figure 7.4 Factors that can influence behaviour

The different ages and stages of development have distinct behaviours. A child between 12 and 14 months can be very angry as their attempts to be independent are restricted. We accept temper tantrums in children of around two years; we may not like the tantrums but we understand that it is a normal part of development. Is a temper tantrum in a five year old acceptable or normal, however? Older children can be very intolerant of adults who they consider weak, but does this developmental stage excuse rude or dismissive behaviours?

Figure 7.5 Children with a positive self image have the confidence to concentrate and complete activities independently

Self-image

The way children feel about themselves will impact on their behaviour. A child's self-image can be negatively affected by abuse and neglect. Parenting styles and expectations for a child can influence self-image. If expectations are too high, or the parenting style very strict, children may feel failures and have a poor view of themselves.

Family

Birth order and the influence of siblings can impact on behaviour. A child will often copy the actions of their older siblings or other family members, and not always the good actions! The values and attitudes of a family will always influence a child's behaviour. It is very difficult, without devaluing the family, to rebuke a child for using an offensive term or swearing if you know this is normal language in their home.

Changes in a child's life

Changes in a child's life are often reflected in their behaviour. All children are unique and how each child reacts to change will be very different. Sometimes a child may not fully understand the impact of the change, such as a relationship breakdown or bereavement. They may take their cues from the adults and other family members around them as to how to behave. For example, if a parent is very angry, the child may believe this is the right way to behave and also be angry; if the parent is distressed the child may also be upset.

Transitions may result in a child becoming very clingy or seeking attention. On the other hand a child can become withdrawn and uncommunicative, and may display comfort behaviours such as thumb sucking and masturbation as a way of dealing with their distress.

A child's personality

Think about how a child's personality develops. Is it developed as a result of the child's experiences and the environment in which they live and grow? Or is a child's personality inherited, like the colour of their eyes or hair? Does it mean that if Granny has a bad temper her grandchildren may also have a bad temper? Or did Granny's bad temper arise because she was always short of money, tired and had a poor standard of living? This of course is the 'nature versus nurture' debate, which has been discussed by many for a very long time.

School and nursery

Starting in a nursery may be the first time a child has experienced large group situations and this can influence how they behave. Schools and nurseries have their own frameworks for behaviour and ways of managing children's behaviour. These may be very different from what the child has experienced before. Transitions can influence a child's behaviour in many different ways and the impact may not always be evident early on.

Children may experience bullying at school and this is a form of abuse. Many children do not tell anyone what they are going through, however, for fear that it will get worse. This can lead to the bullied child being aggressive to family members, withdrawn, uncommunicative, upset or angry.

Peer groups

It used to be thought that the influence of the peer group was evident only in older children. It is now believed that the influence of peer groups can be experienced as soon as children start at group settings. Some peer groups will set their own rules and expectations for behaviour that can have both

a positive and a negative impact on behaviour. The need to belong is very strong in children, even if this brings them into conflict with their parents and carers.

Figure 7.6 Allow children to be independent to develop their self worth

Case study

Jess, aged four years, refused to go to pre-school unless she could wear her designer trainers, which were like everyone else's. Her mum didn't want Jess to wear them to pre-school and put other shoes in her bag. She asked Chris, Jess's home-based childcarer, to make sure the trainers were left at Chris's house. Jess had a screaming temper tantrum, however, when Chris tried to follow the parent's wishes, which upset the other children and embarrassed Chris. Discussions with the parent resulted in the decision that Jess could wear the designer trainers to nursery.

Discussion point

Read the case study:

● How is this an example of peer pressure?
● What would you do in this situation?

Influence of the media

Children copy the behaviour of those people they believe are strong and influential. This could be their parents, or it could be footballers, singers, members of bands. Children can also be influenced by the way the media reports news events. For example, reports of a passenger aircraft crash and everyone on board being killed could give a child a fear of air travel or aeroplanes. We do not always realise that media reports influence children's behaviour until well after the event. Children may, for instance, show a fear of rivers and running water months after news reports of flooding.

Abuse

The effects of abuse on children's behaviour were discussed in Chapter 3, specifically AC 3.5. It is suggested that you look again at this to remind yourself and refresh your knowledge.

AC 7.7 Outline strategies for managing children's behaviour

Strategies for managing any behaviour should all have a common aim: to encourage positive behaviour. We all want to support children to grow into healthy and well-balanced individuals. Developing ways to promote positive behaviour in children will give them a firm foundation for their future.

Strategies for managing children's behaviour must always take into consideration the age and stage of development of the child. Children experiencing a transition at three or four years old will need very different support and strategies from a child aged 11. The older child may need support and strategies to cope with the changes but they must be appropriate to their age and stage of development.

We must maintain a fair and consistent approach when managing behaviour. This does not mean that we treat all children exactly the same way, but that we treat each child in a fair and consistent way. For example, you may have used a strategy that was very effective in managing one child, who always answered back in a rude way. When faced with the same behavioural issue with a different child, however, this strategy was totally ineffective. This does not mean that you are failing in your responsibilities; it is due to the fact that every child is different and unique. It is neither possible nor good practice to say that for one particular behaviour you have the one strategy. A

two-year-old child who bites another child may be supported to stop by distracting them; for another child distraction does not work and you have to react differently.

Your aim when developing a strategy for promoting positive behaviour should always be to de-escalate and divert. Young children find it very hard to control their emotions and cannot easily understand why what they are doing is unacceptable. When negative behaviour escalates it can be more difficult to manage and so you need to think of ways to prevent things getting out of hand.

Diverting their attention or distracting a child can be very successful for young children, especially those with short attention spans. Distraction techniques could include offering a different activity or asking the child to help you to do something. These techniques can stop the unacceptable behaviours very quickly. For example, if two young children are squabbling over one toy, you can do several things: you can take the toy away from them both, or leave them to fight it out between themselves, or offer both children two different but equally attractive toys. Depending on their age and stage of development, leaving children to sort out squabbles themselves can be a learning experience, but younger ones may not have the necessary abilities of negotiation and compromise. In addition, ignoring a negative behaviour can sometimes allow it to escalate and also give the message that by not responding you are condoning it.

Other strategies can include:

● **Giving the child a choice** – for example, saying 'You can stop throwing toys now or I will take them away from you.' Give the child time to respond and if they do not comply then follow through by removing the toys.
● **Trying to ignore attention-seeking behaviour provided no one is being hurt or adversely affected** – if you respond to attention-seeking behaviour you will reinforce it, especially if the behaviour is not one that you want to encourage, such as screaming.

- **Being calm and consistent** – this will help you to control the situation and your responses to it.
- **Firmly repeating a rule of your setting when a child 'breaks' it** – for example, if a child is name-calling or swearing.

The key to developing effective behaviour management strategies is your understanding and knowledge of each child. You must be aware of their needs, likes, dislikes, preferences and abilities. Any strategy that you decide upon must be discussed with the child's parents and ideally there should be consistency in approach between their home and your setting.

You should have a framework that sets out acceptable boundaries for behaviour within your home. You can make this a written policy and procedures (you are not required in England to have a written policy or procedures for behaviour management). Everyone, including the children's parents, should be aware of your framework. Older children can help to draw up your framework and to agree key elements of it. Having a framework will help you clarify your strategies as you will have already defined what you consider to be unacceptable behaviour. Your framework should not be set in stone. It should be thought about and reviewed regularly, especially when new children start with you. Any expectations in relation to behaviour should be flexible and realistic for the children in your care.

The ABC approach

The ABC approach is not a strategy as such, but can be effective in helping you see unwanted behaviour from a different point of view. It is a process that you can reflect on or write down to help you clarify your thoughts and then develop an effective strategy.

- **A is for antecedents**, meaning all the things that happened before a behaviour occurred. Antecedents can be related directly to the child, their state of health, general well-being such as being tired or hungry, and events that have happened in the child's life like a relationship breakdown or the arrival of a new baby sibling.

Antecedents can also be things to do with your setting. If you haven't got enough resources, for example, children could fall out. Maybe you have changed your routines or the layout of the play areas, which could unsettle the child. Sometimes you may not be aware of the antecedents as parents haven't told you about individual circumstances, in which case you may have to use your professional judgement. Don't make assumptions, though. Antecedents are not excuses for unwanted behaviour, but they can offer some possible reasons for it.

- **B is for the actual behaviour** of the child that we want to manage. Very often the unwanted behaviour is the first thing we are aware of and often we have an emotional reaction to it. We don't want to see children upset or hurt by others; we don't like it. When thinking about a child's unwanted behaviour we need to be totally factual and take the emotion out of the situation. Saying something along the lines of 'X won't play with other children, she hits out all the time and I find it very difficult to keep calm' is an emotional response. It doesn't say anything about the child and focuses on your feelings. It is very doubtful that any child hits out *all* the time. It might feel like they do, but it probably isn't the case. It is much better to describe the child's behaviour, such as 'Child X has issues playing with other children. She hits out at them when they try to involve her and she doesn't respond well to my instructions.' This focuses on what the child does or doesn't do; it says exactly when the unwanted behaviour occurs, and is factual, specific and unemotional.
- **C is for the consequences** of the behaviour. You can consider the consequences for the child, the other children, you, the child's parents and anyone else involved. Consequences can be immediate; for example, if a child hurts another the likelihood is that the hurt child will object and cry and make you immediately aware. Consequences can also be delayed; parents may mention to you days after an event that their child doesn't like playing with child X. Whenever you become aware of the consequences you need to react.

Very often children do not exhibit just one form of unwanted behaviour. In the above example, child X hit others, didn't play with others and didn't listen to instructions. It is very difficult, however, to change all unwanted behaviours in one go; so pick the one behaviour that you consider to be the most significant. In the above example it could be to stop hitting other children. So you may want to think about ways that you could help the child to deal with their emotions in a different way. When that has been achieved you could move on to another aspect of the behaviour, perhaps listening skills. By doing this your strategy will have far more chance of being effective, and the child will achieve and be praised, rather than constantly failing. This approach will take time and you will not get instant results.

Read the case study below and see if you can identify the ABCs. Then see if you can think of a strategy to help promote one aspect of positive behaviour in the child.

Case study

Toby is 30 months old and an only child. He has been cared for by Annie four days a week for six months. He was a premature baby and spent a long time in hospital after his birth with complications. He took a long time to settle with Annie. He often refuses to do as he is asked; for example, he will not tidy away toys before lunch. In fact he does the exact opposite and tips more toys out on the floor. He won't sit at the table with the other children at mealtimes and has a violent temper tantrum if Annie tries to put him on a chair. Annie has discussed Toby's behaviour with his mother, but she says that he is only little and still has a lot to learn, and that Annie should be more patient with him. Some of the other children are beginning to copy Toby, however, and not put toys away when asked; others are frightened by his temper tantrums. Annie feels that she is running out of patience and her partner thinks she should give Toby's mother notice and terminate the contract.

pacey says

Remember to refer to non-statutory guidance documents such as Early Years Outcomes as mentioned above and 'Development Matters'. These will both help you to assess/track children's learning. 'Development Matters' includes information on the characteristics of effective learning, Prime and Specific areas of learning, development statements and ideas to guide you to plan for children's next steps.

CACHE Level 3 Preparing to Work in Home-Based Childcare

Assessment links

This assessment task relates to all of Learning Outcome 7 and covers assessment criteria 7.1, 7.2, 7.3, 7.4, 7.5, 7.6 and 7.7.

You have been asked to produce a booklet or guide for parents and carers that will provide information about children's development and learning.

When designing your booklet or guide remember:

- to keep language straightforward and uncomplicated
- to avoid using technical jargon
- to avoid using abbreviations without explaining what the letters stand for the first time you use them
- to try to use text, lists, illustrations, charts, tables or any other appropriate way to present the information so that it is interesting for the reader
- to try not to squash too much information on to each page, as this may make it unappealing and difficult to read
- there is specific information that must be included in your booklet or guide, so it may be helpful to think about including a contents page and numbering your pages.

The booklet or guide will need to:

- identify areas of learning and development in relation to current frameworks (use the framework for the country in which you live, see page 92)
- explain factors that influence children's development
- explain the difference between sequence of development and rate of development
- describe key milestones in development from birth to 12 years in relation to:
  - physical development
  - cognitive development
  - speech, language and communication development
  - social and emotional development
- explain how children's learning is influenced by:
  - positive relationships
  - environment
- describe factors that influence children's behaviour
- outline strategies for managing children's behaviour.

118

Chapter 8

Understand the value of play in promoting children's learning and development

Learning Outcome 8

By the end of this chapter you will be able to:

1 Identify the rights of children in relation to play, as detailed in the UN Convention on the Rights of the Child
2 Explain the innate drive for children to play
3 Discuss how play is necessary for the development of children

4 Explain the benefits of balancing child-initiated and adult-led play activities
5 Identify how children's play needs and preferences change in relation to their stage of development
6 Discuss the need for an inclusive approach when planning play activities

We all play in some shape or form, whether it is a game or sport, or an instrument, and whether we play on our own or with others. Play is one of the most important ways in which children learn. Play allows children to do things that they cannot do in real life, such as pretend to pilot a space rocket, be an elephant or sing in a boy band! The value of play should not be underestimated. It is a very complex activity.

AC 8.1 Identify the rights of children in relation to play, as detailed in the UN Convention on the Rights of the Child

The United Nations Convention on the Rights of the Child (UNCRC) was drawn up in 1989. The UK is a signatory, along with all but two other countries in the world. The two countries that did not sign were the USA and Somalia. The Convention was approved by the United Nations in 1991 and, although it is not legislation nor statutory, all signatories are legally bound to make all laws and policies compatible with the Convention. The ethos of the UNCRC underpins many pieces of UK recent legislation, such as the Children Act (2004) and the EYFS (2014).

There are 54 articles in the UNCRC and they cover four different groups, namely **survival**, **protection**, **development** and **participation**. For example:

● Article 2 states that children have a right to be protected from all forms of discrimination.
● Article 3 states that the best interests of the child must be the primary consideration in all activities and actions concerning children.
● Article 12 states that a child has a right to express his or her views freely and that that view is to be given appropriate weight in accordance with the child's age and maturity.
● Article 16 states that children have a right to privacy.

The right to play is enshrined in Articles 7 and 31; the right to education is included in several others, however. Part of Article 7 states that 'The child shall have full opportunity for play and recreation', and Article 31 states that 'All children have a right to relax and play, and to join in a wide range of activities.'

The Articles that are most relevant to home-based childcarers are Articles 1–4, 12–15, 19, 23, 28–31 and 39.

All of the Articles are important and relevant to home-based childcarers, however, because they should make you think about the ways that you relate to children, how you listen to them, and how you recognise and respond to their comments and views. They underpin your responsibilities and duty of care to safeguard and protect children. The Articles should make you think in more detail about how you can plan inclusive play activities and experiences that are available to the children in your care. The Articles also reinforce that all children are unique and entitled to be treated with dignity and respect at all times.

Links to the EYFS

All of the values and rights of the UNCRC underpin the EYFS. In the introduction to the EYFS (2014) it states that 'A secure, safe and happy childhood is important in its own right'. The four guiding principles of the EYFS can be tracked directly back to the UNCRC, as it states that:

- every child is unique
- every child needs positive and supportive carers
- every child should learn and develop in enabling environments
- the age and stage of development of every child must be taken into account.

Useful resources

UNICEF
The 'What rights?' leaflet from UNICEF clearly explains the rights of children, including the right to play. It can be downloaded from the website: **www.unicef.org.uk**

AC 8.2 Explain the innate drive for children to play

What is play? What do we actually mean by play?

Play can be a way of amusing yourself, either on your own or with others. Play might imply, to some people, just 'messing about'. It may not appear to have any purpose or obvious aim. Play can be taken very seriously by adults, however; consider how some people feel when their favourite football team does not *play* as well as expected and loses a match. We talk about people *playing* games or sport, we go to watch a *play* in a theatre. We use the word 'play' when someone is making music, for example, *playing* the guitar. Play has many different meanings depending on the situation and context. For children, however, it is the most important way of learning and is the basis of all development. It is a huge and deep activity that should be nurtured, valued and supported.

Play is the natural way that children and other young mammals teach themselves and consequently learn. It is spontaneous, unplanned and instinctive. The need to play is innate. The young of all mammals play and those that have the most to learn, play the most. Carnivores, such as lion cubs and puppies, play more than herbivores, such as calves or lambs. This is because hunting for the next meal is harder to learn than is grazing grass. Human children, who have the most to learn of all mammals, spend far more time in play than any other mammal, including primates such as monkeys. A baby's first plaything is a nipple, which they explore with their tongue and lips from the very first time they feed. Without supportive and sensitive adults, however, the play and therefore the learning will not develop.

Key term

Innate – inborn, instinctive, natural

Children everywhere in the world must learn important skills in order to live happy, productive, socially acceptable lives. These skills cannot be taught in schools, in fact, they cannot be 'taught' at all. They are developed, learned and practised by children as they play, either on their own or in groups. These skills include the abilities to think creatively, to get along with other people and co-operate effectively, and to control their own impulses and emotions. While we cannot 'teach' them we can provide activities that support the development of these abilities. For example, we can't teach a child to be creative, but we can support them with activities that help develop creative thinking.

All young children are creative in their own unique ways. No two children will play in exactly the same way with the same toys. In their play and self-directed explorations and investigations, children create individual and unique mental views of the world around them and also of imaginary worlds. These are the foundations of creativity.

We cannot teach creativity as it is innate, but we can, unfortunately and unwittingly, quash it in children. Creativity can be quashed by learning activities that focus not on children's own investigations, explorations, views and thoughts, but focus instead on activities set by an imposed curriculum, for example, one in which all questions have one right answer and everyone must learn the same things. Think of it like this: is there only one way to draw a picture of a house? Is grass always bright green? Or, more controversially, can children learn to read only through learning phonic sounds? We know that the answer to these questions is 'no'. There are numerous different ways to draw a house, grass is many different shades of green, and children learn in many

Figure 8.1 A secure, safe and happy childhood is important in its own right

different ways. We should nurture children's creativity by allowing them to freely play, explore and investigate.

Perhaps more important than creativity is the ability to get along with other people, to care about them and to co-operate with them. Children everywhere in the world are born with a strong, innate drive to have playmates. Children will seek out others and, while they may not actually play with them, they will participate through watching, listening, copying. It is through play that young children develop social skills and practise concepts such as fairness and morality.

Play, by definition, is voluntary; a child cannot be made to play. This means that when children are playing, they are always free to stop at any point. If a child cannot stop playing voluntarily then they are not truly playing, as the free and voluntary aspect of play has been taken away from them. All 'players' instinctively know this. Children know that to keep the play going, they must keep the others happy. Even when playing on their own, children sustain the play by doing things that satisfy and keep themselves happy.

When children disagree about how to play, they must negotiate, discuss, share ideas and listen to each other. For play to continue children have to make compromises. If children cannot do this then the play will end. This is true for young babies: for example, if one baby wants a toy that another has then they cannot verbalise this desire or get the toy themselves, so they cry. You respond to the cry and the original play activity effectively is stopped by your intervention. A child who cannot or will not listen to others, who cannot negotiate or co-operate, will be left out of the play. At this point adults usually intervene, as we seem to have a need to see all children playing happily together. It can be argued, however, that our needs are preventing the child from learning how to co-operate and see things from another's point of view. These skills are fundamental in our future lives and how we develop relationships.

In play, children learn how to control their impulses and to follow rules or conventions. All play has some form of rules, often made up by the children without them realising, especially when very young. In imaginary play such as 'house' or pretending to be superheroes, the first and possibly only rule is that the child must stay in character. If a child pretends to be a pet dog, the 'rule' is to make dog noises instead of talking, and to move around on all fours no matter how uncomfortable that may be. If a child pretends to be a superhero, they and their playmates believe that superheroes never cry, even if they fall over and hurt themselves. Being a human being means that we must control impulses and behave in accordance with social expectations. Play helps children to develop this control and socially acceptable behaviour. Play allows children to test boundaries, explore and control their own fears, and to understand risk and challenge. Play puts children in control.

Children must be allowed to follow their inborn drives to play and explore, so that they can grow into intellectually, socially, emotionally and physically strong and resilient adults.

AC 8.3 Discuss how play is necessary for the development of children

Links to the EYFS

Section 1.8 of the Learning and Development Requirements of the EYFS reinforces the importance of play. It states that each area of learning and development must be delivered through a balance of child-initiated and adult-led play activities. It is strongly recommended that you read this section carefully.

Play is a fundamental means of learning for children. It enables the development of skills in all areas, and to restrict play is to restrict development and learning. It is central to the way that children explore and the way they make sense

Figure 8.2 All young children are creative in their own unique ways

of their environment and the world in which they live. Play enables children to practise and master skills, as well as to develop new skills.

For children to get the maximum benefit from play activities you must understand how valuable play is to children's development (see AC 8.2). You will need to offer play opportunities both indoors and outside, and to offer a balanced mix of opportunities – some that are adult led and some that are initiated by the children. It is quite normal for some adult-led activities to become child initiated as children develop their own ideas. For example, you may have planned a cooking activity, which leads instead to the children making patterns in the flour with their fingers!

In Chapter 7 we considered the different stages of learning and development; play also has different stages. Generally the stages are progressive, in

Find out more

Over the years many people have studied how children play. One person was the German educator Friedrich Froebel (1782–1852). He believed that children needed play in order to grow, and likened them to plants in a garden. He set up a 'kindergarten' (literally 'children's garden') where children could play both indoors and outside. Froebel is recognised as inventing finger play and many traditional songs and rhymes that are still used today. Many of Froebel's ideas still have an influence on modern thinking about play. You can find out more at www.froebeltrust.org.uk.

that one stage leads to another. There will be times, however, when play seems to regress to an earlier stage. This is normal. For example, if a child is feeling unwell or under the weather, they may want the comfort of familiar playthings

Table 8.1 Different stages of play from birth to eight years

Approximate age	Stages of play
0–6 months	Watches others, explores with mouth, plays alone – **solitary play**.
6–12 months	Watches and copies others, explores with mouth and touch, can play simple games, e.g. peek-a-boo – still **solitary play**.
12–18 months	Learns through trial and error, repeats actions that produce a pleasurable response, begins to notice other children playing and copies – still **solitary** but sometimes **parallel play**.
18–24 months	**Parallel play** and sometimes **spectator play** – enjoys playing alongside adults, still learns by trial and error and repeating actions.
2–3 years	**Symbolic play**, imitates and copies others but still mainly **parallel play**.
3–4 years	Begins to have periods of **co-operative play**, but can go back to earlier stages of play if presented with new activities, resources or situations.
4–6 years	Begins to understand the rules of games, engages in **co-operative play**, can take turns.
6–8 years	Develops own games with rules, enjoys competitive games, prefers to play with children of same sex.

and want to play on their own. Sometimes when presented with a new play situation a child who normally plays co-operatively may stand and watch before joining in. The table below summarises the different stages of play.

Key terms

Solitary play – playing alone

Parallel play – playing alongside others, often at the same activity, but not joining in

Spectator play – watching others play

Symbolic play – using objects to represent something else, for example, a plastic block becoming a phone

Co-operative play – playing and sharing with others, developing understanding of rules

There are different forms of play as well as different stages. Generally, play can be categorised into four types: physical, creative, imaginative and manipulative.

1 **Physical play** – play that uses large muscles and exercises the whole body can be described as physical play. Children learn control, co-ordination, balance and spatial awareness, and have opportunities to expend excess energy. A baby kicking its legs at nappy changing is engaging in physical play, so are children who are running, climbing, jumping.

2 **Creative play** – this encourages children to explore and experiment, and to use their senses to discover more. Creative play does not have an end product; it should be totally open ended. This means that a group of children making greetings cards that all end up looking very similar are not engaging in creative play but in an adult-directed activity. Painting, drawing, small world play, using construction toys and bricks are all examples of creative play activities.

3 **Imaginative play** – this play allows children to pretend that they are different people, or are in new and different situations. This play often happens quite spontaneously as children respond to the world around them, for example,

Figure 8.3 Children must be allowed to follow their inborn drives to play and explore, so that they can grow into intellectually, socially, emotionally and physically strong and resilient adults

pretending to be an aeroplane flying through the sky after seeing one overhead. Role play and dressing up are examples of imaginative play.

4 **Manipulative play** – children using and developing the skills of their fingers and hands is very important. Manipulative play enables children to develop co-ordination and concentration. Babies engage in manipulative play as they explore their own fingers and hands. This develops the sense of touch, which in turn leads to greater control of finer muscles and fingers, and development of perception and accurate hand–eye co-ordination. Playing with rattles, banging two objects together, playing with building bricks, Duplo

and jigsaw puzzles are all examples of manipulative play.

Quite often one play activity will provide opportunities for several different types of play. Read the case study over the page and see if you can identify the different types of play.

Find out more

Heuristic play involves playing with natural resources. It stimulates sensory development as well as creativity and problem solving. It is sometimes called 'treasure basket play', especially when referring to babies. You can find out more from the book *Heuristic Play* by Sheila Riddall-Leech.

Case study

Carly cares for two boys, aged three and four years. The younger boy was on a boat at the weekend, so to extend his learning Carly provided two large cardboard boxes and suggested the boys made their own boats. With help the boys painted the boxes and cut 'wave' shapes to stick on the side. They put toy steering wheels inside the boxes, used kitchen rolls as telescopes and put on pirate dressing up clothes. The boys climbed inside their boxes and pretended to sail away, waving their arms as they pretended to row. The older boy led the play for a while, pretending the sea was rough and turning his boat over. The younger boy watched and then did the same. The boys ended up with the boxes on their backs so the play became them pretending to be snails crawling around on the floor. The play session lasted most of the morning, before the boxes collapsed and the boys declared that the snails were dead!

Links to the EYFS

Planning and supporting play opportunities is a form of teaching that enables children to learn. The learning will be unique to each child and it is important that you think about this so that you can be effective in helping children develop. Teaching does not mean formally planning activities following a set curriculum, as perhaps a primary school teacher might do. Teaching is about educating children in many different ways and helping them to learn, develop and acquire skills. There are three characteristics of effective teaching and learning identified in the EYFS. These are:

- **Playing and exploring** – children should be encouraged to have a go, explore and investigate.
  How do you help children achieve new things without doing too much for them?
  How do you encourage children to take risks and challenge themselves?
  How do you help children learn by trial and error?

- **Active learning** – children concentrate and keep on trying if they encounter difficulties; they celebrate their achievements.
  Do you provide an environment and routines that encourage children to become independent?
  Can children move freely between inside and outdoor spaces?
  Do you provide 'open-ended' resources and activities that have no adult-defined learning outcome?

- **Creating and critically thinking** – children develop their own ideas and ways of doing things; they make links between their ideas and develop different strategies.
  Do you ask open-ended questions that encourage thinking, rather than asking questions that can only be answered with a yes or no?
  Do you really listen to the children?
  How do you encourage the children to problem solve?

Key term

Open-ended activity or resource – these are focused on the 'doing' rather than the end result, and can be used in very flexible and adaptable ways

In your setting

Play is a very important aspect of a child's life. Your role is to provide opportunities for play and give support if needed. For children to maximise play opportunities you need to provide:

● **Play space** – while babies and children may not move very much sometimes in their play, they still need to have 'personal space' where they can explore in their own way.

● **Play time** – imagine how you would feel if you had become engrossed in an activity and then were told to stop for whatever reason. Think about how to organise your day and routines so that children have time to play. Obviously there will be times when play will have to be curtailed, such as at school pick-up times. But ask yourself, what is the benefit to the child of packing away a plaything because it is lunchtime? Why can't the child leave it where it is and then go back to it after lunch?

● **Playthings** – you do not have to provide unlimited resources to encourage development, but they should be varied and age- and stage-appropriate. How often have you given a present to a child and they've played with the paper and packaging more than the actual gift? Be inventive, use safe and hygienic domestic items such as pan lids and wooden spoons. Use open-ended resources such as large cardboard boxes, sheets, pieces of material, natural things and treasure baskets. Don't forget you can extend your resources through toy libraries and exchanges.

● **Playmates** – you, as well as the other children, can be playmates for a child. If you care for only one child, think of ways in which you can meet other children, such as at drop-in groups.

AC 8.4 Explain the benefits of balancing child-initiated and adult-led play activities

Children learn more effectively if they are actively involved and doing things, sometimes alone, sometimes with others. Children learn through first-hand experiences rather than just being told to do something.

Child-initiated activities

A child-initiated activity is one where the child leads their own play. It is based on the child's own motivation and is within the child's control. Examples of child-initiated play include:

● a baby playing with and exploring their hands
● an 18 month old playing with wrapping paper
● a three year old playing with sand or water
● a four year old dressing up and pretending to be a superhero.

Child-initiated play does not mean that an adult is not involved. You should be supervising and supporting all activities in which the children are involved. It may be that you are watching and observing them play rather than actively taking part, or you could be responding to their requests for more resources and so extending the play.

Child-initiated play is sometimes referred to as 'spontaneous play'.

Adult-led activities

Adult-led activities are those that you initiate. The children may not view them as play; however, the activities should be playful and as open ended as possible. Adult-led activities may come about because you have noticed a particular need in a child or a skill that could be developed or extended. For example, you may provide magazines, scissors, glue sticks and paper so that children can develop their scissor skills, fine manipulation skills and co-ordination. How the children stick their cuttings on to the paper, however, should be open ended and not directed by the adult. Story time is an adult-led activity, so is singing and often tidying up. Cooking could be classed as an adult-led activity, but it could change later in the course of the activity to a child-initiated one, as children perhaps explore the texture of flour, sugar or eggshells.

Adult-led play is also sometimes referred to as 'structured play'.

Balancing child-initiated and adult-led play activities

Children learn by leading their own play and by taking part in activities that are led by adults. In any setting there should be a balance between the two. A child who only engages in child-initiated play may not develop holistically in the long term, and it is possible that some specific skills could be under-developed. On the other hand, if only adult-led activities are presented to a child they may not develop creativity, imagination, independence, problem solving and social skills.

The younger the child is, the more likely it is that the play will be driven by the child. You cannot, for example, plan for a baby to play with their toes! As children grow and develop, the balance between child-initiated and adult-led play will gradually move to more activities that are led by adults. It is expected that by the time children reach school age, especially Year 1, more activities will be adult led. This does not mean, however, that there is no place for child-initiated play among older children.

Links to the EYFS

The EYFS requires that a balance is achieved between activities that are initiated by children and those that are adult led (Section 1.8 of the Learning and Development Requirements). You must respond to each child's emerging interests and needs. It could be that if you provide resources to develop a specific skill, the activity could be described as adult led, but how the children use the resources is up to them.

Figure 8.4 Adult-led play is also sometimes referred to as structured play

AC 8.5 Identify how children's play needs and preferences change in relation to their stage of development

Babies come into the world ready to learn, and the way they learn is through play. As children grow and develop their play needs change and the things that interest and motivate them also change. Therefore the play opportunities and resources that we provide and the ways that we organise and plan for play must also change.

Play opportunities must be age- and stage-appropriate for the children involved. This means that you need to have a good understanding of children's development (see Chapter 7). You also need to have realistic expectations of what children are capable of at their individual stage of development. Play activities and experiences do not necessarily have to be different for each age or stage of development. You can adapt and modify play experiences and resources to suit the individual needs of a child. For example, a child of two years may happily play alone with Duplo, a child of three years may play alongside another as they play with Duplo, and a child of five years may play with another child to construct something from both Duplo and Lego.

Tip

Providing play opportunities that are just too difficult may not offer challenge, but can instead make a child lose confidence in their own abilities and therefore develop a sense of failure. Conversely, play opportunities that are very easy may not motivate or stimulate a child. They could lose interest and become bored. Be aware, however, that sometimes when children are feeling unwell or emotionally insecure playing with something easy and undemanding can be very comforting.

Figure 8.5 Young children will often play alongside each other. This is called parallel play

Babies need play opportunities to develop their physical skills, to encourage language and communication, sensory development and awareness of their environment. While all children need to develop these skills, these are fundamental to ensure a baby's future growth and learning. Babies and young children are vulnerable and learn to become resilient through meaningful interactions and support from others. Babies may play on their own (solitary play) but need to have the reassurance that a supportive and sensitive adult is close by.

A feature of toddlers' development is their growing need for independence. Play activities should be very open-ended so that the child can take the play in whatever direction they desire. Your role is to be supportive and make sure that they remain safe. Toddlers, and all children, learn from copying adults so it is very important that you are a positive role model. Toddlers are very active and need to explore and investigate, so play should maximise opportunities to do this. Young children are also beginning to learn how to play with others and will engage in parallel play. This can have implications for your resources and toys. If you have only one set of digging tools, for example, then only one child can dig at any time, which would not encourage social skills or learning about how to play with others. To allow parallel play you may need two sets of digging tools.

By the time children are between two and three years old, they are developing greater social skills and awareness of others. They need a wide range of play activities, both adult-led and child-initiated. Children of this age change their minds often and their preferences may also change rapidly. You need to be versatile, adaptable and patient.

Children over the age of three are usually involved in group play activities through pre-school and nursery classes. Many of these settings carefully plan their activities, not only to make sure that they offer a broad and balanced experience but also to ensure that they offer both adult-led and child-initiated activities. Sometimes the child-initiated part is called 'free flow play'. The adult-led play may take place in small focused groups where an adult can teach specific skills such as phonics, numbers and writing skills. This idea can be copied in a home-based setting, where you could plan short one-to-one activities designed to meet a child's specific needs.

School-aged children can usually articulate well their play preferences. By now they have developed social skills and will play co-operatively with others. All children are different, however, and you need to be aware that some children may find it difficult to play with others, are shy, lack confidence in their own abilities or find it hard to make friends. You can provide play opportunities that will support their development in these areas. Consider board games, giving these children responsibilities, and praising even the smallest achievement.

AC 8.6 Discuss the need for an inclusive approach when planning play activities

All children are unique; they have different personalities, interests, needs and abilities. They should be valued and respected for whom they are. Children who feel valued will respond positively to you and will enjoy being in your company. You have to be a positive role model; if you show respect for others children will learn positive attitudes and values from you. Another effective way to encourage children to show respect and have positive attitudes is to create a learning environment in your home that is inclusive.

An inclusive environment is about having materials and resources, and planning activities, that reflect the diversity in our society. This does not mean that you just put out a selection of dolls with different skin tones for the children to play with; that is a start, but not the whole picture.

Reflective practice

A home-based childcarer purchased lengths of material so that children could dress up in saris, as she felt that she needed more 'multi-cultural resources'. When the children saw the material, however, they made cloaks and parachutes, pretended to fly with 'wings', and some used the material to hide underneath. Not one child asked to be dressed in the material as if they were wearing a sari. The adult felt that she still wasn't being inclusive.

● What do you think?

There is a danger that some home-based childcarers may fall into a 'multi-cultural' trap and inadvertently plan activities or provide children with materials, activities and images that do not accurately reflect other cultures. This might mean, for example, having pictures of different homes, including igloos, and telling the children that all Inuit people live in igloos, when in fact many live in towns and urban areas.

How you use and work with your equipment and resources is very important. You should avoid the potential danger of teaching children a little about a culture and then presenting a stereotype. This implies that everyone is the same. It is like believing that the English culture is only about Big Ben and Christmas, and that everyone in England uses Big Ben to set the time and celebrates Christmas.

During your career as a home-based childcarer you will probably care for children from a wide variety of backgrounds. You must show that you value and respect each family and welcome them into your setting. If you are open minded there is much to be gained from respecting different ways of bringing up children. For example, the Indian tradition of massaging babies is now widely used in British health clinics and family centres.

An inclusive play environment, however, is not only about respecting and valuing different cultures. It includes making sure that all children in your care have the same opportunities to access play. It means that you should not have gender-specific activities or resources. It is fine for boys to play with dolls and girls to play with cars. Similarly, you must be aware of any adaptations to play activities and resources that you may need to make for children with impairments or disabilities.

Article 2 of the UNCRC states that children have a right to be protected from all forms of discrimination, and this includes play. Discrimination, as discussed in Chapter 4, impacts negatively on children. It stops them being able to reach their full potential, because they are made to feel that their efforts are not valued. Stereotyping and labelling a child impact on their self-esteem and self-worth. If you tell a child that they cannot play with a certain piece of equipment because it is 'only for the girls', then you are limiting that child's curiosity, explorations, investigations and learning.

In your setting

Planning play activities and experiences for children is a very individual process. As you get to know the children in your care, you may start to plan play opportunities in advance so that you can meet their individual needs. These opportunities and experiences do not all have to be adult led; you can provide resources that will lead to child-initiated play. You do need to take into consideration the following points to make sure that you offer inclusive play opportunities:

● Know about each child's stage of development.
● Understand their likes, dislikes, interests and preferences.
● Take into account children's individual needs.
● Think about the next steps in their development and learning.

Useful resources

Publication

'Early years outcomes'
Download 'Early years outcomes' from **www.gov.uk/government/publications**, reference DFE-00167-2013. This will help you identify the stages of development for children under five years and identify possible next steps.

Website

Play England
This is a charity that aims to support a child's right to play. The website **www.playengland.org.uk** has information about inclusive play opportunities.

pacey says

For further research you could find out more about sustained shared thinking and how it can support children's development. Put simply sustained shared thinking is those lovely moments when you and a child are completely absorbed in something together. This could be a conversation or an activity, for example exploring something new. Research has shown that children learn (and remember what they have learnt) at a higher level through opportunities such as this.

Research suggests the three characteristics of sustained shared thinking are:

● Open – ended questions – asking questions like 'What do you think?', 'What would happen if...?'
● Adult modeling – children watch, learn and imitate those around them. Being aware of this can provide practitioners with an additional tool in supporting learning and development.
● Freely chosen play activities – these provide a great platform for extending and developing children's thinking as they will be motivated and absorbed by their chosen play activity.

Think about how you can encourage or make opportunities for sustained shared thinking. Things you can do to promote this include:

● Listening carefully to what a child is saying – take note of their body language too
● Give all your attention, show that you are genuinely interested – think about your own body language (eye contact, nodding, smiling)
● Share your own experiences (relating to what you are talking about) with the child, for example 'I like to wear a hat too, I wear one to keep my ears warm, when I go out to walk my dog'
● Re-cap – clarify what the child is telling you – 'so you think that...'
● Speculate – stimulate their thoughts further 'What do you think the cat (in the story) was thinking?'

Figure 9.1 Reasons to observe children

Observations can be written down and there are many different ways to do this, depending on what the child is playing with, where they are and who they are with. Any observation should provide enough factual and non-judgemental information for you to make balanced and informed deductions about children. There will be times when you are observing and you will want to record something that a child has done quickly and informally. On the other hand, there will be times when you want to record something in a more organised and formal way. There are many different formats and methods for formally observing children at play. No one method or format is better than any other; it depends on what you are observing and what you want to find out.

Table 9.1 gives you brief details of different formats for collecting information for observations to help build a holistic picture of children's development.

Useful resources

Books
There are many different formats for recording observation information, and many books and websites will give you further details. Two books that you may find useful are:

How to Observe Children
How to Observe Children by Sheila Riddall-Leech

CACHE Level 3 Early Years Educator
CACHE Level 3 Early Years Educator for the Classroom-Based Learner by Carolyn Meggitt

How you carry out an observation depends on many things:

● **What you want to learn about the child** – is it whether an activity is suitable for them, or to look at how they play with certain resources and toys?

It could be that a parent has asked you to make a note of something, such as how often a child sucks their thumb, or for how long they sleep. This is often referred to as the aim of your observation. Having an aim keeps your observation focused and stops you wandering off the point.

- **Where you are observing** – if you are inside watching the children play, it may be easier to write information down. If you are outside, for example, in a park, you could take photographs of the children playing on large equipment.
- **What the child is doing** – you can observe a child to see if they play with others or alone. You may want to think about a particular aspect of development, such as physical skills or language. How the child is playing when observed may help you to reflect on how you organise your day, routines and resources.

Table 9.1 Different formats for collecting information for observations

Format	Brief details
Photographs	Show a snapshot of what a child is doing at one particular moment.
Written	Can be of varying length and detail, must be focused (have an aim). Note: one sticky note is not a detailed written observation.
Checklists and tick charts	Useful for identifying whether a child has or has not achieved certain specific skills or aspects of learning, such as physical skills like kicking a ball, throwing, catching, balancing. Checklists should not be used to compare the development of a child with that of other children, but they can be a useful reference point over a period of time to check on long-term development.
Recordings and videos	Useful for observing language and communication skills as well as social development.
Examples of children's 'work'	Examples of children's drawings, paintings and early attempts at writing or mark making can be useful evidence to assess their skills; these are a form of observation.
Structured	Structured observations are usually ones where you have set up a specific activity so that you can observe a specific skill.
Naturalistic	Observations that are spontaneous and not planned, and often of activities in which you are involved; these can be useful to give a brief holistic view of a child's development at any one time.
Event sampling	These observations are used to record specific information about one event, such as a behavioural concern, and can last all day as you only record something when you see that specific event.
Time sampling	Time sample observations are used to observe a child over a period of time, perhaps a full day or a morning. You observe and note what the child is doing every 30 minutes, for example, and so build up a picture of how the child spends their day.

Figure 9.2 Remember you need written parental permission to take photos of children

Observations are not standalone tasks that in themselves meet a local authority or regulatory body requirement. They are part of a bigger process of planning, assessment and reflection. All of these things are dependent on each other, for example, you cannot reflect on the success or efficacy of an activity if you have not got information in some format relating to how the children responded to the activity.

The information, or evidence, that you collect from any form of observation can be invaluable for several reasons:

- It can show that you understand how children learn, grow and develop, and that the play activities you plan and provide take all of these things into consideration.
- Observations of children at play will give you information so that you can check that the activities and experiences are at the right level, and whether the children have learned and progressed in any way. This is called assessment.

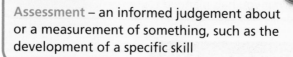

Key term

Assessment – an informed judgement about or a measurement of something, such as the development of a specific skill

- The information that you gain, together with your own professional knowledge and experiences, will help you plan appropriate and inclusive activities and experiences. Your observations may have made you more aware of a child's particular need or interest. You will then be able to use the observation to plan appropriate activities to support that child.
- Information learnt from the observation will help you identify a child's next steps so that their learning and development will progress.

Key term

Next steps – the things that a child could do next in order to progress in their development; for example, the next step from completing a ten-piece jigsaw could be to tackle a 15-piece one

- Observations can help you develop a long-term picture of a child's development, and can show progress and development across all areas of learning.

Reflective practice

Any professional home-based childcarer should reflect and evaluate the play activities and experiences that they plan and provide for children. You want to make sure that everything you do is for the benefit of the children. Sometimes when you are working closely with children it can be difficult to see if the play activities you are providing actually do meet their needs; so at times you need to step back and reflect on what you are doing. One way that you can reflect on your practice is to make observations of the children as they are playing. This will then provide you with evidence that in a quieter moment you can look at and decide if the play activities and experiences really do what you had planned for.

Links to the EYFS

Assessment of children's progress is a key component of the EYFS (Section 2 Assessment). You are expected to undertake some form of observation, but not necessarily written, in order to understand children's levels of achievement, interests and different ways of learning. You must also share the observed information with the parents. If you care for children between the ages of two and three years it is highly likely that you will complete the two-year progress check. This check is based on your observations and assessments of the child in the prime areas of learning. If you have developed the habit of observing children, you will find that this check is not an onerous task.

AC 9.2 Explain how observations are used

You need to explain how observations are used for the following purposes:

- To plan for children's individual needs
- For early intervention
- To review the environment
- During transitions
- When working in partnership.

Explain how observations are used to plan for children's individual needs

Every child is different, unique and has their own set of needs. The needs of a child will change as they grow and develop, so how you respond to those needs should also change. It is obvious that play activities that stimulate a nine-month-old baby will not sustain the interest of a three-year-old child. Also, children will become disinterested if they are presented with the same play experiences day after day. To meet the need for stimulation you must be flexible and offer play experiences that are varied and motivating. You will know through watching and observing the children if your planned play activities are meeting this need.

It is essential that you consider a child's individual needs if you are to offer a truly inclusive setting where all children and their families are valued and welcomed. It is very important that any observation you make is accurate and factual, and does not make assumptions about a child's needs. You should not be judgemental, but use your observations to help you create an inclusive environment.

Once you have gathered information about a child's individual needs you will be able to plan appropriate play activities for them, which motivate them and offer them challenge. It will also help you to develop effective routines to support the child's development and progress.

Explain how observations are used for early intervention

In general, the earlier a concern, whether confirmed or potential, can be identified with a child's development, the better the chance is of dealing with it and successfully supporting the child. Observations will help you identify how the child is progressing and if their development is following expected patterns. Sometimes development may be delayed or temporarily interrupted, for example, if a child has a bad cold and blocked ears and so cannot hear clearly. If you are alert and observing these things, you can react quickly and support the child. On the other hand, early intervention for a child with a long-term difficulty can significantly support both the parents and the child and help put the necessary professionals and agencies in touch with the family.

If you start observing the children in your care as soon as possible after they start, you build up a detailed and comprehensive picture of their development. You will be able to see evidence of their progress but also be able to identify areas where development is not as expected. You can use your observations as a basis for discussions with parents and help them to decide what support would benefit their child.

Explain how observations are used to review the environment

Sometimes it is all too easy to become complacent about how you organise your home and the children's learning environment. We become comfortable with the way things are, almost saying, 'Well, it works, so why change it?' To a certain extent that is human nature, but ask yourself: does it really create a stimulating learning environment for the children in your care?

Observations do not always have to focus on the children playing. It is sometimes very useful to change the focus to what they are playing *with* and how are they using the toys and resources. You could notice, for example, that the girls in your care do not often play with balls outside, or the boys do not look at the books in the book box. As a result you could introduce different coloured balls of different sizes so to make them attractive to the girls, or could plan an outdoor adult-led activity with balls where your encourage the girls to join in. You could look at the range of books in the book box and perhaps plan a visit to your local library where all the children could choose books that capture their individual attention. This could lead to a story telling session when you get back.

Figure 9.3 Do observations in different situations and of different activities

Explain how observations are used during transitions

Transitions can be planned, such as starting a new setting, or unplanned, such as a bereavement. If you have already built in to your everyday practice that observations are common place, you will be in a very strong position to support the child through changes, whether planned or unplanned. Your observations can be shared with parents and offer them reassurance that their child's needs are being met, especially if they are finding the separation from their child difficult when they start at your setting.

Reflective practice

Using the knowledge that you have gained from observing other children, you may find that you adjust your settling-in procedures for a new child or change how you support children who are starting school. The transition will then be much smoother, and this knowledge will also help you plan supportive activities. This is reflective practice in action and ultimately will make you a more professional home-based childcarer as you will be very responsive to a child's individual needs.

Explain how observations are used when working in partnership

Partnership working was discussed in Chapter 6 and it may be useful to read this chapter again as you think about observations. Partnership working is very valuable as it often helps to develop a holistic picture of a child. For example, you may have observed that a child has a language difficulty. After discussing this with the child's parents, expert help could be sought. A speech and language therapist could become involved with the child and their family. They will also undertake observations of the child. If these can be shared with you the child will receive continuity and consistency of care and their development will be effectively supported. Confidentiality and the child's right to privacy must be adhered to, however.

If you have concerns that a child is in need of protection you should make observations and gather information as appropriate. These observations should be shared with other professionals when, or if, requested. It is not, however, usual practice to share such observations with the child's parents or carers if you suspect that they may be involved in the allegations.

Tip

You must keep all observations of children confidential and securely stored. You should never share an observation of a child with other parents and carers, or indeed with other children.

In your setting

It is essential that you have a parent's written permission before your share observations of their child with another professional. If, however, you have serious concerns about the well-being of the child you do not need parental permission to share your observations.

Find out more

The Leuven Involvement Scale is a way of assessing a child's involvement in an activity and the quality of their learning. It is based on short, two-minute observations. It is widely used in group settings to look at the overall quality of the setting. If you put 'Leuven Involvement Scale' into a search engine you should be able to find out more information.

AC 9.3 Discuss how early intervention supports children's development

Early intervention is an approach that aims to offer extra help and support to a child and their family before the child starts to fall behind the expected pattern of development. Early intervention can work effectively only if you work co-operatively with the child's parents and carers and have a range of information to share with them. This means that you should aim to have undertaken several observations of the child involved in different activities; these observations would, ideally, be in several different formats.

The way that you and the child's parents will know if early intervention is required is if you have observed the child's development and learning over a period of time and discussed your findings with the parents or carers. Your observations need to have information that can show whether progress has or has not been made over a period of time, and you cannot do this if you only have a week's worth of observational material. It is not possible to say if observations over one month, or two or three, are sufficient. It will completely depend on the child and the specific concern that you have about development. Early intervention, however, is about preventing problems occurring in the first place and your observations should support this. It is better to act before a problem develops into a major concern than to do nothing at all.

It is good practice to look at a range of ways of collecting information and observing children's development. For example, if you rely entirely on photographs you will only have limited information about what the child has been doing; you will not have information about what the child has said or how they have played with others over a period of time. The information that you gather does need to be holistic as all areas of development and learning are connected and inter-related.

Early intervention will often mean that other professionals become involved with the child and their family. With the parents' written permission you could share the information gained from your observations. Once the early intervention programme has been established to support the child's development, you must continue to observe and record information. This will help you, the parents or carers and the other professionals involved to reflect on and evaluate the early intervention programme.

AC 9.4 Explain how to work with others to plan the next steps in relation to the needs and interests of children

Chapter 6 looked at working in partnership with others to support children's outcomes. It is suggested that you look again at this chapter.

The key principles of working with others are openness, trust, honesty, effective communication, and shared goals and values. We all want the best possible outcomes for children and one of the best ways to achieve this is to respond to and meet their needs and interests. As children grow and develop their individual needs and interests will change.

All children have universal needs that are biological or physical, and that are essential to survival. These include the need for food, drink and shelter. Other universal needs can be classed as psychological and these are essential for maintaining the quality of life. These needs are for love, affection, secure and stable relationships, friendships, intellectual stimulation and independence. Biological needs do not really change, as we all need to survive, and they can dominate other needs. For example, if someone is starving then their need for food is more important than their need to have friendships. Psychological needs can change as we develop and grow; for example, a young child's need for independence will develop and grow as they gain skills.

Key term

Universal needs – the basic requirements to ensure survival and quality of life

A child's interests will also change as they grow and develop. You could be caring for a young child who comes to you with an avid interest in a particular cartoon character. As the child learns more and develops, so will their interests.

Providing activities that involve their interest can help with the settling-in process; that interest may change to something completely different, however, as they gain more confidence and independence.

You will be able to identify needs and interests through your observations, especially as the interests change. You will also use your observations to identify a child's next steps. You will be doing everything that you can to meet a child's individual needs, interests and next steps. You will be sharing information with the child's parents/carers and working with them to support the child.

Sometimes it can be highly beneficial to work with other professionals to support a child. For example, a child in your care might also attend another setting, such as pre-school, playgroup or nursery class. If you can work with these settings, you will be able to offer a consistent approach that will benefit the child. Your observations will provide factual information that should clearly show the child's development and learning. Next steps can be discussed and shared. Changing interests can be identified and needs be met more effectively.

Do not breach confidentiality, however, and always make sure that you have the written permission of the parents before you share or discuss information about their child with another professional.

pacey says

Observations can also be reflections. They can help you to evaluate your role as a home-based childcarer and help to identify areas for improvement or development.

PACEY have a range of resources that can support you to carry out effective observation, assessment and planning for the children in your setting.

Assessment links

This assessment task relates to Learning Outcome 9 and links to assessment criteria 9.1, 9.2, 9.3 and 9.4.

You are asked to produce a resource that will help you when undertaking observations of children. There is no set format for the way that you present the evidence for this task. Think carefully about what you learn from observations and what helps you to remember information. It may be that you use lists or write notes. You might retain information better if it is presented in charts, tables or diagrams. You may prefer information to be presented in short 'bite-sized' chunks or to be written out like a report. You could write information on cards and store them in an indexed box or in different folders, or you could store files electronically on a memory stick.

The point is that this assessment task should be useful and meaningful to you. Your resources must:

● Explain what can be learned about children by observing them at play.
● Explain how observations are used:
  ● to plan for individual children's needs
  ● for early intervention
  ● to review the environment
  ● during transitions
  ● when working in partnership.
● Discuss how early intervention supports children's development.
● Explain how to work with others to plan next steps in relation to the needs and interests of children.

UNIT 2

Preparing to set up a home-based childcare business

Chapter 10

Understand how to lead and manage a home-based childcare setting

Learning Outcome 10

By the end of this chapter you will be able to:

1 Identify the skills, attributes and behaviours required to lead and manage a home-based childcare setting

2 Discuss the roles and responsibilities of a home-based childcarer when leading and managing a setting

3 Identify sources of support for the home-based childcarer

People who work with and care for children, in any setting, need to have very specific skills and attributes. The considerations are different, however, when the care takes place in your own home. As you work through this unit you should become aware of how special your chosen career path is.

AC 10.1 Identify the skills, attributes and behaviours required to lead and manage a home-based childcare setting

People decide to become home-based childcarers for many different reasons. Sometimes it is a total career change, sometimes a shift of focus, for example, from working in a day nursery to working at home. Whatever the reason, however, caring for other people's children requires total commitment to the huge responsibilities involved.

Many home-based childcarers and private nannies enjoy the freedom and flexibility that working for themselves can bring. It can be quite liberating to not have to answer to a boss or manager, but you are in a position of accountability – you are answerable to the

children, their families and to the regulatory bodies. There are still very clear legal requirements with which you must comply.

You may think that as a lone worker you do not lead or manage. You may believe that you can only lead a setting if it involves more than one person. For you, 'managing' may mean organising other people, such as the manager of a nursery does. This is not strictly true.

'To lead' can mean to set an example and guide. You must be a positive role model for the children for whom you care and they will learn from your example. You will guide their learning in many different ways. So in this context you do lead.

It is vital that you manage your time or things will become chaotic. You will develop routines to help you manage your time; you will develop ways to manage and promote positive behaviour; you will plan and supervise appropriate activities to meet the children's needs. This means that you *do* manage your setting. It may be that you decide to take on an assistant or a co-worker, in which case your leadership and management roles will develop and change. This will be discussed in more detail in Chapter 11.

Figure 10.1 You must comply with the Welfare requirements at all times

Skills, attributes and behaviours needed to be a successful home-based childcarer

- **A genuine love of children** – sounds obvious, but how many people do you know who are doing jobs that they actually don't like? You must enjoy being with and caring for children. If you don't, you may find it hard to fulfil your responsibilities. As a lone worker you may only have children for company some days, so if you don't enjoy their company you could have a problem.

- **Good communication skills** – these are necessary with both children and adults. Communicating with children can take many different forms and will impact on how well they settle with you initially. Effective communication with parents and carers is vital for establishing positive working partnerships. Communication also includes listening. You must listen carefully, sensitively and with full attention to children and their parents/carers. This will help you to understand their needs, organise your routines and manage your day effectively. See Chapter 6 for more information on communication.

- **Good organisation skills** – you are not just organising yourself and other family members, you have responsibilities to others. If you care for children before and after school, you will need to organise your day so that they are not late in the morning nor waiting for you after school. You need to organise and manage your day so that the needs of all the children can be met, for example, their rest, mealtimes and sleep times. Part of your job will include record keeping from a business perspective and also about the children in your care. Lack of organisation could mean that your finances are not accurate, which will impact directly on your income. Lack of organisation of children's records could lead to breaches of confidentiality and/or to their needs not being met.

- **Awareness of the need for confidentiality** – being aware of and respecting confidentiality is highly significant when considering ways to safeguard children (see Chapter 3). It shows that you respect children, understand their rights and are aware of safeguarding issues.

- **Understanding of how children learn and develop** – this is a huge topic and you will probably always be learning something new about children's learning and development. In order to plan for and provide appropriate play activities and experiences you must – as an absolute minimum – understand the stages of development. You can take active steps to increase your knowledge and awareness, however, by undertaking additional training, going on courses and keeping abreast of current developments.

- **Understanding of how to meet children's needs** – as with learning and development, meeting individual needs is crucial to the role of the home-based childcarer. It is an ongoing and very large topic. It is about being aware of and respecting differences, having an inclusive setting where all are welcomed, and providing routines that keep children safe and healthy and support their learning and development. Look again at Chapter 4 for more about inclusive practice.

- **Understanding of how to keep children safe** – this award covers safeguarding of children in Chapter 3. Many local authorities, however, offer this training as well. While safeguarding training is not a regulatory requirement for registration, it is good practice to make sure that you have some knowledge and understanding of it before applying to be registered.

Undertaking this training is only the beginning, however, and you must be constantly vigilant and aware. Keeping children safe also includes making sure that your home and places where the children play are clean and hygienic and that you do everything reasonable to prevent the spread of infections. You are also required to provide healthy, balanced and nutritious meals and snacks; this is part of keeping children protected.

- **Patience** – patience is essential when working with children. For example, it can be much quicker for you to put on a child's socks and shoes for them, but they will learn much more if you let them do it for themselves. This requires patience as the child will take longer. If you are patient, children will learn tolerance and respect from you. Good organisation supports patience. For example, if you do not plan ahead you may not give children enough time for independent dressing. It can be very hard to be patient with a child dressing themselves when you have only given yourself five minutes to get everyone in the car and off to do a school pick up.

- **Having a sense of humour** – being able to laugh with children and appreciate the lighter side of situations is not disrespectful, quite the reverse. It shows that you are realistic and happy. Having a sense of humour will also help you cope with stressful situations more effectively.

- **A calm temperament** – this links to being patient. Even in an emergency it is important that you can remain calm. A calm manner can be very reassuring for an anxious child or even for parents. Staying calm when you feel challenged can be difficult, but it is an essential attribute.

- **Having a flexible approach** – being flexible is not the same as being inconsistent. Having a flexible approach means that you are responsive to children's changing needs, interests and preferences. It means that you are open minded and willing to listen to other people's points of view and opinions. An inconsistent approach to your work leads to insecurities and sometimes a lack of inclusive practice. You will also learn more if you are flexible, as you will be willing to change your views and take into consideration different ways of doing things. If you are flexible you will be more willing to seek out training opportunities and will value the importance of keeping up to date and continuing professional development.

- **Being a positive role model** – one way children learn is from copying others. If you are patient, calm, have a sense of humour and show respect for others, children will learn these attributes from you.
- **Being professional** – defining what it means to be professional is really a book in itself! It is more than having a uniform, business cards, a sign on your car or highly organised records. Being professional is about your personal skills and attributes. Part of being professional is being self-aware and understanding the impact of your own behaviour, attributes and skills on others. It is about how you show that you respect individuals. It is about how you fulfil your legal responsibilities and duty of care. It is about having all of the above skills, attributes and behaviours.

AC 10.2 Discuss the roles and responsibilities of a home-based childcarer when leading and managing a setting

The roles and responsibilities of a home-based childcarer have been discussed in relation to safeguarding in Chapter 3 and in relation to equality, diversity and inclusion in Chapter 4. In both these cases your roles and responsibilities are defined by the legal requirements of your country. If you work in England you are legally required to meet the requirements of the EYFS. In other words, you have legal responsibilities to do everything that you can to safeguard the children in your care. You must support all children and their families with equal respect.

Your roles and responsibilities in relation to leading and managing a setting are defined by legal requirements. In England, these are the Safeguarding and Welfare Requirements of the EYFS. In Wales, you must comply with the National Minimum Standards for Regulated Child Care. In Northern Ireland, you are expected to provide the standard of care outlined in the Childminding and Day Care Standards for Children Under Age 12. In Scotland, you must pay heed to the National Care Standards for Early Education and Childcare.

> **Tip**
>
> Although the countries of the UK have differently named requirements, essentially they are underpinned by the same values – that the welfare of the child is paramount.

You have a responsibility to respect confidentiality. Within your setting you must manage all information with consideration of confidentiality issues. This includes how you store information, what information you share and how you manage sensitive information that you are given.

You have a responsibility to meet the needs of all the children in your care. This is the most important part of your role and so you must treat all children and their families with dignity and respect. Your day will have to be managed in ways that allow you to meet individual needs; so you will need to think about your routines and procedures and how you manage your time. Children will learn about dignity and respect from you so it is vital that you are a positive role model at all times and lead your setting by example.

Even though you may be a lone worker, you do have responsibilities and are accountable to others. In the first place you are accountable to the regulatory body. You are also accountable to the parents and carers of the children for whom you care. If you join a professional organisation such as PACEY, you are accountable to them to uphold professional standards. If you decide to take on an assistant or a co-worker, you have responsibilities towards them. With an assistant you have a responsibility to pay them and if you are their employer to make sure that you keep up to date with National Insurance contributions. As an employer you become subject to employment law and you must follow fair practices with regard to holiday, sick and maternity pay rights. Becoming an employer is discussed in greater detail in Chapter 11.

Useful resources

Website
HMRC
For information about becoming an employer:
www.hmrc.gov.uk

Reflective practice

Monitoring and evaluating the service offered is an important aspect of the leadership and management of any setting.

Some home-based childcarers send out questionnaires to parents and carers, they ask children for their views on activities and the provision, and they evaluate activities and experiences themselves. Some childcarers complete a self-evaluation form and use this to highlight their strengths and weaknesses and to develop an action plan (there is a self-evaluation form on the Ofsted website at https://online.ofsted.gov.uk/OnlineOfsted/public/launchportal.aspx; it is not a legal requirement for you to complete it but doing so is considered good practice).

This is all part of being a reflective practitioner. It helps you to develop your skills and practice and is one of the signs of a true professional.

Ask yourself: how could you monitor and evaluate the service that you offer?

Figure 10.2 Make sure equipment that is used is safe and fit for purpose. Check all equipment regularly

Links to the EYFS

Leadership and management is one of the three main sections that inspectors look at when doing an Ofsted inspection. Inspectors look for evidence in the following areas:

- How you safeguard children.
- Your understanding of the EYFS and how you meet the Learning and Development Requirements, including assessing children's progress.
- Your training and qualifications and how these impact on your work.
- How you work with others, such as schools, other settings, parents and carers.
- How you evaluate and monitor all aspects of your service.
- How you hope to improve and develop your service.

AC 10.3 Identify sources of support for the home-based childcarer

Everyone working with children will need support at some point. The role of providing home-based childcare can be quite isolating and there may be times when you feel quite alone. In such cases it is essential that you know from where you can get appropriate help and support. You must, however, make sure that when you do seek support you do not breach confidentiality, unless of course the welfare of a child is causing concern.

Professional Association for Childcare and Early Education

The Professional Association for Childcare and Early Years (PACEY) is the professional association for those working in childcare and early years. A standard-setting organisation, they promote best practice and support childcare professionals to deliver high standards of care and learning. PACEY is committed to promoting quality childcare services and to improving the status and conditions for home-based childcarers. Membership of this organisation is not mandatory but it is strongly advised. PACEY offer a wide range of support services and supports its members to grow their own professionalism and to be part of a sector-wide organisation representing their views and experiences. It is also very effective in liaising with government departments on issues concerning childcare generally, and also specifically home-based childcare.

Groups or drop-ins

Caring for children is a very demanding job and being self-employed means that you do not always have another professional childcarer close at hand. Many home-based childcarers set up informal groups or drop-ins where they can socialise, share new ideas and get support. These groups can sometimes be in different home-based childcarers' homes or in local facilities, such as Children's Centres, community halls, sport and leisure centres. Some local authorities support drop-in groups either by providing a venue or by providing a person to lead the group. Meeting with other people in the same profession can be highly supportive. They understand the issues that you may encounter and may be able to suggest different ways of approaching situations. It is also an opportunity to meet home-based childcarers who are more experienced than you, and you can benefit greatly from their experience.

Local authority

Your local authority will have a department or team that deals with childcare and early years education. The people in these teams will have different titles, but are essentially a useful source of support and help. They can often put you in touch with other local authority personnel and social services staff if needed.

Health visitors

Health visitors, either your own or those of the children for whom you care, can be a valuable source of support and help. Health visitors have a very good understanding of children's growth and development, which they gain through carrying out child health surveillance and developmental checks. They can also help put you in touch with other professionals, particularly in the medical world, if you have a concern about a child. When you carry out a child's two-year progress check, it is very good practice to liaise with the health visitor through the child's parents so that useful information can be shared.

Qualified teachers, early years teachers and people with Early Years Professional Status

Qualified teachers, early years professionals and people with early years teacher status have trained in and studied topics relating to children's care, learning and development for lengthy periods of time. They are often very well placed to offer you support and help with children's learning and behaviour. More and more home-based childcarers are offering places for two-, three- and four-year-old children as part of local authorities' provision of free early education and childcare for 15 hours per week. It can be very beneficial to establish a positive working relationship with these professionals, as ideas for activities and experiences can be shared, help with possible learning difficulties can be addressed and a shared approach established for those children who attend more than one setting in order to promote consistency.

Figure 10.3 Everyone working with children will need support at some point

Family and relatives

Your family and relatives can be supportive of your business. Hopefully you will have discussed your career plans with your family and anyone else who may be affected, before you actually begin work. Anyone who works full-time and has family responsibilities and commitments can find, at times, that it is difficult to meet all the demands placed on them. It can be difficult to balance the needs of your family against your professional responsibilities. This can be more complex for home-based childcarers as they are working in their home and using the same spaces as their family. Many self-employed people work from home, but often have a separate work area, so that their business life does not encroach on their family life. This is not the case for most home-based childcarers, however. There will be other people's children and their families in your home. There will be changes to your family routines and you may not be able to spend as much time with your own family. If you have discussed all of these issues with your family before you start working, they will be in a stronger position to offer you support.

> **Tip**
>
> You must remember not to breach confidentiality when talking about your work, even with your family.

> **Discussion point**
>
> Read the case study on the next page:
>
> ● How can you make sure that all of your family is supportive of your business?
> ● From whom else could Amirah have sought help and support?

Case study

Amirah decided to become a home-based childcarer after she stopped working following the birth of her daughter. She also has a son of school age. Amirah and her husband live with his parents in a large two-storey house with a conservatory leading to a big back garden. Amirah plans to use the conservatory as a play room and to use the big kitchen to prepare and serve the children's meals. There is a downstairs bathroom with a separate toilet. Amirah's husband is very supportive of her plans.

At first Amirah's in-laws were concerned that the house would be full of noisy children and that they would lose their privacy. Amirah tried to reassure them that the children would not have access to the family sitting room or any upstairs rooms. Her in-laws agreed she could try for six months and they would see how things go.

At a briefing meeting Amirah met an experienced home-based childcarer and explained her concerns. The other home-based childcarer suggested that Amirah brought her in-laws to her house to see how she ran her business and also how she kept some rooms private.

A few weeks after Amirah was registered, she noticed that her father-in-law was often around as the children were leaving and would wave goodbye to them. Her mother-in-law began to come into the kitchen to help at mealtimes. It became clear that Amirah's family was very supportive of her business and that her in-laws actually enjoyed having the children in the house. Amirah was very grateful for the support of the experienced home-based childcarer.

pacey says

If you employ an assistant you are also responsible for their work and actions. You will have to ensure that they follow the EYFS and this includes ensuring they undertake appropriate training and that you carry out effective supervision.

Networking and keeping in touch with other home-based childcarers is important because:

● childcare is a demanding job and can be lonely working from home by yourself
● training and learning can help you to develop professionally
● running your own business can be challenging
● the childcare sector is changing frequently and networking with others is a great way of keeping up with changes to legislation and regulations.

PACEY Local is a volunteer-led initiative, aiming to bring together like-minded childcare professionals to alleviate isolation, empower newly qualified professionals and share in best practice. There's a free online peer support site, where you can connect with other childminders, nannies and nursery workers in England and Wales to share advice, concerns and best practice. To find out more visit www.local.pacey.org.uk.

Assessment links

This assessment task relates to Learning Outcome 10 of Unit 2. This assessment task has two parts.

Part 1 links to assessment criteria 10.1 and 10.2. Part 2 links to assessment criteria 10.3. Both tasks must be completed in order to achieve this unit.

Part 1 requires you to produce information that:

- identifies the skills, attributes and behaviours required to lead and manage a home-based childcare setting
- discusses the roles and responsibilities of a home-based childcarer when leading and managing a home-based setting.

There is no set format for how this information should be presented. It must, however, be clear and legible. The language that you use should be straightforward and not contain jargon, too many technical terms or abbreviations without explanations.

There is no word limit, but read through your work regularly as you produce it. This will help to prevent you repeating yourself. Focus on the key words – in this case these are:

- skills
- attributes
- behaviours
- roles
- responsibilities.

Part 2 requires you to produce a fact sheet that identifies sources of support for a home-based childcarer. Sources of support may be different for each individual, but there will be some common ones.

As with Part 1 there is no set format for your fact sheet, so you could use illustrations, tables or charts as well as text, for example.

Chapter 11

Understand how to comply with financial and taxation requirements when setting up a home-based childcare service

Learning Outcome 11

By the end of this chapter you will be able to:

1 Explain how the home-based childcarer registers as: self-employed/an employer

2 Explain the Self Assessment process

It is very important that you start your home-based childcare service as you mean to go on and take a professional approach from day one. Part of your professional responsibility is that you comply with taxation and financial requirements, whether you work alone or with an assistant.

AC 11.1 Explain how the home-based childcarer registers as: self-employed/an employer

Registering as self-employed

You are working for yourself, not anyone else, therefore you are classed as self-employed. A home-based childcarer must register as self-employed with Her Majesty's Revenue and Customs (HMRC) for taxation purposes. You will be committing an offence if you do not do this within three months of starting to receive payments for looking after other people's children.

If you were previously employed by someone else, you should ask them to provide you with a P45 form. A P45 has three parts; part 1 is for you, and parts 2 and 3 are for your new employer. Although you will need part 1 only, it is advisable to file the other parts of the form safely.

Part 1 has details of:

● your National Insurance number
● your full name, address, date of birth
● if you had a previous employer, the date you finished
● details of your previous employer
● how much tax you paid in the tax year you ended employment with them (a tax year runs from 5 April to 4 April the following year).

You will need all of this information to fill in a (Self Assessment) tax return.

There are two ways to register as newly self-employed:

● Look in your local phone book under HM Revenue and Customs for your local office. Phone them and ask to be sent a copy of booklet SE1 'Are you thinking of working for yourself?'
● Or, go to www.hmrc.gov.uk and download a copy of booklet SE1.

There is a range of products and services on the HMRC website, including online presentations (webinars) and e-learning resources to help you understand the different aspects of starting and running your own business:

- www.hmrc.gov.uk/startingup/help-support. htm has a range of help and support articles.
- You can also find 'bite-sized' information on tax issues in video format at www.youtube.com/ user/HMRCgovuk.

Once you have looked at the information you can register as self-employed at www.gov. uk/new-business-register-for-tax. On this site there is a form to complete and submit online. Once you have submitted this form you will be sent a letter by HMRC with your Government Gateway account details. You will need this letter in order to complete your Self Assessment (see AC 11.2).

Registering as self-employed is straightforward, provided you have all the necessary information to hand. The required information will all be on your P45.

Figure 11.1 It is important that you maintain accurate financial records

Tip

In order to access all the online services of HMRC, you will need to have a Government Gateway account. This enables you to access government services online. Part of the process for registering as self-employed includes setting up this account. Your Government Gateway account will require a user ID (which it creates) and a password, which you will use every time you log on to the site.

National Insurance

Once you have registered as self-employed you will have to adjust your National Insurance contributions. The number of years and the amount of contributions paid in to National Insurance will impact on your pension once you reach the national qualifying pension age. There are different charges for National Insurance and, depending on what rate you decide to pay, your entitlement to certain benefits, such as sick pay or maternity pay, will be affected.

Most home-based childcarers who are self-employed pay Class 2 National Insurance contributions. This is a flat rate of £2.75 a week (information correct for 2014–2015). You are encouraged to pay monthly by direct debit, so you pay £11 or £13.75 every month. Alternatively, you can choose to pay every six months, with payments due on 31 January and 31 July.

If your expected earnings are below £5885 per year (information correct for 2014–2015), however, you might not need to pay. In this case you can apply for a Certificate of Small Earnings Exception, but a lack of contributions could affect your State Pension and other benefits in the future.

You do not have to pay National Insurance Class 2 contributions for any complete week when you cannot work due to illness, or when you are caring for someone and are receiving certain benefits. You may be entitled to National Insurance credits instead, which would maintain your National Insurance record and so protect your State Pension and certain other benefits.

To register to pay National Insurance Class 2 contributions you need to use your 18-digit reference number. You can find your reference number on the letter that HMRC send you when you register as self-employed. The first two digits are always '11' and the last digit can be an 'X'. You can pay by direct debit as mentioned before, by Bank Giro, at a post office or by post.

It is highly unlikely, but possible, that you will need also to be registered for VAT. You must have a turnover of more than £81,000 per year, however, for this to apply (correct for 2014–2015).

Registering as an employer

Once your home-based childcare service is established you may decide to expand by taking on an assistant. This effectively means that the number of children that you can care for at any one time is doubled if you have one assistant, or tripled if you have two. Bear in mind that there are clear requirements for the amount of space available in your home for caring for children – so expanding requires more than just taking on more assistants.

There are basically two ways that you can have an assistant:

- Your assistant works at your home, but is registered with the regulatory body in their own right and is self-employed.
- Or, you become an employer and your assistant works as your employee.

If you employ other people, you are responsible for paying their tax and National Insurance contributions. Page 11 of the booklet SE1 'Are you thinking of working for yourself?' gives you all the information that you need to know about this.

You will need to register as an employer with HMRC. This links to Pay As You Earn (PAYE). You can download from the HMRC site a software package (Basic PAYE Tool), which is designed for employers with nine or fewer employees. The software gives Real Time Information (RTI) so all you need to do is input all payments made, at the time that they are paid to your employee. The stoppages are then displayed immediately on the screen. More information can be found at www.gov.uk/paye-for-employers. Online presentations for small or new employers can be found at www.hmrc.gov.uk/webinars/employers.htm.

Your employee is entitled to the National Minimum Wage, holiday pay and other benefits. The National Minimum Wage (correct for 2014–2015) is:

- £6.50 per hour for employees aged 21 and over
- £5.13 per hour for employees aged between 18 and 21 years.

You must also make sure that you use the correct tax code for your employee. A tax code is usually made up of several numbers and a letter. Everyone, whether employed or self-employed, has a personal tax allowance of £10,000, provided that they are legally entitled to live in the UK and are a registered taxpayer (information correct for 2014–2015). This personal allowance is automatically given to you.

AC 11.2 Explain the Self Assessment process

Everyone in the UK who is working has an account with HMRC. This is so that HMRC can calculate the amount of income tax you must pay. If your tax affairs are straightforward you may already pay all of the tax due on your earnings or pensions through your tax code.

You may need to complete a tax return if you have more complicated tax affairs, even if you already pay tax through your tax code. There are also certain circumstances in which you will always need to complete a tax return – for example, if you are:

- self-employed
- a company director
- a trustee
- receiving foreign income.

In order to calculate the tax due if you are self-employed, you must supply information on a tax return. This is called Self Assessment.

Self Assessment involves completing a tax return each year. You can do this online or on a paper copy that HMRC can send to you. You show your income and capital gains (profits on the sale of certain assets) on your tax return, as well as claiming tax allowances or reliefs.

How to get a Self Assessment tax return

You need to register for Self Assessment before you can get a tax return (see AC 11.1, page 153). When you register as self-employed online,

you will also be registered for Self Assessment. HMRC will use the information you provide to set up the right records for you. They will then send you a ten-digit tax reference, called a Unique Taxpayer Reference. You'll need to keep this safe.

HMRC will send you a reminder each year, usually in April or May, telling you to complete your tax return (Self Assessment). If you haven't received this letter or a tax return by the end of May, you should get in touch with HMRC.

You can choose to fill in your tax return either online or on paper. There are lots of benefits to sending it online. It's quick, easy and you have three months longer to send it.

If you send in a paper tax return, it must reach HMRC by midnight on 31 October. If you miss this deadline you have three months more to send your return online instead.

If you send in your tax return online it must reach HMRC by midnight on 31 January. You'll have to pay a £100 penalty if HMRC doesn't receive your tax return on time. The later you file your return, the more penalties you're likely to have to pay.

Sending your tax return online

Completing and submitting your tax return online has many advantages. For example, your figures are calculated automatically and you'll know right away how much tax you owe (or what HMRC owes you). Most tax returns can be sent online.

You need to sign up for HMRC Online Services first. Once you've signed up, you can use HMRC's free Self Assessment service or you can buy commercial software to send your tax return. You sign up for the online service through the Government Gateway (see page 154).

Useful resources

Websites

HMRC and tax support

www.hmrc.gov.uk

www.gov.uk/new-business-register-for-tax

www.hmrc.gov.uk/startingup/help-support.htm

www.youtube.com/user/HMRCgovuk

www.gov.uk/paye-for-employers

www.hmrc.gov.uk/webinars/employers.htm

Publication

'Are you thinking of working for yourself?'
Booklet SE1 'Are you thinking of working for yourself?' published by HMRC can be downloaded online or is available from your local tax office in print form and several languages.

pacey says

Top finance tips

● Keep on top of your accounts – do them weekly or at least monthly
● Number all your receipts – use this number to cross reference to the item in your accounts book or spreadsheet
● It is good practice to use a cash book and attendance register to manage payments from parents – you could ask parents to pay by direct debit, standing order or online transfer
● You should have a separate bank account for your childcare business – your bank can advise you on business banking.
● Remember also that you can accept payments by childcare vouchers (there is more information about childcare vouchers on the HMRC website). There are many different childcare voucher companies and you will have to fill out the forms to join each one as necessary.

You will find the PACEY Essential Business tools on the PACEY website.

Assessment links

This assessment task relates to Learning Outcome 11 of Unit 2 and links to assessment criteria 11.1 and 11.2.

You are asked to produce a leaflet as a guide to tax and Self Assessment for home-based childcare workers. You may find it helpful to look at other leaflets that are freely available. For example, leaflets on health care issues are freely available at health and medical centres; leaflets on food are freely available in shops and supermarkets.

These leaflets are often colourful and eye catching; they use illustrations, charts and tables as well as text to get the message across. These features should also be included if possible in your leaflet.

Your leaflet must explain:

● How a home-based childcare worker can register as self-employed.
● How a home-based childcare worker can register as an employer.
● The Self Assessment process.

Chapter 12

Understand how to create a business plan

Learning Outcome 12

By the end of this chapter you will be able to:

1 Discuss steps to take when planning your own home-based childcare business

2 List types of insurance required for a home-based childcare setting

3 Create a business plan

As a home-based childcarer you are running a professional business, albeit a relatively small one, but you must keep account of your finances and be aware of financial planning. This is so that you can run a business that at the very least covers your costs.

AC 12.1 Discuss steps to take when planning your own home-based childcare business

Chapter 10 discussed the support that your family and relatives could give you as you start your business. It may sound obvious, but you must discuss your plans with all of your family and those living in your home, before you take any steps towards becoming a home-based childcarer.

Your family life

Working as a home-based childcarer can impact your family life. For example, your own children will not be able to come in from school or activities and have your undivided attention if there are other children around. Toys and activities will need to be available for all children. Your children may have to share mealtimes with others. However, your children will always have playmates at home.

Reflective practice

Many home-based childcarers do not use their own children's bedrooms for their business, meaning that toys their children do not want to share can be kept in their bedrooms so they are not accessible to others.

- Is this reasonable?
- Are your children entitled to keep some things 'private'?
- Do you think that all children should be encouraged to share?

Your house, or at least the rooms used for childcare, may have more toys and equipment than before. You will need to decide how best to store toys and resources so that your family does not feel that their home has been taken over!

Contact your local authority or local Family Information Service

Once you have had an initial discussion with your family, you need to contact your local authority or local Family Information Service and sign up for a briefing session. These sessions are called slightly different names by different authorities, but basically have the same aim – to inform you as a potential home-based childcarer. The number of sessions you'll attend will vary between each local authority; however there will be a lot of information given out and opportunities to ask questions.

Useful resources

England
The website **www.gov.uk/find-family-information-service** will help you find out information about briefing/information sessions in your area in England.

Tip

Take something with you to the briefing sessions so that you can make notes. There will be a lot of information and possibly dates shared, so if you write things down you will be able to refer to your notes and remind yourself of the information later on.

The briefing session will give you information about how to register with your regulatory body (see Chapter 13).

Training

You will also be given information about training that you must do before you are registered. Pre-registration training is mandatory regardless of your previous qualifications. While it may be excellent preparation, if you have a degree, an NNEB, DNN, BTEC Diploma, NVQ Level 3 or gained any other qualification in childcare at any level, you are **not** exempt from the pre-registration training for home-based childcarers.

Compulsory training will include:

- safeguarding children
- Paediatric First Aid
- your local authority-approved pre-registration course (if you are reading this book then there is a very strong possibility that your approved pre-registration training course is this one).

Some of the training may be provided online, while other training will be face to face. Training will be held at different times of the day. In some

cases you may be able to get help with costs, but you must be prepared to pay some, if not all, of the initial costs of training prior to registration, however.

In your setting

It is good practice to train for a qualification in food hygiene before you are registered. This can be arranged through your local authority or PACEY. PACEY (the professional organisation for home-based childcarers) offers this training online. Further details can be obtained by calling PACEY on 0300 003 0005.

Tip

Your First Aid training is valid only for three years and you must renew your qualification to remain registered. It is good practice, however, to renew all of your training on a regular basis.

Other training that you will have to do will be in relation to the legislation and education frameworks.

Links to the EYFS

In England you will need to undertake training on the EYFS. You *must* be conversant with the EYFS before your registration visit from Ofsted or a childminder agency, as you will be asked in detail about it. You will need to prove to the inspector or agency that your knowledge is good enough for you to meet the statutory requirements on the day you are inspected. If you do not understand all of the statutory requirements or have not had appropriate training, there is a strong possibility that you will not be registered.

Vetting

Everyone who cares for children, works with them or comes into contact with children in their work is required to have a criminal record check. Anyone over the age of 16 years who lives in the house where you will be caring for children will also need to have a criminal record check. These checks are carried out through the Disclosure and Barring Service (DBS).

In your setting

After registering with the regulatory body or childminder agency, it is your responsibility to organise a criminal record check for anyone in your household who reaches the age of 16 (in England). You will not be sent a reminder.

The criminal record checks are not portable; this means that if you were working in a day nursery or a school before you decided to become a home-based childcarer, you are not able to use that check. From September 2014 everyone working with children has to reapply to the DBS. You will not be allowed to start to care for other people's children in your home if you have not got a current check, even if you had one previously.

In England, checks are carried out by Ofsted, or an agency, on behalf of the Disclosure and Barring Service. Your DBS check does not have a set period for validity. You must inform Ofsted or a childminder agency, however, if your circumstances, or those of your household or your assistant, change. For example:

- if your teenage child is arrested for drug offences
- if your assistant's partner is arrested for offences against children
- if your partner is arrested for domestic abuse or bodily harm against another individual.

This list is not exclusive; if in doubt contact Ofsted or your childminder agency.

DBS checks can be completed online via the Ofsted website, www.ofsted.gov.uk. You can email customerservices@dbs.gsi.gov.uk for more information. The DBS check needed by a childminder costs £44 (correct as of September 2014). You will be given relevant forms at your briefing meetings or pre-registration session if you wish to apply on paper and not online.

References and health checks

You will need to provide character references before you become registered. References from a previous employer are ideal. References should not be family members or personal friends. You will also need to have a health check from your doctor. Some doctors will charge for this service. Further details will be given at the briefing or pre-registration meetings.

Transport

If you plan to use your own car for transporting children, you must have a valid driving licence, MOT (if required, depending on the age of your car) and up-to-date road tax. It is good practice to join a motoring organisation that offers car rescue cover so that you and the children will not be stranded if your car breaks down.

Contracts

You must not start to care for any child before you have agreed a contract with the parents/carers. A contract is a legal document between you and the parents/carers. It covers, at a minimum, personal details, fees to be charged, when and how children will be collected, hours of childcare, holiday and sickness arrangements. If you join PACEY you can purchase contract forms from them that have been checked by their legal team.

You should discuss the details of the contract after the first meeting with the parents/carers, and before the settling-in period. It will take time to complete a contract properly, and neither you nor the parent/carer should rush this. It is not good practice to meet a child and their parents and to complete the contract at that first meeting.

Contracts are very important and should be updated every time there is a change in a child's circumstances, such as different days of care or hours they will be attending your setting. Contracts must be signed and dated by both you and the parents/carers. You must keep one copy of the contract securely, such as in the child's file, and give one copy to the parents or carers.

Join a professional organisation

A professional organisation will give you a huge amount of support and information. The most well known, but not the only one, in England and Wales is the Professional Association for Childcare and Early Years (PACEY). It was previously known as the National Childminding Association (NCMA). PACEY offers advice in relation to insurance and other aspects of the home-based childcare business. You can also purchase your contracts, child record forms, accident record books, attendance records and many other very useful business tools. Members of PACEY also have access to a wide range of resources including factsheets, practice guides, best practice videos, free online training and advice lines including legal, health and well-being and early years and childcare support.

Useful resources

PACEY
PACEY's website is **www.pacey.org.uk**

Northern Ireland Childminding Association and Scottish Childminding Association
Northern Ireland and Scotland also each have a professional organisation, linked to PACEY. These are the Northern Ireland Childminding Association (NICMA) **www.nicma.org** and the Scottish Childminding Association (SCMA) **www.childminding.org**

Independent Childminders' Social Enterprise
In 2013 the Independent Childminders' Social Enterprise (ICM-SE) was formed. More details can be found at **www.icm-se.org.uk**

AC 12.2 List types of insurance required for a home-based childcare setting

Public liability insurance

It is a legal requirement that you have public liability insurance in place before you start to care for other people's children. Public liability insurance will not stop or prevent accidents, but having it in place will provide you with legal liability cover against unforeseen accidents or incidents that occur to you, the children or other people. Public liability insurance will help you if you find yourself in the unfortunate position of being sued by another person over a professional matter, for example, if a child is injured or dies while in your care. Public liability will also cover any claims against you for damage that may be caused to other people's property by the children for whom you care.

There are several companies or organisations that will offer you public liability insurance and premium charges do vary. The differences between the costs of various companies may be due to the other services that are offered. On average you can expect to pay about £50 per year at the time of publication. However you may be able to find it cheaper, especially if you join a professional organisation.

Public liability insurance ideally should have a limit of indemnity of £5 million. Some policies will also include employers' liability insurance, which you should have if you employ an assistant. The limit of indemnity for employers' liability is usually £10 million.

Some policies will also offer:

- Legal expenses – limit of indemnity £100,000
- Loss or damage to third party property – £1000
- Debt recovery and contract dispute cover for amounts over £100.
  Debt recovery and contract dispute cover can be very useful if you get into the unfortunate position of parents and carers owing you money.

House and contents insurance

You should also make sure that your own house and contents insurance company knows that you are running a business from home. Some do not charge an excess, but some do.

Class 1 business insurance

You must have class 1 business insurance for transporting children in your car. Your vehicle insurance cover should be fully comprehensive, not third party, fire and theft. Your vehicle's insurance certificate should state that the insured individual is covered to drive a vehicle used for transporting children.

In your setting

You are required by law to display your public liability insurance certificate in your home, so that it is visible to parents and carers, visitors to your setting and inspectors. Other insurance certificates should be stored securely. It is good practice, however, to keep a copy of your car insurance certificate or insurance details in your vehicle.

AC 12.3 Create a business plan

Putting together a business plan will help you to organise the financial side of your business. There is not a set or correct format for a business plan; it is a matter of personal preference. If you decide to get help from a small business advisor at your bank you may be given their forms. Banking forms can often be more complex, however, and seek more information

than is necessary for you, such as financial projections for three years ahead.

Also, you may not want to or need to set up a business banking account. It is a good idea, however, to have a separate current account for all financial matters concerning your home-based childcare business.

In your setting

PACEY has produced a cashbook that is available for members to buy. PACEY has made an agreement with HMRC that the format of the cashbook is an adequate record of trading. There is no reason, however, why you could not take the format and transfer it to a computer program. Do remember that any records stored on your computer should be password protected.

It is very important that you develop a routine for recording your income and expenditure. It is important to do this once a week, monthly or every time you receive a payment. There is no right or wrong way to do this; it is a matter of personal preference.

Case study

Sam and Anya are a husband-and-wife home-based childcare team; both are registered with Ofsted. They have a current account in both their names that is used only for their childcare business; they can both access this account online or by telephone.

They have set up a simple accounts record on their laptop, using Microsoft Excel. They have one sheet where they record all payments made to them, including the date and the name of the person paying them. These entries are cross referenced to the numbered invoices that they give to parents/carers. Parents/carers are invoiced at the end of each month and are encouraged to pay by online or telephone banking, as this reduces the amount of cash Sam and Anya keep in their home. Invoices are produced and saved in a folder on their laptop.

They have a second sheet where they record all money that they spend on their business, including the date and a general description of the expenditure, for example, 'fruit for snacks'. All receipts for each month's expenditure are dated and kept in order in a plastic wallet. By the end of the financial year they have 12 plastic wallets of receipts. Sam and Anya also record on another sheet any mileage that is connected to their business, such as school runs or trips out during the school holidays.

When discussing how they organise their financial matters, it is clear that they have a simple but effective system that works for them. It is kept secure and password protected on their computer.

The business plan format at the end of this section (page 168) is a suggested one only, but it does include all the main information points that you should include in your plan.

Part 1 Introduction and marketing

It is a matter of personal preference if you give your business a name. If you decide to do this, your business name should be short and simple and easily memorable. Alternatively, your business does not need to have a name at all.

Description of the services

The description of the services you plan to provide should be concise and say exactly what you plan to do. For example:

I can provide care and early years education for children from six months to five years old, and before- and after-school care for children between five and 12 years. I am registered on both the Early Years and Childcare Registers.

Background

The background section could be written as if you are telling another person why you have decided to set up your business. It can also be used as an introductory leaflet for parents and carers when they make enquiries.

In this section you could include:

- What training you have had or plan to have and when it was completed.
- For how many children and of what ages you can care.
- Which insurance policies you have in place, including for your car.
- To which professional organisations you belong.
- Hours and days of business.
- Which framework you follow (e.g. in England this would be the EYFS).
- How you will assess and record child development and progress.
- When you will provide parents and carers with written reports on their child's progress.

Mission statement

A mission statement is a formal summary of your aims and values. It does not have to be long, just a clear and succinct sentence. For example:

I aim to provide a high standard of childcare for children and their families at an affordable price.

Unique selling points

Your unique selling points (USPs) are the things that make you and your service different from other people offering similar services. You might be a vegetarian (or another dietary/lifestyle choice) and offer only vegetarian meals and snacks – that could be a USP. You might be bilingual – that could be a USP. Another USP could be the schools or other settings you are prepared to drop children off at and collect them from. You may be prepared to work at the weekends, or to offer flexible hours to meet the needs of parents and carers who work shifts. That is a USP.

Other USPs could be to do with your home; for example, you might have a huge outdoor space, you might have a vegetable garden that children can help you tend, you might have excellent access and facilities for children with disabilities.

You might also have skills that could be classed as USPs. You might have experience of working with children with learning difficulties, with twins, with specific medical conditions; you might be competent at using sign language or Makaton. Other USPs could be that you are prepared to take childcare vouchers, that parents can set up direct debit payments for convenience, or that you have a webcam system in your home that parents can log on to.

Remember that your USP should not inadvertently be discriminatory; for example, you cannot have a USP that you will care only for children of a certain religion.

Situational analysis

A situational analysis considers your strengths and weaknesses, and the opportunities and threats to your business. This is sometimes

Table 12.1 Example of a SWOT analysis

Strengths:	Weaknesses:
Registered with Ofsted or an agency	Very new to home-based childcare
Completed initial training	Not yet had a judgement grade from Ofsted
Open every weekday	Don't know many people in the area
Have own family, including child with dyslexia	
Walking distance to local pre-school, nursery and primary school	
Large garden for outdoor play, and easy access to facilities such as the adventure playground in the local park	
Opportunities:	**Threats:**
To access more training	Other providers in the area
To offer longer hours, such as weekends or overnight	Changes to legislation or the EYFS
To develop links with other settings	Vacancies not filled
To develop more links with schools	
To join childminder drop-in groups	

also called a SWOT analysis and it can be very useful to do this as you start your business and to review it every three months or so to see what has changed. An analysis like this helps to focus your mind on the real issues that impact on your business. An example of a SWOT analysis is shown in Table 12.1.

Market research

Market research is essential for any business, and home-based childcare is no different. You need to ask yourself:

● Is there a need for home-based childcarers in my area?
● How do I know this?
● Who are my competitors? (Not just other home-based childcarers.)
● Who are my customers?

Market research takes time and effort, but it could mean the difference between a successful business and one that just 'ticks along'.

You will need to get out and ask the questions. Find out what other childcare services there are in your area, including day nurseries and other home-based childcarers. Why is the one you are planning different? Why should you be successful when, for example, a day nursery in your area is operating at only 60 per cent capacity?

Who are your customers, and what is your target market? Consider how many primary schools and nursery classes there are in your area. Most working parents do not work only in school term-time or school hours, so maybe you could aim to cater for school holidays, or for before- and after-school care. Can you be flexible and offer morning, afternoon or full-day sessions as well as before- and after-school care? This could be your USP.

Marketing and advertising

Marketing and advertising is not something you do only before you start or at the beginning of your business. It is something that you will need to be aware of all the time if you want to fill vacancies and run a successful business. There are lots of different ways that you can advertise and market your business, including through the media or using business cards, fliers and leaflets.

You can market your business through the **media** by using:

- the Family Information Service or your local authority equivalent
- free ads newspapers
- local evening and weekly newspapers
- parish newsletters; church and places of worship noticeboards
- school newsletters and special events programmes, such as summer fairs
- local groups and clubs (but make sure that they understand that they are not necessarily endorsing your business)
- the internet: set up your own blog or website, use social media and appropriate forums (but be very aware of issues of confidentiality)
- your local radio station.

hope that you will place more orders with them for which you will pay. In some cases you initially pay only for packaging and postage.

Give your cards and leaflets out to:

- parents/carers that you already know through your own children
- Children's Centres
- health centres
- friends and neighbours
- midwives and health visitors
- staff at local schools and pre-school groups
- crèche managers
- people running antenatal classes, and those specialising in classes and courses for pregnant women
- local employers.

Other ways to advertise and market your business:

- Put a sign up in your house and/or car windows.
- Register with an online childminding or childcare group that matches settings to parents/carers.
- Put business cards, leaflets or fliers in local shops, libraries, colleges, schools, leisure and health centres.

In your setting

It is not a good idea to put your address on any advertising material. You could get unwanted and nuisance callers, or put yourself, the children and your family at risk. It is better just to put your name and contact phone number. It is also worth considering investing in a mobile phone that you use only for your childcare business.

Using **business cards, fliers and leaflets**: If you decide to have business cards, leaflets or fliers, try to make them eye catching. Keep them fairly simple, with only essential information.

You can organise business cards, leaflets and fliers relatively cheaply, especially if you create them yourself on your own computer or if a family member or friend helps you. Some websites will print free advertising material for you – in the

Reflective practice

Think about some of the print adverts that you remember noticing recently.

- Can you identify what made them memorable?
- Was it colour, size of print, font, the service being advertised, or something else?

Remember that nothing looks more unprofessional than a handwritten notice on a scrap of paper, with incorrect spellings and scruffy handwriting.

Part 2 Financial planning

Start as you mean to carry on and keep track of your finances on a very regular basis. When running any business it is essential to keep track of the money coming in and going out. Look again at the case study of Sam and Anya on page 162.

The most effective way to keep track of money is to set a budget and monitor how closely you are able to stick to it.

> **Key term**
>
> **Budget** – a detailed statement of what you expect to receive and spend

When you first set up your business your budget will be based on informed estimates. Talk to other home-based childcarers and ask about their expenditure and income. For example, what are their hourly or daily rates? Do they charge for nappies, sun cream, and meals and snacks? How do parents/carers pay them?

Start-up costs

Start-up costs will be different for each home-based childcarer; there will be some common costs, however, such as:

- pre-registration course
- travel to courses and training venues
- Ofsted or childminder agency registration fee (Ofsted currently charge £35)
- membership to a relevant professional organisation
- Paediatric First Aid training
- First Aid kit
- safeguarding training
- Food Safety training
- manual handling training
- health check
- public liability insurance
- car insurance
- business cards, leaflets and fliers; stationery, printer ink
- health and safety equipment
- registration with Information Commissioner's Office (ICO) (fee is currently £35 and is required if you plan to take and use photographs of children).

Annual expenditure

Your annual expenditure will include:

- Ofsted or childminder agency registration fee
- membership of relevant professional organisation
- renewal of insurance policies
- renewal and replacement of toys, equipment and resources
- council tax
- electricity and/or gas
- water
- telephone (landline and mobile), internet.

You may have monthly direct debits set up for your gas, electricity, water, telephone and council tax. For accounting purposes, however, these are regarded as annual expenditures.

The table below shows some of the allowable expenses specific to home-based childcarers who work at least 40 hours per week, which PACEY has agreed with HMRC.

Table 12.2 Allowable expenses specific to home-based childcarers who work at least 40 hours per week

Expense	Amount allowed of total expense
Heating and lighting	33.3 per cent of costs
Water rates or meter charges	10 per cent of costs
Council tax	10 per cent of costs
Wear and tear	10 per cent of gross income
Rent	10 per cent of costs
Free milk	You can claim 189ml (a third of a pint) for each child who attends your setting for at least two hours per day.

> **Useful resources**
>
> **Website**
>
> *Nursery Milk*
> For more information on free milk you can contact your local authority or **www. nurserymilk.co.uk**, where you can make a claim online, or call them on 0844 991 4444.

Table 12.2 is not exhaustive and HMRC may still refuse an allowance if the cost is not 'wholly exclusive and necessary' for the purpose of your business.

Larger items such as car seats, buggies and high chairs will be treated as assets for your business, and as such are subject to capital allowance. This means that the cost of these items can be spread over a number of years as an allowable expense.

When claiming income-related benefits – such as housing benefit, council tax benefit or income support – home-based childcarers can have a special concession called the 'two-thirds disregard'. This means that two-thirds of your income from your childcare business is disregarded when your entitlement to these benefits is calculated. Expenses such as heating, lighting and food are not taken into account. For other benefits and tax credits, the amount you may receive will be based on your net income. Your net income is your total (gross) income less your actual business expenses.

Income support is normally available only to people who work fewer than 16 hours a week. You should check with the Department for Work and Pensions, however, if you think you may be eligible. Go to www.gov.uk/browse/benefits for more information.

Approximate weekly expenditure and income

There are some basic calculations you will need to do in order to work out your approximate weekly expenditure and income.

These calculations are for example purposes only.

1 First of all, work out your approximate **weekly costs** using this formula:
Total yearly expenditure ÷ Number of weeks working = Weekly costs
For example: £5000 ÷ 48 = £104
This figure may not, of course, take into consideration food and drinks for meals and snacks.

2 Next, work out exactly how many hours you will be able to work each week, counting each child separately. To do this, first work out the total number of **hours per week** that are available to be 'sold', that is actual hours that you can care for children and be paid:
Hours per day × Days open per week × Registered places = Total hours per week
For example: 10 × 5 × 6 = 300 hours per week
If you offer sessional places use the hours in each session in the above calculation.
It is unrealistic to expect that you will fill all your available places at the start of your business. So repeat this calculation with a lower number of registered places 'sold'. This will give a more realistic figure initially. If you estimate 80 per cent occupancy, your total hours would be 240 hours.

3 Next, work out what you need to **charge per hour** in order to cover your costs when you have achieved a realistic number of hours 'sold'.
Weekly costs ÷ Realistic hours sold per week = Break-even hourly fees
For example: £104 ÷ 240 = £0.43
This is the absolute minimum you could charge.

4 When you have decided on an hourly fee you can work out **how many children** you will need to have attend in order to meet your costs.
Number of hours that need to be sold per week ÷ Hours per day ÷ Days per week = Number of children needed at all times to break even
For example: 240 ÷ 10 ÷ 5 = 4.8 children at all times
There will be a limit to the number of children you can have at any one time due to the conditions of your registration. You must also remember that you must include your own children, if you have any under five years, in the number of children that you can care for at any one time.

In the example above you would need five paying children at all times to meet your minimum costs, more than five to make a profit, and fewer than five would mean you would make a loss. It is highly unlikely that you will be registered for six children under five years old, including any of your own. This would mean that you could achieve a break-even figure if you charged 43p per hour for each of the six children.

If you had six paying children for ten hours a day, five days a week and charged 43p per hour you would have an income per week of £129. Over 48 weeks this would be an income of £6192, before expenses. You cannot, however, count your own children under five years as fee-paying.

If your expenses were £5000, as in the example above, your profit would be £1192 per year. Your profit is effectively your wage. So it is obvious that 43p per hour is not feasible. In addition it is very unlikely that you will have six paying children for ten hours, five days a week, especially at the start of your business or if you have children of your own under five years old.

So, your hourly rate needs to be set at a realistic figure in order that you have a decent income or a wage. What should you set as your hourly rate? There is little point having an hourly rate that is considerably higher than other home-based childcarers in your area, as you will not fill your vacancies. If you undercut other providers who are charging £4 per hour by charging £3, for example, would you make a profit?

Find out as part of your market research what the other providers in your area are charging. What do they include in their fees? For example, are there extra charges for nappies, meals, snacks, trips, sun cream?

On the face of it, it would seem that if you had an hourly rate of £4 you would be making a massive profit: £4 per hour for ten hours for six children is £240 per day.

This is an income of £1200 per week, £57,600 per year and a profit of £52,600.

But, are you going to be operating at full capacity right from day 1 and for all 48 weeks of the year? And what about your own children when calculating numbers?

Realistically you may start with three children, for whom you care for three days a week for five hours per day per child for 32 weeks of the year:

£4 per hour × 5 hours × 3 children × 3 days = £180 per week = £5760 per year

This realistically means an initial profit of £760 as you start your business (if your annual expenses are £5000).

Part 3 Sources of support

Sources of support could include:

- your local authority
- other home-based childcarers
- the small business advisor at your bank
- PACEY and/or other professional organisations
- websites and forums.

Sample business plan format

This is only a suggested business plan format, but it includes all the main information points from this chapter.

Table 12.3 A possible business plan template

Part 1 Introduction and marketing
Name of business:
Description of the service to be provided:
Background:
Mission statement:
Unique selling points:
Situational analysis:
Market research:
Marketing/advertising plans:
Part 2 Financial planning
Start-up costs:
Annual expenditure and income:
Approximate weekly expenditure and income:
To cover expenditure it will be necessary to have…:
Part 3 Sources of support
Support and contact details:

pacey says

Remember you need to ensure that your house and car insurances are covered for business use. Check with your insurance providers to ensure that they will cover you for childcare in your home. Some insurance companies will not insure you at all and some may restrict the numbers of children you can care for.

Writing a business plan may be a little daunting. Don't be afraid, it's really very simple and you are probably already doing something similar. You know how much income you receive into your household, you will be paying bills, budgeting, planning holidays and so on. For your own interest, note down your current monthly or weekly income and expenses. A business plan is a way for you to set out the key things that you would like to achieve with your business and how you can achieve them. You can also use the plan as a way to identify how much you will need to earn to pay for the cost of your outgoings and start to earn an income. You need to know that your childcare business is sustainable so give your business the best chance of success by beginning with a strong business plan. Over time your business plan may change and develop as you and your business change and you will need to regularly review and update your plan. PACEY provide support and guidance to help you plan for the challenges of managing your own business at the same time as meeting the requirements of the Early Years Foundation Stage (EYFS) in England, and the National Minimum Standards in Wales.

Assessment links

This assessment task relates to Learning Outcome 12 of Unit 2 and links to Assessment Criteria 12.1, 12.2 and 12.3. This assessment task has three parts.

1 You need to discuss the steps that you will take when planning your business. You cannot do this in a written piece of work. Remember, you are not just writing out a list – it is a discussion; so you may want to give more

explanation of why you plan to do something.
2 Make a list of the different types of insurance that you will need for your setting. As this is only a list, you could use bullet points; remember, however, to give your list a title, for example, 'Insurance types needed for a home-based childcare business'.
3 Using a format that suits you, produce a business plan.

Chapter 13

Understand how to register with the appropriate regulatory body

Learning Outcome 13

By the end of this chapter you will be able to:

1 Describe how to register with the appropriate regulatory body

As a home-based childcarer it is a legal requirement that you register with the appropriate regulatory body. If you do not and you receive payment for caring for other people's children, you are committing a criminal offence. You can be fined £5000, sent to prison, or both, if you provide childcare services without being registered. You do not have to register if you are doing only occasional babysitting.

AC 13.1 Describe how to register with the appropriate regulatory body

The regulatory body will carry out an inspection of your premises before you are registered and assess you as a suitable person for delivering childcare. They will then inspect you at regular intervals to make sure that you are meeting the required statutory standards.

In England

In England you have a choice between registering with Ofsted and registering with a childminder agency if you are planning to care for children under eight years old. You cannot register with both. Ofsted published a childminder agency handbook in September 2014. You can download this from the Ofsted website – www.ofsted.gov.uk. The registration process can take two to three months. You must

undertake and complete mandatory training before you can continue with your registration.

To register with Ofsted you need to do the following:

● Contact your local council or local Family Information Service for help with your application and advice on training.
● Download from Ofsted the guide to registering on the Childcare Register – www.ofsted.gov.uk/resources/guide-registration-childcare-register.
● Apply online at the Ofsted website – https://online.ofsted.gov.uk/OnlineOfsted/default.aspx. The application fee was £35 at the time of publication. Or you can contact Ofsted by phone on 0300 123 1231.

After you have applied to Ofsted they will check your references and carry out the checks with your doctor, the local council and the DBS. They will also carry out checks on any other people living or working in your home.

You will then be contacted by an inspector who will arrange to visit your home. Once you are approved you will receive a certificate that shows you are registered. You must display your certificate, or a copy of it, where it can be clearly seen by parents/carers.

If you want to care for children only up to five years old, you should apply to join the Early Years Register. Many home-based childcarers, however, also provide care for children over five years and so are registered on both the Early Years Register and the voluntary and compulsory parts of the Childcare Register (see below).

> ### Useful resources
>
> *Ofsted*
> Search this website for information on the registration guide **www.ofsted.gov.uk**

The Childcare Register

The Childcare Register (compulsory and voluntary) has specific requirements that must be met at all times by people providing childcare. There are 15 requirements, which are subdivided and clearly listed in the fact sheet 'Requirements for the Childcare Register: childcare providers on non-domestic or domestic premises'.

The requirements are:

1 Welfare of the children being cared for
2 Arrangements for safeguarding children
3 Suitability of persons to care for, or be in regular contact with, children
4 Qualifications and training
5 Suitability and safety of premises and equipment
6 How the childcare provision is organised
7 Procedures for dealing with complaints
8 Records to be kept
9 Providing information for parents
10 Providing information for Ofsted
11 Changes to premises and provision
12 Changes to people
13 Matters affecting the welfare of children
14 Insurance
15 Certificate of registration

You must also comply with other relevant legislation, including health and safety, disability discrimination and food hygiene.

The Early Years Register

The early years age group is for children aged from birth until 1 September following his or her fifth birthday. The legal requirements that you must meet for the safeguarding and welfare, and learning and development, of young children are set out in the Statutory Framework for the EYFS.

> ### Useful resources
>
> **Publications**
> *EYFS Statutory Framework*
> The EYFS Statutory Framework can be downloaded at **www.gov.uk/government/publications**, reference DFE-00337-2014.
>
> *Early Years Register*
> The fact sheet for records, policies and notification requirements of the Early Years Register can be downloaded from **www.ofsted.gov.uk**

Preparing for your registration visit

Ofsted has produced a guide designed to help you prepare for your registration visit. It has a list of questions that you could be asked by the inspector. This list is not definitive but is a selection of possible questions to help you think about how you intend to deliver your home-based childcare service.

> ### Useful resources
>
> **Websites**
> *Ofsted*
> **www.ofsted.gov.uk/resources/childcare-registration-form-early-years-register-preparing-for-your-registration-visit**
>
> *PACEY*
> Go to this website and search for the registration visit information page **www.pacey.org.uk**

In England

You will need a copy of the EYFS Statutory Framework (see AC 7.1). It is also good practice to have a copy of 'Development matters in the Early Years Foundation Stage' and 'Know how materials', which are also available from www.gov.uk/government/publications.

Many local authority pre-registration training courses use the booklet from Ofsted – 'Preparing for your registration visit' – during the sessions. This booklet is divided into three sections:

1 Learning and Development Requirements
2 Safeguarding and Welfare Requirements
3 What do I need to do to develop my service further?

As you work through the questions there are spaces for you to make notes and consider possible answers.

It is a good idea also to prepare some of the documents that you will need to meet the requirements and to think about some of the resources that you will use to assess children's starting points, their progress and the educational programme that you will offer to meet their needs.

It cannot be stressed enough that the more prepared you are, the better chance you have of having a successful visit and being registered.

In Scotland

If you want to register as a home-based childcarer in Scotland and care for children under 16 years of age, you must register with the Care Inspectorate. All adults living or working at the home where you will be based must also be registered.

You can download an application form from: www.careinspectorate.com. Alternatively you can contact the National Enquiry Line on 0845 600 9527 and ask for an application pack.

After you have applied for registration the Care Inspectorate will:

● check your references
● carry out Protection of Vulnerable Groups Scheme checks and Disclosure Scotland criminal records checks
● check anyone else who lives in your home
● inspect your home.

If you have a successful inspection for registration you will be issued with a certificate. You must display this certificate where it can be clearly seen.

The registration process normally takes between two and three months.

Useful resources

Scottish Childminding Association
The Scottish Childminding Association's website has plenty of guidance and help on the registration process: **www.childminding.org**

In Wales

In Wales you must register with the Care and Social Services Inspectorate Wales (CSSIW) if you want to care for children under the age of eight years. First of all you must attend a pre-registration and information session. You can find out where the nearest session to you is by contacting your local CSSIW office. You also need to download and read the guidance for applicants, and an application form. You must also complete mandatory training before you can continue with your registration.

Useful resources

Pre-registration sessions
To find out about pre-registration sessions go to the following website and search for the appropriate information **http://wales.gov.uk**

Guidance document
The guidance document can be downloaded from: **http://wales.gov.uk**

Application form
The application form can be downloaded from: **http://wales.gov.uk**

Once you have completed the application form you must return it to your local CSSIW office. There is no application or registration fee. Once you have submitted your application form the CSSIW will:

● check your references
● carry out checks with your doctor, your local council and the CRB (DBS)

- check anyone else living or working in your home
- carry out an inspection of your home.

If you have a successful inspection for registration you will be issued with a certificate. You must display this certificate where it can be clearly seen.

The registration process normally takes between two and three months.

Useful resources

Websites
Registration
Guidance on registration can be found at **www.gov.uk/register-as-childminder-wales** and also at **www.pacey.org.uk**

In Northern Ireland

Under the Children (NI) Order 1995 you are required to register with your local Trust if you want to provide a childcare service in your home. There is no charge for registration. There are three parts to the registration process – training, vetting and assessment. The registration process normally takes about three months.

As with the other regulatory bodies you will be invited to attend an information and pre-registration session. This is then followed by mandatory training, which must be completed before you can continue with your registration.

You and all members of your household over the age of ten years will be subject to the following checks:

- criminal records (AccessNI checks)
- Social Services records
- identity checks
- medical reports
- references from two people
- a health visitor reference if you have a child under five years.

Social work visits will be made to assess your home for safety and to assess your suitability and fitness for childminding. Checks will also be carried out in the outdoor environment. You will also be expected to provide the standards of care as outlined in Childminding and Day Care Standards for Children Under Age 12 – Minimum Standards. It is essential that you are familiar with these standards before you are assessed. They can be downloaded from http://www. dhsspsni.gov.uk.

The guidance document for the registration process can be downloaded from: www.nicma. org. This document contains a health and safety checklist that should be used to address any issues in advance of the assessment visit.

Useful resources

Website
Northern Ireland Childminding Association
The professional organisation for home-based childcarers in Northern Ireland has a wealth of information on its website: **www.nicma.org**

Assessment links

This assessment task relates to Learning Outcome 13 of Unit 2 and links to assessment criteria 13.1.

Before you can operate a home-based childcare business, you must register with the appropriate regulatory body. This task asks you to describe how you will register. This task could be completed through a written report or with a flow chart showing steps that you need in order to register.

Common dietary habits

Food	Buddhist	Hindu	Jewish	Mormon	Muslim	Rastafarian	Roman Catholic	Seventh day Adventist	Sikh
Alcohol	✗	✗	✓	✗	✗	✗	✓	✗	✓
Animal fats	✗	Some	Kosher only	✓	Some (halal)	Some	✓	✗	Some
Beef	✗	✗	Kosher only	✓	Halal	Some	✓	Some	✗
Cheese	✓	Some	Not with meat	✓	Some	✓	✓	Most	Some
Chicken	✗	Some	Kosher only	✓	Halal	Some	✓	Some	Some
Eggs	Some	Some	Without blood spots	✓	✓	✓	✓	Most	✓
Fish	Some	With fins and scales	With scales, fins and backbone	✓	Halal	✓	✓	Some	Some
Fruit	✓	✓	✓	✓	✓	✓	✓	✓	✓
Lamb/ mutton	✗	Some	Kosher only	✓	Halal	Some	✓	Some	✓
Milk/ yoghurt	✓	Not with rennet	Not with meat	✓	Not with rennet	✓	✓	Most	✓
Nuts	✓	✓	✓	✓	✓	✓	✓	✓	✓
Pork	✗	Rarely	✗	✓	✗	✗	✓	✗	Rarely
Pulses	✓	✓	✓	✓	✓	✓	✓	✓	✓
Shellfish	✗	Some	✗	✓	Halal	✗	✓	✗	Some
Tea/coffee/ cocoa	✓ (no milk)	✓	✓	✗	✓	✓	✓	✗	✓
Vegetables	✓	✓	✓	✓	✓	✓	✓	✓	✓

✓ will eat or drink ✗ do not eat or drink

Fasting is often a matter of individual choice; however, the following times are often observed: Jews fast at Yom Kippur, Muslims fast at Ramadan, Mormons fast for 24 hours once a month. Some Roman Catholics prefer not to eat meat on Fridays.

Glossary

Accident – an unforeseen, unplanned mishap, calamity or mistake that may cause distress or injury to another individual

Allergy – an abnormal reaction in the body to certain foods that are usually harmless

Attachment – a unique emotional tie between a baby and another person, usually an adult such as the mother or primary carer

Assessment – an informed judgement about, or measurement of, something, such as the development of a specific skill

Assessment criteria – evidence that you must produce to show that you have understood all aspects of a learning outcome

Budget – a detailed statement of what you expect to receive and to spend

Child protection – part of the safeguarding process; the actions that you take when you suspect a child is at risk of significant harm

Confidential – keeping things private, not disclosing any personal information about children or their families

Co-operative play – when a child plays and shares with others, developing an understanding of rules

CSSIW – Care and Social Services Inspectorate Wales, the Welsh regulatory body

Describe – write in detail about an idea, topic or subject, using language that is straightforward and does not contain jargon

Developmental norms – see Milestones

Disclosure – when a child has told an adult or another child what has happened to them; this can include evidence of abuse or neglect

Discrimination – treating someone unequally or differently due to their age, gender, sexual orientation, race, religion or beliefs, disability

Discuss – write about or consider the key features or main points

Diversity – the variety of values, beliefs, cultures, life experiences, knowledge and skills of each individual in any group of people

Duty of care – a requirement to exercise a reasonable amount of caution and attention to avoid negligence that could lead to harm of others

Echolalia – echoing the last part of what others say

Emergency – a situation that is urgent; a crisis or real danger

Enforcement – implementation of actions that can lead to prosecution

Environment – the surrounding, setting or situation where you work and care for children

Equality – being fair or impartial, and making sure that all people are treated appropriately

Evaluate – look at information from different viewpoints, and make a reasoned conclusion or judgement

Explain – give details, make clear, put into plain words

EYFS – Early Years Foundation Stage (England only)

First-hand experience – doing something or finding out something yourself

Food intolerance – an adverse reaction to a food or ingredient, which happens every time a food is eaten

Green Paper – a tentative government report and consultation document of policy proposals for debate and discussion, without any commitment to action; the first step in changing the law

Hazard – a potential risk or something that could harm or damage a child

Holistic – all-inclusive, whole, overall

Holophrase – one word that is used to express more than its meaning

Impairment – loss, deficiency, weakness

Incident – something that happens; an occurrence, either minor or serious

Inclusion – making sure that every person has the opportunity to access education and care, participate in activities and belong

Infection – disease, virus, illness

Innate – inborn, instinctive, natural

Learning outcome – a topic or series of topics that you are expected to study

Legislation – laws, rules and regulations that have been made statutory by Acts of Parliament

Milestones – assessable measurements that provide typical values and variations in height, weight and skills development; sometimes referred to as developmental norms

Motherese (or fatherese) – high pitched 'sing song' tone of voice, describing what is going on

Next steps – the things that a child could do next in order to progress in their development, for example, the next step from completing a ten-piece jigsaw could be to tackle a 15-piece one

Observation – watching, studying, examining or scrutinising the actions of others

Ofsted – the Office for Standards in Education (England), the government department responsible for the inspection of childcare settings

Outline – to give a brief and concise summary

Parallel play – playing alongside, often at the same activity, but not joining in

Partnership – a collaboration or relationship based on trust and respect in the best interests of the child

Policy – a strategy, plan, course of action in given situations, or a set of guidelines

Prejudice – a judgement that is made without careful consideration of accurate or relevant information, which can lead to narrow mindedness, bigotry and unfairness

Primitive reflexes – actions that originate from the central nervous system that new-born babies do, but that disappear as the baby develops

Procedures – ways, practices, methods, systems to help carry out an action or policy

Rate of development – the speed or time it takes for a child to develop

Regulatory – governing, monitoring

Risk – the possibility or chance of danger, or threat to safety

Risk assessment – a check that is carried out to identify any hazards and find out the safest way to deal with them

Routines – ways of doing things that follow a sequence or pattern, usually planned and carried out regularly

Safeguarding – includes everything that we can do to keep all children and young people safe, promoting children's well-being, welfare and putting measures in place that will improve children's safety and prevent abuse

Sequence – an order or succession of actions or skills

Solitary play – playing alone

Spectator play – watching others play

Statutory – legal, part of the laws of the country that must be followed

Stereotype – to label, put into artificial categories, typecast

Sudden infant death syndrome (SIDS) – also known as cot death; the sudden and unexplained death of an infant

Summarise – provide a brief account that reviews the key points or features

Supervision – management, care, protection

Symbolic play – using objects to represent something else, for example, a plastic block becoming a telephone

Theory – a well-researched and unique idea or perspective on a particular subject or topic

Transitions – times of change, or moves in a child's life; can be big, such as starting school, or small, for example, moving from one activity to another

Universal needs – the basic requirements to ensure survival and quality of life

Well-being – safety, comfort, security, happiness

Bibliography

Books

Amnesty International (2008) We Are All Born Free: The universal declaration of human rights in pictures. London: Frances Lincoln Children's Books.

Meggitt, Carolyn (2014) CACHE Level 3 Early Years Educator for the Classroom-based Learner. London: Hodder Education.

Pound, Linda (2014) How Children Learn: Educational theories and approaches. Salisbury: Practical Pre-School Books.

Riddall-Leech, Sheila (2008) How to Observe Children. London: Heinemann.

Riddall-Leech, Sheila (2012) Heuristic Play. Salisbury: Practical Pre-School Books.

Documents and publications

'Are you thinking of working for yourself?' – www.hmrc.gov.uk/leaflets/se1.pdf

'Birth to five' – www.nhs.uk/Planners/birthtofive

Development Matters – www.foundationyears.org.uk/files/2012/03/Development-Matters-FINAL-PRINT-AMENDED.pdf

The Early Years Foundation Stage (EYFS) – www.gov.uk/government/publications, reference number DFE-00337-2014

'Early years outcomes' – www.gov.uk/government/publications, reference number DFE-00167-2013

'Safer food, better business' – www.food.gov.uk/business-industry/caterers/startingup/childminders/#.U6qvDP9wbIU

'What to do if you are worried a child is being abused' – www.gov.uk/government/publications/what-to-do-if-youre-worried-a-child-is-being-abused, reference number DFES-04320-2006

'Working together to safeguard children' – www.gov.uk/government/publications/working-together-to-safeguard-children

Websites

Barnardo's – www.barnardos.org.uk

BRAKE – www.brake.org.uk

Care and Social Services Inspectorate Wales:

- http://cssiw.org.uk/?lang=en
- www.gov.uk/register-as-childminder-wales
- http://wales.gov.uk/docs/cssiw/publications/111014cmappen.doc
- http://wales.gov.uk/docs/cssiw/publications/120502cmguidanceen.doc
- http://wales.gov.uk/cssiwsubsite/newcssiw/aboutus/contactus/location/?lang=en

Care Inspectorate (Scotland) – www.careinspectorate.com, 0845 600 9527

Childline – www.childline.org.uk, 0800 1111

The Children's Commissioner for England – www.rights4me.org

Common Assessment Framework (CAF) – www.dcsf.gov.uk/everychildmatters/strategy/deliveringservices1/caf

Early Years Register – www.ofsted.gov.uk

The Equality and Human Rights Commission (EHRC) – www.equalityhumanrights.com

Family Information Service (England) – www.gov.uk/find-family-information-service

Food Standards Agency – www.food.gov.uk

The Foundation for the Study of Infant Deaths – www.lullabytrust.org.uk

Foundation Phase – http://wales.gov.uk/topics/educationandskills/earlyyearshome/foundation_phase/?lang=en

The Health and Safety Executive (HSE) – www.hse.gov.uk

HM Revenue and Customs (HMRC):

● www.gov.uk/new-business-register-for-tax
● www.gov.uk/paye-for-employers
● www.hmrc.gov.uk

Independent Childminders' Social Enterprise (ICM-SE) – www.icm-se.org.uk

The Information Commissioner's Office (ICO) – www.ico.org.uk/for_organisations/data_protection/registration

Meningitis Now – www.meningitisnow.org

National Care Standards – www.nationalcarestandards.org/files/early-education.pdf

National Domestic Violence Freephone Helpline – www.nationaldomesticviolencehelpline.org.uk, 0808 2000 247

National Society for the Prevention of Cruelty to Children (NSPCC) – www.nspcc.org.uk, 0808 800 5000

Northern Ireland Childminding Association (NICMA) – www.nicma.org

Northern Irish Minimum Standards – www.nicma.org/cms/docs/ChildmindingandDayCareMinimumStandardsJuly12.pdf

Nursery Milk – www.nurserymilk.co.uk, 0844 991 4444

Office for Standards in Education (Ofsted) – www.ofsted.gov.uk

Parents, Early Years and Learning (PEAL) – www.peal.org.uk/resources.aspx

Play England – www.playengland.org.uk

Professional Association for Childcare and Early Education (PACEY) – www.pacey.org.uk

Public Health England (formerly the Health Protection Agency) – www.gov.uk/government/organisations/public-health-england

Rethinking Childhood – www.rethinkingchildhood.com

The Royal Society for the Prevention of Accidents (RoSPA) – www.rospa.com

Scottish Childminding Association (SCMA) – www.childminding.org

SunSmart – www.sunsmart.org.uk

Team Around the Child (TAC) – www.education.gov.uk/a0068944/team-around-the-child-tac

The United Nations Children's Fund (UNICEF) – www.unicef.org.uk

Women's Aid – www.womensaid.org.uk

Index

abuse
  allegations of 43, 44–5, 54–5
  disclosure 53
  domestic violence 47–8
  emotional 50–2
  neglect 48–9
  physical 49–50
  reporting suspicions 46, 53–4
  sexual 52–3
  signs of 42, 47–53
  suspected 8
  see also safeguarding
accident book 7
accidents 36–7, 97
  preventing 16
  reporting 7
acronyms 176
active learning 126
adoption 3, 5
adult-led play 123, 127–8
  see also child-initiated play
adult modelling 132
adult-to-child ratios 17–18
advertising 164–5
allergies 67, 77, 94, 98
anaemia 74
anoxia 96
antecedents 116
antenatal influences 96
antiseptic cleaners 30
anxious parents 85
assessment 137
asthma 21, 98
asylum seekers 48
attachment 110
attendance 97
attention 102
  diverting 115
attention-seeking behaviour 115
babies
  bottle feeds 30–1, 33
  cuddling 110–11
  feeding 30–1, 33, 67–8
  nappy changing 72
  personal care 69–70

play 130
  sleep position 71
  sleeping 16, 17
  supervising 18
  weaning 67
baby monitors 16, 18
bacteria 29–30, 32–3
balance 99
bathroom, risk assessment 26
bedwetting 48
behaviour
  ABC approach 116–17
  attention-seeking 115
  influences on 112–15
  managing 115–17
birth order 113
bodily waste 34
body image 74
body language 88
body temperature 75
books 139
boredom 14
bottle feeds 30–1, 33
boundaries 116
brain damage 96
breast milk 33
  see also bottle feeds
briefing session 158–9
British Safety Standards 25
Buddhist diet 175
bullying 114
business plan 162–9
capital allowance 167
car insurance 161–2
car travel 19, 27
care, children in *see* looked-after
  children
care standards 66–7
Care Standards Act (2000) 8
cashbook 157, 162
child development
  cognitive 51, 95, 102–5
  delayed 112
  factors influencing 94–8
  holistic 95

milestones 98–109
  personal, social and emotional
    46, 94, 95, 97, 105, 108–10
  physical 95, 99–102
  and play 122–6, 129–30
  rate of 98
  sensory 102, 125
  sequence of 98
  speech, language and
    communication 95, 98, 105,
    106–7, 111
  spiritual and moral 95
child-initiated play 123, 127–8
child protection 42
  see also safeguarding
Childcare Act (2006) 3–5, 8
Childcare Register 171
childcare vouchers 157
childcarer
  attitudes, skills and values 62–3,
    145–7
  household members 43–4
  own children 17–18
  as positive role model 28, 62–3,
    111, 147
  roles and responsibilities 147–8
  sources of support 149–51
childminder agency 10, 170
children
  individual needs of 141–2, 146
  looked-after 3, 5, 48, 97
  rights of 2, 4, 10, 119–20
  visually impaired 17
  vulnerable 3, 5, 48
  with special educational needs
    and disabilities (SEND) 3, 5,
    50, 75
Children Act (1989) 2–4, 7
Children Act (2004) 2–3, 7, 9, 44,
  45, 119
Children and Families Act (2014)
  3, 5
Chinese New Year 76
class 1 business insurance 161–2
cleaning products 29, 30

Climbié, Victoria 3
climbing frames 16
close supervision 16
coeliac disease 67, 77
cognitive development 51, 95, 102–5
Common Assessment Framework (CAF) 45
Common Core of Skills and Knowledge for the Children's Workforce 67
communication 88, 111, 145
concentration 102, 125
confidentiality 5, 90–1, 140, 146
consent 3
    see also written permission
consequences 116
constant supervision 16, 17
contracts 85, 160
Control of Substances Hazardous to Health (COSHH) Regulations (2002) 8
cooking, as play 127
co-operative play 124
co-ordination skills 99, 102, 125
creative play 124
creativity 102, 121
criminal offences 9
criminal record checks see Disclosure and Barring Service (DBS)
Criminal Records Bureau (CRB) 9
critically thinking 126
cultural diversity 96, 131
danger 14
    see also risk management
Data Protection Act (1998) 3, 5–6, 90
dental decay 75
Development matters 16, 117
diabetes 67, 77, 83
diarrhoea 47
diet
    healthy eating 32, 75–6
    planning meals 67–9, 73–4
    poor 96
    vegan 77
    vegetarian 77
dietary restrictions 67, 76–7, 175
digital cameras 6

digital photographs 87
    see also photographs
dignity 120
disability 98
    see also special educational needs and disabilities (SEND)
Disability Discrimination Act (1995) 5
disclosure 53
    see also abuse; safeguarding
Disclosure and Barring Service (DBS) 9, 44, 160
discrimination 3, 5, 10, 60–3, 119, 131
distraction techniques 115
diverse environment 7
diversity 10, 58–64
Diwali 76
domestic violence 47–8, 50
dressing 71
drinks 32, 67
duty of care 42
early intervention 138–9, 140–1
Early Years Foundation Stage (EYFS) Framework 3, 4–5, 93
    expressive arts and design 105
    learning goals 102
    literacy 105
    mathematical development 105
    personal, social and emotional development 46
    physical development 102
    prime areas of learning and development 94, 102
    Safeguarding and Welfare Requirements 7, 9, 31, 43, 65, 69
    specific areas of learning and development 94
    understanding the world 105
    unique child 58, 120
Early Years Register 9, 170–1
eating disorders 51
echolalia 105
education 97
education, health and care (EHC) plan 5
emergencies 7, 35–9
emotional abuse 9, 50–2

emotional security 110
enforcement 11
English as an additional language 62
environment
    definition 14
    diverse 7
    inclusive 130–1
    indoor 18–19, 24–7
    influence on learning 111–12
    outdoor 19, 27
    reviewing 139
    risk-free 14
    safe and secure 16
    stimulating 111
environmental health service 32
EpiPen 21, 22
equality 3, 10, 58
Equality Act (2010) 3, 5, 10
equipment
    bottle feeding 30–1
    risk assessment 26–7
evacuation procedure 7
event sampling 136
Every child matters 3–4
eye contact 88
fabricated illness 50
Facebook 87–8
family
    environment 96–7
    influence on behaviour 113
    structure 59–60
fatigue 47
festivals, and food 76
financial management 157
financial planning 165–8
fine motor skills 99
finger foods 75
Fire Precautions (Workplace) Regulations (1997, amended 1999) 7
fire safety 7, 8, 38
fireguard 25
first aid box 36
First Aid qualification 7, 35, 159
first-hand experience 14
food
    hygiene 32–3, 159
    preparing 33

safety 31–3
storing 33
waste 34
see also diet
Food Information for Consumers Regulation (Regulation (EU) 1169/2011) 78
food intolerances 67, 77, 94, 98
food poisoning 32
Food Standards Agency 32
formula feeds 30–1, 33
free flow play 130
Froebel, Friedrich 123
fussy eaters 75
gender-specific activities 131
gluten 77
Green Paper 3–4
gross motor skills 99
hair care 69
hallway, risk assessment 26
hand–eye co-ordination 125
hand washing 28, 29, 70, 74
hazardous substances 8
hazards 23
head lice 69
headaches 47
Health and Safety Executive (HSE) 7
Health and Safety (First Aid) Regulations (1981) 7
Health and Safety at Work Act (1974) 7
health checks 160
health visitors 149
healthy eating 32, 75–6
hearing impairment 94, 98
heuristic play 125
high chair 68
Hindu diet 175
holiday pay 155
holophrase 105
home learning environment 88–9
home-to-setting diaries 87
hospital stays 83, 98
house insurance 161
household members 9
hyperactivity 74
illness 38–9, 50, 98
imagination 102

imaginative play 124–5
inactivity 73
incidents 35–7
inclusion 10, 58
barriers to 60–3
inclusive environment 130–1
income-related benefits 167
independence 71, 73, 130
Independent Safeguarding Authority (ISA) 9
indoor environment, risk assessment 24–7
indoor supervision 18–19
infection 28–9
information
security of 6
sharing 3, 45, 83, 87–8, 90, 140
storing 6, 90–1
see also confidentiality
Information Commissioner's Office (ICO) 5
inhalers 21
injuries 7
inspections 11, 65
see also Ofsted
insulin 21, 77, 83
insurance 161–2
investigation 11
Jewish diet 175
kindergarten 123
kitchen, risk assessment 25
Kitemark 26
labelling 131
lactose intolerance 77
Laming Report 3
language, offensive 112, 113, 116
language development *see* speech, language and communication
learning
active 126
and environment 88–9, 111–12
and positive relationships 110–11
through play 120–6
see also child development
legislation 2–10
equality 10
health and safety 7–8
safeguarding 8–9
see also regulatory bodies

Leuven Involvement Scale 140
library 139
lifestyle choices 97
lifting 7
listening 88, 145
literacy 105
see also speech, language and communication
Local Authority Designated Officer (LADO) 44–5
Local Education Authority (LEA) 66
Local Safeguarding Children Board (LSCB) 9, 43, 44
lone working 46, 54
see also childcarer
looked-after children 3, 5, 48, 97
manipulative play 125
Manual Handling Operations Regulations (1992) 7
market research 164
marketing 164–5
masturbation 113
meals
planning 67–9, 73–4
see also diet
media, influence of 114–15
medication
administering 22
record keeping 22–3
storing 21
memory skills 102
meningitis 39, 98
menstruation 75
mental harm 9
see also emotional abuse
missing child 37
mission statement 163
mobile phones 6
morality 122
Mormon diet 175
motherese 105
motor skills 99
multiple births 96
Muslim diet 175
nappy changing 72
National Care Standards Committee 66
National Insurance 154–5
National Minimum Wage 155

naturalistic observations 136
'nature versus nurture' 114
neglect 48–9
negotiation, through play 122
newsletters 88
Northern Ireland
    care standards 66
    frameworks for learning and
        development 94
    regulatory body 11
nursery, starting 114
obesity 75
observations
    formats 136
    purposes of 138–40
    written 135, 136
off-site trips 19, 21
offensive language 112, 113, 116
Ofsted 43
    inspections 65, 148, 171
    registering with 10, 170–1
open-ended play 124, 126
open-ended questions 132
organic food 77
organisation skills 145–6
outdoor environment, risk
    assessment 27
outdoor supervision 19
over protection 13
P45 153
Paediatric First Aid qualification
    7, 35
parallel play 124, 130
parents
    anxious 85
    first meeting 84–6
    with mental health issues 48, 50
    separating 5
    working in partnership with 80,
        81–2, 84–90
partnership working see working
    in partnership
patience 146
Pay As You Earn (PAYE) 155
Payne, Sarah 9
peer groups 114
perception 102
perinatal influences 96
permission see written permission

personal care 69–71, 74
personal hygiene 28–30, 47, 72–3, 75
personal information see
    information
personal protective equipment
    (PPE) 7, 34, 72
Personal Protective Equipment at
    Work Regulations (1992) 7
personal restraints 19
personal, social and emotional
    development 46, 94, 95, 97,
    105, 108–10
personality 113–14
pets 27, 34–5
photographs 6, 87, 136, 137
physical
    abuse 49–50
    contact 110–11
    development 95, 99–102
    play 124
physical punishment 9
plants, toxic 27
play
    adult-led 123, 127–8
    child-initiated 123, 127–8
    co-operative 124
    creative 124
    and development 122–6, 129–30
    free flow 130
    heuristic 125
    imaginative 124–5
    inclusive approach to 130–1
    learning through 120–6
    manipulative 125
    open-ended 124, 126
    parallel 124, 130
    physical 124
    planning 138
    right to 119–20
    self-directed 121
    solitary 124, 130
    spectator 124
    stages of 124
    supporting 127
    symbolic 124
positive relationships 110–11
positive role model 28, 62–3, 111, 147
postnatal influences 96
poverty 96

praise 71
prejudice 60–3
prematurity 96
pre-registration training 159, 172
primitive reflexes 99
privacy 72–3, 75, 119
procedures 21, 43
Professional Association for
    Childcare and Early Years
    (PACEY) 23, 149
professional organisations 161
professionalism 147
Protection of Children Act (1999) 9
Provision of Learning and
    Childcare Order (2014) 94
puberty 74–5
Public Interest Disclosure Act
    (1998) 54
public liability insurance 4, 161–2
public transport 19, 27
qualifications 7
questionnaires 148
Race Relations Act (1976) 5
Rastafarian diet 175
ratios, for supervision 17–18
recordings 136
records, keeping and storing 3, 5–6
    see also information
references 160
reflexes 99
registration 11
    childminder agency 10, 170
    as employer 155–6
    as food business 31–2
    Ofsted 10, 170–1
    regulatory bodies for 10–11,
        170–3
    as self-employed 153–5
    registration visit 171
regressed behaviours 47–8
Regulation of Care (Scotland) Act
    (2001) 66
regulatory bodies 10–11, 170–3
Regulatory Reform (Fire Safety)
    Order (2005) 8
reins 19
religion, and diet 76, 175
Reporting of Injuries, Diseases and
    Dangerous Occurrences

Regulations (RIDDOR) (1995) 7, 36
residential care homes 8
respect 120
responsive care 110
rest 71–2, 74–5
restraints 19
rickets 75
rights, of children 2, 4, 10, 119–20
risk, definition 13
risk assessments 7, 8, 23
    checklist 24–7
    indoor rooms 24–7
    outdoor areas 27
risk-free environment 14
risk management 13–16
road safety 19–21, 27
role play 112
Roman Catholic diet 175
routines 28, 65
    sleep 71
Royal Society for the Prevention of Accidents (RoSPA) 37
safeguarding 41
    allegations of abuse 43, 44–5, 54–5
    child protection 42
    duty of care 42
    legislation 8–9
    local authority procedures 44–5
    and lone working 46, 54
    policy 55–6
    regulatory requirements 43
    reporting suspicions 46, 53–4
    sharing information 45
    see also abuse
safety harnesses 19
safety marks 26
Sarah's Law 9
school
    absence from 98
    drop-off and collection 19, 83
    starting 114
scissor skills 16, 127
Scotland
    care standards 66
    frameworks for learning and development 94
    regulatory body 11

security 6, 91
Self-Assessment 153, 156
self-care 102
self-confidence 51, 61
self-directed play 121
    see also child-initiated play
self-employed, registering as 153–5
self-esteem 51, 61, 110, 131
self-harm 51
self-help skills 105
self-image 61, 113
self-worth 131
sensory development 102, 125
settings, drop-off and collection 83
settling-in 86
Seventh Day Adventist diet 175
Sex Discrimination Act (1975) 2
sexual abuse 52–3
sharing information 3, 83, 87–8, 90, 140
siblings 18, 113
Sikh diet 175
situational analysis 163–4
skin care 70
sleep 16, 71–2, 74–5
smoking 71
snacks 67, 73
social media 87–8
social skills 120–2
solitary play 124, 130
special educational needs and disabilities (SEND) 3, 5, 50, 75
Special Educational Needs and Disability Act (SENDA) (2001) 10
Special Educational Needs Co-ordinator (SENCO) 10, 91
spectator play 124
speech, language and communication 95, 98, 105, 106–7, 111
spontaneous play *see* child-initiated play
stair gates 24, 25, 26
stairs, risk assessment 26
start-up costs 166
stereotyping 63, 131
sterilising, feeding equipment 31

stomach aches 47
story time 127
structured observations 136
structured play *see* adult-led play
substance abuse 50
sudden infant death syndrome (SIDS) 71
supervision 16–21
    indoor 18–19
    legal requirements 17–18
    outdoor 19
    ratios 17–18
    types of 16
sustained shared thinking 132
swearing 112, 113, 116
SWOT analysis 163–4
symbolic play 124
tantrums 113
Team Around the Child (TAC) 45
teeth 70
thumb sucking 113
time management 16, 144–5
time sampling 136
toddlers 130
toilet 26
toileting 72–3
toy libraries 112
toys, risk assessment 26
training 159
transitions 66, 82, 110, 112–14, 140
transport 160
'treasure basket play' 125
trust 46
twins 18
two year progress check 83
undressing 71
'unique child' 58
unique selling points (USPs) 163
United Nations Convention on the Rights of the Child (UNCRC) 4, 10, 66, 119–20
universal needs 141–2
vegan diet 77
vegetarian diet 77
vetting 159–60
videos 136
visual impairment 17, 98
voluntary organisations 81
vulnerable children 3, 5, 48

Wales
  care standards 66
  frameworks for learning and
    development 94
  regulatory body 11
washing hands 28, 29, 70, 74
waste disposal 34
weaning 67

welcome pack 85–6
well-being 16, 65, 110
whistleblowing 54
Williams, Keanu 49
working in partnership 80
  barriers to 89–90
  benefits of 81–3
  with other childcarers 81

with other professionals 81, 82–3
with parents 80, 81–2, 84–90
Working together to safeguard
  children 9, 43
wrist bands 19
written permission 19, 21, 22, 83,
  87, 140